Marketing the Frontier in the Northwest Territory

Marketing the Frontier in the Northwest Territory

Land Sales, Soils and the Settling of the Great Lakes Region in the 19th Century

Robert E. Mitchell

McFarland & Company, Inc., Publishers
Jefferson, North Carolina

ISBN (print) 978-1-4766-8067-5
ISBN (ebook) 978-1-4766-3906-2

LIBRARY OF CONGRESS AND BRITISH LIBRARY
CATALOGUING DATA ARE AVAILABLE

Library of Congress Control Number 2020017421

Front cover image: Chicago in 1820,
Chicago Lithographing Company,
circa 1867 (Library of Congress)

Printed in the United States of America

McFarland & Company, Inc., Publishers
Box 611, Jefferson, North Carolina 28640
www.mcfarlandpub.com

Acknowledgments

Many national, state and local archivists and reference librarians helped make this new evidence-heavy social history possible. Thanks to the Bureau of Land Management's archives housed in Springfield, Virginia, the National Archives and Records Administration, several offices within the Library of Congress, the Michigan State Archives and Library, the libraries and archives of University of Michigan, Michigan State University, and Central Michigan University, as well as courthouse records in Michigan's Midland County and a Virginia Family History Library. Other national, state and local experts who kindly responded to my questions are referenced throughout this study.

In the recent past, this kind of academic history was limited to journals and an occasional book publisher favorable to the French Annales school of history. Charles Perdue, my editor with McFarland, saw how this multi-disciplinary region-focused study could open new approaches to understanding American history. For that I am much appreciative.

But why five Great Lakes states and a microanalysis of one case study Michigan county? The same question could be asked about my recent book *Human Geographies Within the Pale of Settlement: Order and Disorder During the Eighteenth and Nineteenth Centuries.*

Before retiring from the Foreign Service in May 1995, my children asked me why I knew so much about my maternal Protestant ancestors, pioneer farmers in the middle of Michigan, but so little about my paternal ancestors who left the Pale of Settlement for Michigan shortly after the end of the American Civil War. My children and others now have partial histories for both sides of my own ancestors.

These books are dedicated to proponents of new social histories as well to my two ancestral lines and the areas they left and later settled.

Table of Contents

Summary, Overview and Next Steps

Preface

Whereas Russia expanded from west to east, America moved east to west.

> Westward the course of empire takes its way;
> The first four acts already past,
> A fifth shall close the drama of the day;
> Time's noblest offspring is the last.[1]

American frontiers were closed by on-the-move eastern farmer-investors who trucked, traded and settled land. Emanuel Leutze captured a slice of this settlement history and America's supposed manifest destiny in his large mural that adorns the western staircase in the U.S. House of Representatives' chambers.

The narrative historian Frederick Jackson Turner argued that American democracy was formed on the frontier by those who settled it. "American democracy," he wrote, "was born of no theorist's dream.... It came out of the American forest, and it gained new strength each time it touched a new frontier."[2]

Turner and others, it seems, thought they had discovered why American culture and politics were different from those in Europe. That is not the focus of the present study. Instead the following chapters draw on multiple disciplines to explore

- How frontier lands were mapped, legally defined and trucked-and-traded in imperfect markets;
- How different soils on the land as well as access to markets for harvests from different quality soils influenced human geographies on the frontiers "over time";
- How farmers cultivated their soils; and
- Farmers' financial returns on the investments they made in imperfect markets.

Although there is much traditional storytelling in the following chapters, this study is not concerned with personal or national character. Instead, this is a number and evidence-heavy new institutional and market-based history of soils and those who cultivated and either remained or wastefully abandoned them on the frontiers of the original five pre–Civil War states carved out of the northwest territory that England surrendered to the American victors in the new nation's war for independence.

The physical geographies of soils will be linked to the human geographies of those who invested in and cultivated frontier soils. These two separate geographies are also linked to legal institutions, administrative agencies, and antebellum America's imperfect markets for land so that it is possible to track and analyze relationships between land-related independent and dependent variables from the late 1790s through to 1870 as one of several ways to understand how individual investment decisions were made by the farmers who closed and often stayed on the frontier. We also have accounts of how individual settlers personally coped with their new lives as pioneer farmers.

The present study separately explores the settlement histories of three separate spatial units: five individual states, sixty-eight counties in one state, and the individual farmers in one case-study multi-soils county. Readers and follow-on researchers will be introduced to where to find and then use quantitative evidence on the soils, farms, harvests and residential moves. There is still much history to be written on imperfect markets for land, the decisions that different investors made, and how local communities were created out of newly arrived strangers.

We will explore the information that potential investors had about land on the frontier, how that land was marketed, what soils could be most profitably cultivated, and the pre-modern farming technology available at the time.

Narrative historians seldom dwell on the evidence they use. Because quantitative evidence on soils, acreages, investments and harvests is central to the present study, follow-on researchers are provided information on where to locate and record evidence on the lands that settlers closed on the pre–Civil War American frontier.

There are several anticipated readerships for this combined narrative and technical history:

- Economists and social scientists interested in how individual farmer-settlers made their investment decisions in newly created imperfect markets for land on the antebellum frontiers.
- Historians interested in the origins and operations of antebellum laws, the agencies that implemented them, and how

these laws and agencies influenced the investment decisions made by individual farmer-settlers who closed the frontier.
- Soil scientists, physical geographers and human geographers interested in how their technical languages and approaches can add to our understanding of America's settlement history.
- Historians and general readers who can tolerate technical terms and statistical arrays in the course of a traditional narrative history of how the farm frontiers were closed in five antebellum Great Lakes states with particular attention to one illustrative quantitative-evidence-rich state, Michigan.
- The new breed of quantitative historians interested in how to link top-down to bottom-up histories.
- Readers interested in how imperfect markets can both influence and be influenced by a nation's system of democratic governance.

Chapter 1 introduces many technical terms and statistical evidence absent in most general narrative histories. Readers might begin this chapter with its summary (and do so with all other chapters as well). Number-heavy social histories make demands on both authors and readers.

Introduction

In his *Historiography in the Twentieth Century,* George Iggers covers "The arrival of Narrative" history with its "renewed emphasis on the experiences of concrete individuals." He "posited a clear line of distinction between historical scholarship and imaginative literature."[1]

I reference Iggers to draw some of the differences between traditional narrative and more recent social histories. Because the present study covers topics and hypotheses found in several social science disciplines, this introduction identifies the analytical (explanatory) and narrative challenges that are explored in the following chapters. Some readers, of course, find the social sciences to be pseudo-science. Those readers and others are invited to start with Chapter 1.

This book explores how 156,678,000 square miles of highly diverse Amerindian lands in the five states of the Old Northwest Territory were imperfectly privatized, traded, settled, farmed and often wastefully abandoned. We will cover the federal, state and private markets for land as well as the farmers who invested in and cultivated the many different soils on the expanding frontier.[2]

Two inter-related market themes are covered in the following ten chapters:

- We focus on the diverse public owners and "rational" private investors who intended to make wise investments in the lands they bought, sold, settled and farmed.
- These investment and settlement decisions were made in "information-poor markets" that did not link the price of an acre of land to the potential of that land to be profitably cultivated.

By focusing on the consequences of cultivating different classes of soils purchased in information-poor markets, this book adds to our understanding of why and how the frontier was wastefully closed.

Investors and farmer-settlers were presumably rational decision-makers. But there was sparse trustworthy information on the potential value of the lands that were being trucked and traded. Soil science and agricultural economics arrived after much of the frontier was closed.

Farm settlement on the frontier was for many investors a game of roulette. This is a book on how that game was designed and operated as well as the price that farmers paid for their unwise investment bets.

"Land" has multiple meanings that include an exact legal location on a map, number of acres, growing season, drainage, access to markets and, most importantly for the present study, "soils."

Just as land has many dimensions and meanings, so did the "markets" that priced, financed and traded the land that was being closed on the antebellum farm frontiers of Ohio, Michigan, Indiana, Illinois and Wisconsin.

We will record and analyze how cultivating different classes of soils influenced two dependent variables: crop yields and whether a farmer in 1860 was still cultivating the same soils in 1870.

The multiple disciplines informing this study include soil science, cartography, standard market economics, physical and human geographies, legal and institutional economics, public administration and political science as well as a dollop of ethnography and sociology. Each of these disciplines has its own dictionary of technical terms, questions and modes of interpretation.

Both traditional narrative history and the more recent quantitative followers of Clio are found in the following chapters on imperfect markets for land and the antebellum farmer-settlers who closed farm frontiers in the five states of the Old Northwest Territory.[3]

The chapters in this top-down book begin at the national level before moving down to five individual states, with particular attention given to Michigan, followed by its sixty-eight lower-peninsula counties, and then a case study of sixteen townships in one county, ending in an analysis of individual farmers in that single multi-soils county.

This top-down approach can also be read from the other direction, one that begins with individual farmers who made investment decisions based on incomplete and often deliberately false market information.

Soil endowments and farm settlement histories of five newly created states are placed in the context of the national legislative history on how markets were designed and implemented followed by the same general histories and profiles of Michigan's lower peninsula counties.

Because state-level and county-level quantitative evidence is subject to what statisticians label a potential "ecological fallacy," we move to individual farm-level soils, crops cultivated, crop yields (returns on investment) and the ability of farmers cultivating different soils to survive from 1860 to 1870 in one case-study county. At all spatial units of our analysis, narrative histories are linked to statistical profiles of soils, farmers who cultivated those soils and population trends over time.

These chapters are much more than litanies of numbers. Our interest is also in why there was so little reliable information on soils and why the market for land suffered so many imperfections. We offer some answers to these questions by reporting on the publicly available notes prepared by the surveyors who mapped the lands taken from Amerindians. This inadequate and sometimes fabricated information was supplemented by speculators and local boosters who solicited far-distant farmer-investors to move west and close the American frontier.

Unfortunately, there is little local ethnography to help us understand the decision-making histories of individual investors and the social lives of strangers who met one another on the frontier. There is still much history to be written on the closing of the American frontier.

The present history builds on the contributions of legions of outstanding narrative historians as well as a growing number of "quants" who use numbered "facts" (such as the number of acres of differently-productive soils as well as returns on investments from cultivating them) that can be related to one another as independent and dependent variables over time.

Multiple references have already been made to rational decision-making, a key assumption underlying much of modern economic thinking about how real-world markets should operate. Behavioral economists such as Nobel Award–winner Daniel Kahneman explored different dimensions of rationality that a decision-maker attempts to maximize.[4] The present book narrowly focuses on the financial returns from the investments that farmer-settlers made.

But there are returns other than financial ones, as will be explored in later chapters that reference the wisdom-of-crowds and gravity models relevant to one powerful pulling force that drew settlers to the frontier. And as Morson and Schapiro reminded us in their *What Economics Can Learn from the Humanities: Cents and Sensibility*,[5] individuals base their decisions on more than selfish financial gains. Unfortunately, there is minimal reliable quantitative evidence on the relative importance that competing interests had on the decisions that investors made on where to settle on the closing frontiers. With apologies to Morson, Schapiro, humanists and social scientists, the present book is constrained by the quantitative evidence available for analysis.[6]

Readers will find more than a quantitative exercise relevant to different academic disciplines. It is also a narrative history, one that begins with two evidence-inviting questions that Madison Kuhn asked in 1966:

> Why was the restless pioneer [who bypassed Michigan in the second decade of the nineteenth century] so reluctant to settle there? ...
> Would they then be as well off as Ohio or Kentucky farmers?[7]

He could have added Indiana, Illinois and Wisconsin to Michigan and Ohio, the five states that the Northwest Ordinances of 1785 and 1787 carved out of the of the vast area that England ceded to the new United States of America in the 1783 Treaty of Paris. Each of these five states had internal differences that invite questions such as "Would a farmer in one of Michigan's mid-state counties have been as well off as farmers cultivating land in the state's more southerly counties?"

Kuhn's phrase "as well off" requires numerical measures on returns that farmer-settlers could realize from their investments in land on the closing frontiers. We also need to understand some of the reasons that help explain inter and intrastate differences in these returns on investments.

Kuhn's unnamed imaginary pioneer could have been Mr. and Mrs. John Doe struggling on their small 1850s farm near Waitsfield, Vermont. Some of their neighbors gave up cultivating crops to join the Moreno sheep mania[8] or to breed horses destined for New York City's large transportation sector. Other neighbors re-started farming in New York State where, according to Donald Parkerson, local farmers were relocating both within as well as outside that state.[9] Still other farmer-investors moved south in search of promising soils.[10]

Settlers-on-the-move had multiple investment possibilities beyond the five new states carved out of the Northwest Territory, the limited focus of the present study.

Early on-the-move investors came from the different cultures that David Hackett Fischer covered in his *Albion's Seeds: Four British Folkways in America*.[11] And just as not all farmers, soils and physical geographies in America were the same, there were differences in how parcels of land were legally defined (metes and bounds vs. rectangular surveys adopted for the Northwest Territory's five new states), the amount and location of publicly-owned land as well as the folkways and cultures of farmer-investors.

The many different American frontiers that were being closed did have one important common feature: land, a potentially productive resource that

1. was not man-made but was a
2. natural resource that was trucked and traded in imperfect markets. And that like many other tradables,
3. was not a consumable but was an asset to be profitably exploited year after year, and

4. lands differed in their potential to yield high returns that would justify the investments made in owning, settling and managing soils.

We will see that the initial "prices" "governments" placed on the privatization of individual acres did not recognize these differences. With exceptions that are clearly explored (swamplands, for example), the markets created to privatize the former lands of Amerindians did not assign different per-acre prices to different investment-quality soils. However, as will be noted in this book's summary chapter, we do not have sufficient information on how speculators, railroads and other intermediaries priced their land holdings. Some of these private entities had credit features not included in the federal privatization programs, but it appears that both the public and private markets for frontier farmlands were absent reliable information on the potential investment value of different soils.

Recapping the above: this market-focused study explores

- how the antebellum imperfect markets for Amerindian lands were created and operated,
- the many different kinds of land (soils) that were privatized and then re-sold,
- how those soils were used (crops sown and harvested), rates of return on financial and human investments, and
- how the different soils in the case-study's county were wastefully closed.

Linking Top-Down to Bottom-Up Histories

Quantitative evidence is aggregated at different geographical (spatial) levels: five individual states followed by sixty-eight counties in Michigan's Lower Peninsula.

The conclusions drawn from these top-down aggregated (ecological) numbers are reinforced by an analysis of 1860s farm-specific soils, individual farmers, the crops they cultivated, harvests reported and the ten-years life-trajectories (1860 to 1870) of individual farms that had different soils in the single case-study Michigan county that had a mixture of scientifically-classified soils. This bottom-up history, it is assumed, "generally" represents the history of each individual state within the five-states of the Old Northwest Territory. Of course, that is an untested although reasonable assumption that will be revisited in the summary chapter.

Focusing on individual farmers, their soils, crops and yields in a single county required much time-consuming archival research dealing with soil and vegetation maps, land patents and deeds as well as the individuals and farms listed in the 1860 population and agricultural censuses.

Linking a bottom-up to a top-down quantitative and narrative history parallels the logic of Robert Darnton's *The Great Cat Massacre*, a bottom-up micro social history that helps us to better understand top-down French social and cultural life in the 1730s.[12] The present study's bottom-up evidence includes the field notes made by the surveyors who mapped the county, follow-on remedial surveys, archive-based information on specific farms, their soils, harvests and farmers as well as how changing legislation and economic conditions influenced both the markets for land and the farm settlement history of a single evidence-rich antebellum county.

References will also be made to authors and works in multiple genres of America's settlement history and markets for land including:

- Frederic Jackson Turner's often-criticized top-down narrative history of the closing of the American frontier,
- the pathbreaking historical quantitative research by agricultural economists such as Jeremy Atack, Fred Bateman and others,[13]
- the new institutional economic history's questions and methods introduced by Robert Fogel, Douglass North and others,[14]
- Douglas Helms, one of the earliest historians who suggested how soils might have influenced American settlement history,
- Paul Gates and other legal scholars who added to our understanding of how laws and institutions shaped the imperfect markets for land that farmers were privatizing and cultivating on the frontier,
- legions of economists and sociologists who have written on the history, operations and adverse effects attributable to imperfect markets,
- literature more generally on historical geography, soil science, regional science, cartography, demography, bottom-up and top-down American history, rural history and historiography as a field of study as well as the
- muckrakers who helped expose the dark side of how America's frontiers were closed.

Each of these genres and disciplines has its own vocabulary, questions, units of analysis and ways to understand how the American frontier was closed.

We will see that few histories of American agriculture, rural life and the closing of the American frontier reference the limited and often deliberately fallacious information that farmer-investors had on which soils could, if properly managed, provide the highest returns on a farmer's financial and human investments. The present study attempts to fill this information and analytical gap by

- introducing scientific classifications of different farm-level soils,
- describing the limited and sometimes fallacious information that farmer-investors had on which soils were most productive,
- explaining why both public and private markets for land lacked accurate information, and
- assessing the settlement consequences of investing in and cultivating different quality soils purchased in information-poor markets for land.

Both soils and settlers can be mapped as physical and human geographies that in an information-full market would coincide with one another. This book explores reasons for the lack of overlap and the associated wasted investments.

Again, readers are reminded that America's agricultural and spatial histories involve market transactions executed in information-poor markets that did not link the price of land to the soils on it. The absence of such linkage helps explain why so many farmers wasted their investments on the frontier. And the linkages also provide answers to the earlier-referenced questions that Kuhn asked.

Prisms of markets, investors and managers of farm operations are not the only keys to understanding how and why frontiers were closed. Chapter 10 will revisit how the present study relates to the other scholarly traditions. We begin here with some of the assumptions and aims of these studies.

Assumptions Made by Earlier Historians

The present study builds on the contributions of earlier historical research on the closing of the American frontier.

Frederic Jackson Turner's narrative school of history argued that cheap land was a financial magnet that drew settlers west to close the American frontier formerly occupied by Amerindians.[15] Rather than the pull of cheap land, Stephen Thernstrom argued that migration was a safety valve for surplus labor from Eastern urban centers.[16] In either case, pull or push, land in the five states of the Old Northwest Territory and the cultivation of that land was an investment presumably made by rational economic men making decisions within a newly invented market for the disposal of the property formerly belonging to Amerindians. (We will see later that these original residents apparently did not consider land to be privately owned but, instead, occupied and used for different purposes.)

Both the Turner and Thernstrom theses seem to assume that antebellum farmer-settlers (including some of my own maternal ancestors) who closed the frontier were rational decision-makers both in their selection of land and in how best to cultivate it in order to justify an investor's financial and human commitments. Cultivating land would not only cover initial investment costs but also yield an excess to reward farm families for continuing to cultivate their soils. The Turner thesis also seems to have incorrectly assumed that the market for land was fairly transparent with adequate information so that unwise investments would be an exception.

Thanks to Paul Gates and other historians we know how federal and state authorities created and managed the privatization of public lands. We will supplement this earlier work with information on how the State of Michigan marketed the land that the central government awarded this state for its own disposal.

What we discover in Michigan's history no doubt has parallels in other states as well. And what we find in a single multi-soils Michigan county is also likely to be found in other counties and in other states. There was incomplete and sometimes deliberately erroneous information on the investment potential of place-specific lands.

Once a farmer settled on his land, he[17] was challenged to rationally manage his crops and soils. (Many farmers were also speculators who profited by selling some of their acres at a higher price than what was originally paid for them.) "Sustainable" farming depended on how well farmers managed their crops and livestock. That "how well" requires giving attention to the history of farming during the mid-nineteenth century, a micro-evidentiary focus that will be adopted in the case-study Michigan county.

We will overlook the alternatives to how the American Frontier could have been closed. For example, instead of privatizing land, it could have been leased by the state to individual cultivators. Polanyi and others argued that because land is not man-made it is not like other goods that are trucked and traded. Instead, it was argued, land was a public good inherited from the far past.[18]

Adam Smith might have questioned whether land should be included in his definition of the wealth of a nation.[19] But in America, Amerindian land became a tradable commodity bought and sold in the imperfect markets. Those imperfections, we will see, resulted in wasteful human and financial investments made during the closing of Michigan's agricultural frontier. They also resulted in similar wasted investments in other states. Michigan was not unique.

One indicator or test of waste will be seen in how the physical geography of soils differed from the human geography of farmer-settlers over time.

Again, readers are reminded that America has many different physical geographies that include hills, mountains, deserts, prairies and swamplands as well as soil-rich areas. Not all regional histories are necessarily the same. They evolved under different legislative and land-market conditions. The present study covers one antebellum region only: the five states carved out of the Old Northwest Territory. But this study is not limited to this one mid–America region only. Instead, our focus is more generally on how the design and operations of markets for land influenced the investment decisions made by antebellum farmer-settlers who closed one series of American frontiers.

Agricultural economists explored many of the questions that are covered in the present study by taking counties or townships, not individual farmers, as the unit of analysis. In order to overcome the ecological fallacy associated with aggregating statistics at these higher spatial levels, the present study also tracks individual farmer-investors in the single case-study county.

In addition to addressing the challenges of ecological fallacies by analyzing individual farms, this study is also aware of the post hoc ergo propter hoc logical fallacy that states "Since event Y followed event X, event Y must have been caused by event X."[20] Alternative ways to possibly close the American frontier all faced the same pre-science lack of understanding of soils and how to price them.

Before searching for answers to Kuhn's questions or with how closing Michigan's frontier was distorted by the imperfect market for land, we will draw on the contributions of institutional economists and legal historians who have written on land-privatization laws and those responsible for transferring land to individual investors. We will see that there were several different markets for land including

- the national market with headquarters in Washington and local offices within individual states,
- those operated by the states themselves,
- others who received pass-through land grants (such as railroads) and then
- sales by private investors, both farmer-settlers and speculators.

Paul Gates' path-breaking research on America's incongruous land laws[21] covers several of these markets.

Later chapters will explore these larger trends as they were experienced in the case-study Michigan county.

Soils, Not Land

A focus on soils rather than on land requires ways to scientifically classify soils according to their potential for high crop yields. Chapter 2 introduces a scientific soil classification system that is common to all five states of Ohio, Michigan, Indiana, Illinois and Wisconsin along with state-level statistics on per-acre corn and wheat yields, new farms added from 1850 to 1860 and other related numerical evidence. These numbered facts on soils and settlers allow us to explore how the imperfect market for land influenced the closing of the American frontier and how states were settled by farmers.[22]

Number-based geographies will be represented by statistical profiles and maps that display the geographical distribution of different quality soils within the five states of the Old Northwest Territory followed by the distribution of soils within the sixty-eight counties in Michigan's Lower Peninsula. This kind of information on soils was not available to mid–1800s settlers, the antebellum period covered in the present study. The sign on the market for land at that time might have emphasized caveat emptor.

A second set of statistical profiles identifies the soils that individual farmers in 1860 were attempting to cultivate in the case-study county. Individual farms are then linked to the 1860 federal agricultural census to discover the crop (investment) returns on farming different quality soils at the micro level of individual farms.

Other Considerations

This concludes an overview of the present research. But historians are aware of the dangers of "presentism," also known as the fallacy of *nunc pro tunc*.[23] We cannot assume that the markets for land were what economists consider ideal (transparent, information-rich and low transactions costs) and would automatically avoid unwise investments. That was not the nineteenth-century market when the American frontier was closed. Nor can we accept the common belief in American exceptionalism and genius.

There was more than one way to open and occupy the lands taken from Amerindians. We focus here on the institutions created to privatize the lands that England ceded to the newly independent United States of America. That focus includes how individual settler-investors responded to imperfect market signals.

Although we only have ersatz information on the actual criteria that different farmer-settlers used in their investment decisions (for example, the feel of the soil when pressed between the forefinger and thumb), we cannot assume that nineteenth century farmer-settlers were intentionally irrational. Nor can we assume that individual farmers compared different sets of soils before investing in them. Reliable information on soils did not become available until soil scientists many decades later conducted their detailed on-the-ground field surveys followed by field studies that linked crop harvests to the specific soils being cultivated. In retrospect, we will see that science does matter in how markets operate and how the American frontiers were closed.

In lieu of reliable information on soils, some settlers no doubt headed to states and counties where earlier farmer-investors had already settled. New aspiring farmers were following the assumed wisdom of the crowd. But since local supplies of the potentially most valuable soils were limited, later arrivals were left with less promising sites to begin farming. Large proportions of those who invested in lower quality soils, we will see, did not survive. They were not enumerated in the 1870 agricultural and population census.

Gravity models rather than standard financial models can contribute to our understanding of farmer settlement patterns during the 1800s. However, the settlement process and pattern relevant to mid-nineteenth century might not fully apply to later generations that had access to modern soil maps as well as reports on what earlier farmers were able to harvest. There could have been a changing congruence over time between soil maps (the basic physical environment) and those who farmed the soils (human geography).

A Reader's Guide to the Chapters

The ten chapters in this study are grouped under four descending geographical (spatial) units of analysis followed by a summary.

Geographic Level 1: A National Overview

Chapter 1: The Invented Markets for Land on the Frontier looks at how the United States of America acquired vast new lands available to settlers moving from east to west as they closed the American frontier during the first half of the nineteenth century. This narrative chapter also references organizations, mapping requirements and privatization procedures involved in the transfer of ownership of this land to new farmer-investors and others who closed the American frontier.

Geographic Level 2: The Old Northwest Territory

Chapter 2: The Five States of the Old Northwest draws on modern classifications of soils to compare inter and intra-state variations in promising soils available to new farmer-settlers over time. Trends in new farm-formation, general populations and crop yields are introduced as well.

Although economists' estimated rates of return on farms do not standardize for variations in productive soils, it seems reasonable to assume that some of the interstate differences in new farm formation and returns on investment were responses to inter-state differences in their soils, not just to the total acres each state had in all soils. The significance of these differences within Michigan are explored in Chapter 3. We will see that many farmers did in fact make wise decisions to invest in Michigan soils thereby providing a partial answer to Kuhn's questions.

Geographic Level 3: Michigan's Lower Peninsula

Chapter 3: The Privatization of Land in the State of Michigan takes the state of Michigan as an example of how the frontier was closed by farmer-settlers and others. This history begins with the displacement of the original Amerindian residents followed by a summary of major national and state laws and institutions governing the transfer of public lands to private owners. We will see that there were multiple markets, not just the federal and state ones. And markets are more than laws. Financial systems and implementing agencies are also involved. What happened in Michigan had parallels in other states where the frontiers were also being closed.

Chapter 4: Soils and Settlements in the State of Michigan Lower Peninsula Counties moves down the spatial unit of analysis from five different states to the sixty-eight counties within Michigan's Lower Peninsula. Differences among these sixty-eight are analogous to differences among states. This analysis also provides answers to the question added to Kuhn's two: would some farmer-investors have been better off in some individual Michigan counties than in others? Chapter 4 compares the legal responsibilities assigned counties with those assigned individual states. After describing the legal establishment and early history of counties, the focus shifts to time trends in the number of farms and farm acres added over time to suggest how soils influenced settlement histories. This analysis also suggests that productive soils were not the only force drawing settlers west. Earlier settlers seem to have signaled the relative attractiveness of a local farm environment. Both soils and settlers were magnets that influenced the closing of the American Frontier. This chapter, however, does not attempt to build a gravity model to assess the relative importance that earlier settlement patterns and the availability of unfarmed productive soils had on farm-settlement histories.

Chapter 5: Rates of Return on Investments in Farming recognizes that not all counties in Michigan offered equal farm-investment opportunities. This number-heavy chapter covers the economics of cultivating different crops within different sections of the state. Farming involves exploiting soils with crops best suited not just to soils but to other physical features as well. And pioneer farmers also had the upfront costs of clearing their land so that it could be plowed and cultivated. Farmers were exploiting a natural resource, soils, that could be depleted if not adequately managed. This meant that returns on investment could decline if the cultivator was a poor manager of his soils, crops and livestock. That this happened both in Michigan and in other earlier-settled states could be one of several reasons why American farmers were not as productive as those in several European countries. Inter-county differences within Michigan parallel those found at the inter-state level and also help us to better understand how Michigan's agricultural frontier was closed. This chapter tags several questions that are pursued later in this study.

Geographic Level 4: One Multi-Soils County

Chapter 6: Moving from Macro to Micro-Level History lays the basis for topics that will be explored in the following three chapters. No new evidence is introduced, just some of the issues that lend themselves to simple quantitative arrays and analysis. Archives both in the nation's capital and in Michigan itself house information on soils, crops and cultivators that were incorporated in a single spread sheet making it possible to estimate how harvests are related to soils as well as why some farmers rather than others were able to continue farming from 1860 to 1870. This case history allows us to explore relationships between physical and human geographies over a ten-year period.

Chapter 7: The County's Physical Geography draws on physical land surveys and other information on the county's physical geography of soils, wetlands, topography, climate, growing season and access to outside markets for farm products. Some of this information was recorded by the private contract surveyors who mapped the county. They were required to note wetlands, vegetation, and the agricultural potential of soils. Some of this information was fabricated by surveyors whose work was not adequately overseen. The surveyors' summary assessments of individual townships did not present a favorable agricultural investment picture of the county. Yet the county did have promising soils (along with major wetland challenges) and a river system that provided access to the outside world. The antebellum market for these mid–Michigan soils was probably not too different from what existed elsewhere in Michigan and in other states. The soil information presented in this chapter will be related in later chapters to farm harvests and the sustainability of farming particular soils.

Chapter 8: The Market and Privatization of Land in a Case-Study Frontier County introduces the reader to individual land patents and deeds that are used to identify specific farmers who cultivated different quality soils privatized under different federal and state privatization statutes in this case-study county. Copies of these official documents are provided along with time trends in patents issued under different statutes. This is a history of land-privatization, not human settlement. Information from the 1860 population and agricultural censuses are linked in the following chapter to patents and deeds that identify the predominant soils that individual farmers were cultivating. This soil information refers to an entire 640-acres section, not just to the exact subsections that were being cultivated. The unit of analysis to be used in the following Chapter 9 is an entire section, not the actual soils within a sub-section, such as the back forty. Farmer-settlers accounted for only a small minority of the privatized land. This information base leads to the following chapter's analysis of how crop yields were related to different classes of soils and to the likelihood that a farmer would survive on his holdings during the 1860–1870 decade.

Chapter 9: Those Who Farmed or Left Their Soils introduces new evidence to what was covered in earlier chapters thereby adding to our understanding of how closing the American frontier was not the same as planting a stable population of immigrants, farmers and non-farmers. Linking crops to the soils on which they were cultivated found that farmers who had good soils were more likely than their neighbors working poorer soils to cultivate two important crops (wheat and Indian corn) and to have higher earnings from their market gardens. Farming was more profitable on good rather than on other soils. This linkage leads back to Kuhn's questions on whether Michigan farmer-settlers made wise investment decisions. Profitability also resulted in sustainability as suggested by the higher persistence rates of farmers cultivating the county's best soils. This chapter covers many other topics relating to how farmers, some of whom were new to their occupation, were able to survive the farm-making process when early-year crop yields were not sufficient to support a farm family.

Summary, Overview and Next Steps

Chapter 10: Looking Back revisits selected earlier research on America's settlement history, questions the present study's assumptions and objectives, reviews the methods used to pursue these objectives and then summarizes the study's major "findings" and interpretations. As with so many other books, readers are advised to begin the present one with the final chapter. It places the market for land in a larger time-ordered perspective that gives attention to how the micro-economics of farming in one soils-diverse county can be elevated to the settlement history of the five states carved out of the Old Northwest Territory and thereby provide answers to Kuhn's two questions. And consistent with Paul Gates's writings on American laws that privatized new lands, we find that farmer-investors were minor landowners in many newly opened markets. Outsiders certainly accounted for a fairly large proportion of all acres patented in one antebellum multi-soils county. Almost all of these early large investors were outside lumbermen and speculators. Many mid-nineteenth-century settlers in this county bought their land from speculators rather than from public agencies responsible for the privatizations of millions of newly acquired American lands. Gates, as with the present study, placed privatization and migration within a larger institutional and legal context—or what might be labeled institutional economics.

Themes Underlying the Present Study's Approach

Number-heavy books, including the present one, tend to focus on fairly narrow discipline-specific questions. But as Mary Poovey has argued, facts and numbers have their own narrative histories of interest to a broader readership. That too is one of the present book's intentions, one that places a somewhat narrow technical market-oriented topic within a larger institutional and historical context on how markets for land influenced the closing of American frontiers.

Several themes or organizing principals are used to answer Kuhn's two questions that are placed in the larger narrative historical tradition of how the American frontier was closed. Instead of answering his own questions, Kuhn reported some of the questionable market information available to investors in land on the frontier. In addition to this kind of questionable information, the present study links specific soils (lands) to the returns on investing in these soils. This linkage allows us to relate the physical geography of soils to the human geography of farmer-settlers at three different spatial units of analysis: five individual states, sixty-eight counties within a single state followed by individual farms within a single multi-soil county.

Soils are classified according to their potential to produce high yields of different crops. The findings at the higher ecological levels of states and counties are also found at the level of individual farmers cultivating different quality soils.

The study's two geographies are placed in the larger context of how the imperfect markets for land (soils) influenced which lands (soils) were most likely to have been privatized to provide sufficient returns on investment to keep a farmer in place from 1860 to 1870.

Different quality soils are treated as independent variables that help explain different rates of return on the investments made by individual farmer-settlers who closed the American frontier. Those farmer-settlers trucked and traded land in imperfect markets. Making these various connections combines two analytical traditions for an understanding of the closing of the American frontier: (1) narrative history and the (2) independent-dependent variable approach common to many social sciences.

At the end of this study, market economists, geographers, soil scientists, institutional and legal scholars, political scientists, demographers and both sociologists and ethnographers will have a better appreciation of what each discipline can contribute to historical research. And narrative historians will again hear the voices of land surveyors, federal, state and local officials as well as investors, market-makers and farmer-settlers who helped close America's antebellum land frontiers.

Geographic Level 1: A National Overview

1

The Invented Markets for Land on the Frontier

Although identifying productive soils was the key to successful investments in farming and an understanding of population movements, earlier historians focused on land in general as well as the legislative history on how congress structured the market for public lands that were acquired over time by the new national government. The present chapter summarizes migration-relevant information related to various antebellum land-disposal acts passed by congress relevant to the five states of Ohio, Michigan, Indiana, Illinois and Wisconsin (not the prairie and other states farther west towards the ultimate frontier, the Pacific Ocean).

We begin with the thirteen founding states of the new United States of America and their Anglo-Saxon market rules that included metes and bounds used for mapping purposes. The Northwest Territory challenged congress to invent a new mapping system along with laws and implementing procedures to divide and then privatize or grant land that began as the public property of the national government. Once established, America's highly imperfect land markets were constantly amended as settler-investors closed the frontier. Amended laws and the mechanisms to implement them are covered in this and in several following chapters.

But before moving there, the present chapter summarizes some of the de-nationalization challenges and responses to them during the closing of the frontier. Frequent reference will be made to other writings linked to the same challenge. All these studies rely on both accepted as well as questionable evidence that later chapters will revisit.

The Legal and Geographical Context

In the Treaty of Paris signed in 1783, Great Britain ceded to the new United States approximately 541 million acres (156,678,000 square miles) of which 230 million were west of the Appalachian Mountains. In 1785 and 1787 the short-lived Continental Congress passed the Northwest Ordinances that set the initial terms for the privatization of approximately 159 million acres of unmapped and largely unknown Amerindian lands in what became the five states lying northwest of the Ohio River Valley. Settlers had already begun crossing south of this vast territory in sufficient numbers to qualify Kentucky for admission to the Union in 1792. Tennessee was admitted four years later in 1796.

Ohio in 1803 was the first of the five Old Northwest states with sufficient residents to qualify for admission to the Union. It was followed by Indiana in 1816, Illinois in 1818, Michigan in 1837 and Wisconsin eleven years later in 1848.

These five candidate states differed in many ways: number of acres, soils, vegetation, ease of access for incoming settlers, the Native Americans already living there, and much more.

Amerindian cultures did not recognize private property rights in land that had borders and legal titles that could be easily and securely transferred to newly arriving settlers. Legal rights to specific lands were part of Anglo-American and other cultures, although there was an option of treating this new land as a public latifundium that would lease land to renters. Instead, the Continental Congress expropriated local land rights (as understood by the native peoples), forced the native residents to relocate without compensation, and then created a legal and institutional system to transfer land ownership to non-natives for whatever uses they might choose.

The new United States of America began its westward expansion by nationalizing (expropriating without compensation) lands "taken" from their original settlers, those who were both stationary and others who moved within their general unmapped boundaries. Some leading American political figures including George Washington had already claimed large swathes of land beyond the Appalachian mountain range. At his death, he owned over 50,000 (mostly undeveloped) acres in Virginia, Ohio, Pennsylvania, New York, Kentucky and the Northwest Territory.[1] These landowners were speculators, not settlers.[2]

Land was not freely given to settlers and speculators. Instead, an ever-changing system of national and state-level payments and legal-transfers was created as part of an agreement that moved the heavy debts that individual state governments (colonies) incurred (public, not private debt) during the war for American independence to the new national government. States that had claims to pan-Appalachian lands transferred their claims to the post–Continental Congress.

A settler needed legal title to identifiable unique spaces. Hence "mapping" along with how land-payments were both financed and processed. A massive new but information-poor market for Amerindian lands was created with adverse economic and family-farmer effects that will be explored in later chapters.

All that is necessary background for understanding how the five states of the Old Northwest Territory were settled, how lands with different soils and vegetation were financed and exploited, and why the unchanging maps of the physical geography of this large area were not the same as the human settlement patterns on the land. The initial chapters in this research move from five different states down to the sixty-eight counties in Michigan's Lower Peninsula followed by a history of how one illustrative Michigan county was settled by newly-arriving farmers who privatized land formerly occupied by Chippewa farmers and hunters.

Farmer-settlers are assumed to have been interested in the most productive soils. Lumbermen were interested in the forest vegetation on land. Farmers and lumbermen who made wise investments in land were more likely to financially benefit than those landowners whose decisions were less sagacious.

We will be exploring who some of these east-to-west investor-settlers were but not how they moved west other than to note that some followed the Wilderness Road through the Cumberland Gap. Those heading to more northerly areas had a more difficult overland route before the Erie Canal and lake travel in 1825 provided settlers with an alternative passage. We await new histories of how transportation networks influenced the closing of different American frontiers.

Of course, migrants in search of good farmland were not limited to the Old Northwest. From 1790 to 1860, the new United States added 2,105,985 square miles to its original 867,980. The Louisiana Purchase increased the national total by another 827,000 square miles, nearly 3.4 times more land than in the present five states of the Old Northwest.[3] Most of these new unmapped lands became available for sale as soon as the original inhabitants of diverse native peoples were coerced to cede their patrimony to the federal government and the new nationalized areas were surveyed.

Settlement history is not limited just to the U.S., for Canada was opening new territories and attracting American settlers as well. Migration, new farms, and the extension of national boundaries (especially in Russia where migration was more centrally-managed unlike the voluntary movements found in America) were also experienced in Europe.[4] However, the United States was a special case because of its vast expanse of land, differences in the potential productivity of soils, the arrangements for privatizing soils (land), and the large movement of settlers from east to west.

Early Legislative Acts

Much had to be done before the newly nationalized public lands northwest of the Ohio River could be sold and settled. East Coast states with claims to lands west of the Appalachians had to cede them to the federal government. Virginia's Act of cession in 1783 anticipated both this and the Northwest Ordinance by stating that the territory Virginia claimed was to be "laid out and formed into states" that would, when admitted to the Federal union, have the same rights (and, presumably, obligations) as the other states. Equally important for subsequent privatization schemes, Virginia stated that the ceded territory "shall be considered as a common fund for the use and benefit of such of the United States that are or might become members of the confederation."[5] None of these areas had been adequately mapped.

To assure that the benefits would accrue to the country as a whole, it was necessary to establish guidelines for the governance of the territory, states created within it, and clear property rights that benefited buyers, sellers and the public (not the original Amerindian migrant and stationary occupants).

The Land Ordinance of 1785 and the Northwest Ordinance of 1787 created the initial institutions and laws that provided the guidelines that would help protect the public against unscrupulous individuals. That there were such individuals and that they were a threat to the public is reflected in Richard Henry Lee's letter of 1787 to George Washington complaining that a "strong toned government" was necessary for the territory because of the "uninformed, and perhaps licentious people" who would take advantage of a situation without clearly defined property rights.[6]

The new institutional structure specified in the 1787 ordinance was spelled out in six articles covering freedom of religion, a bill of rights that made contracts inviolable, the encouragement of education that required, among other things, that Section 16 in each township be set aside for the support of public education, the equal rights and obligations of new states of which between three and five could be created, and that "There shall be neither slavery nor involuntary servitude" except for those convicted of a crime.[7]

To avoid the development of a feudal land system, primogeniture and entail were made illegal. Two tax features were specified as well: states could not tax federal property, and non-residents were not to be taxed at a rate higher than what was imposed on residents. For decades, much land was held by the federal government.

In (partial) recognition that these states were the home territory of numerous native groups, the ordinance's third article stated that

> The utmost good faith shall always be observed towards the Indians; their lands and property shall never be taken from them without their consent, and in their property, rights, and liberty they shall never be invaded or disturbed unless in just and lawful wars authorized by Congress; but laws founded in justice and humanity shall from time to time be made for preventing wrongs being done to them, and for preserving peace and friendship with them.[8]

"Good faith" is a loose term without strict standards for holding settlers and governments responsible for the harm they caused native peoples. Americans in and out of government were large speculators whose profits could be severely damaged if good faith was honored. George Washington, Thomas Jefferson, Patrick Henry, Supreme Court judges, congressmen, senators, governors and men with money were early land speculators before and after the Revolution.[9] At a later time, Daniel Webster owned extensive land holdings in Michigan, Illinois and Missouri.[10] Some land was already owned or at least claimed by pre–Revolutionary settlers—for example, French-Canadian settlers bordering Lake St. Clair in Michigan. But there were also fabricated claims ranging up to 130,400 acres.[11] A federal Board of Land commissioners created in 1812 found "incredible forgeries, fraud, subornation and perjuries" in Illinois.[12] Mancur Olson might have classified these invaders as bandits.[13]

Richard Henry Lee's fears of licentious people were well founded—then and still today. The then questionable land holdings and their soils had yet to be mapped or analyzed. Nor do we know what criteria the alleged owners used in selecting their holdings.

Land was not to be auctioned or sold until it had been surveyed. To accomplish this, the Land Ordinance of 1785 established the rectangular system of surveys. It took time to work out the administrative structures and technical procedures for implementing this ordinance. To this end, the Act of 1796 established the Office of the Surveyor General who in turn was to appoint a corps of surveyors.

Private contractors performed actual on-the-ground surveys. They were to divide land into congressional townships that in theory were to be 36 square miles (six by six miles). A township's position (its "number") was exactly located as north or south of a "baseline" and east or west ("range") of a prime meridian. Townships were in turn subdivided into 36 squares, each theoretically one square mile or 640 acres. (This was in theory, not in fact.) The resulting sections were numbered from

1 to 36 beginning with Number 1 in the northeast corner of the township and from there running west to Section 6, dropping one section south to Section 7 and then running in a systematic zigzag manner to Section 36 in the far southeast border of the township.[14] An east-west, north-south and fractional (¼ and ½) system is used to identify any specific parcel of land within a section.[15] This system and the history of the rectangular survey are covered in a number of excellent volumes.[16]

These are man-made grids with the borders marked by blazes in forested areas. The corners had four marked trees.[17] The grid was displayed as a plat (map) so that prospective settlers and investors could more easily find and accurately define the sections of interest to them. Equally if not of more immediate importance to prospective investors, the public had open access to the notes that the private surveyors were required to prepare relating to

> all rivers, creeks, springs and smaller streams of water, with their width, and the course they run in crossing the lines of survey, and whether navigable, rapid or mountainous, the kinds of timber and undergrowth with which the land may be covered, all swamps, ponds, stone quarries, coal beds, peat or turf grounds, uncommon natural or artificial productions, such as mounds, precipices, caves, etc., all rapids, cascades or falls of water, mineral, ores, fossils, etc., the quality of the soil and the true situation of all mines, salt licks, salt springs and mill seats, which may come to your knowledge are particularly to be regarded and noticed in your note books.[18]

In addition, the private sector surveyors included in their notes their observations regarding specific types of trees, their diameters, and whether the soil was of first, second or third quality for agricultural purposes. That is, there was some minimal but questionable information on the physical geography of these five new states each of which had its own internal variations of soils and growing conditions.

To the degree this information was accurate and uniform throughout the Old Northwest, prospective settlers and speculators had the then-best available admittedly squishy and often invented information on which to make their investment decisions. (Some of the limitations of the evidence used in this and later chapters will be noted elsewhere.) Of course, not everyone took advantage of these notes, and there were errors and outright frauds in the surveys, notes, and plats. Some errors were corrected over time through re-surveys.

Each State's Endowment of Soils

Kuhn's questions included comparisons between Michigan and four other states. What he did not provide was information on inter-state differences in total size (square miles), the quality of soils, the pace at which these soils were privatized and trends in the number of acres that farmers were cultivating. Trend information indicates past settlement histories and the availability of promising soils still available for new farmer-settlers. That settlement-related information is summarized below.

There were approximately 239,345 square miles (over 153 million acres) of land available for privatization in the five states of the Old Northwest as summarized state by state in Table 1.1.

Table 1.1: Three Estimates of the Number of Acres in Each State in the Old Northwest

	Statistical Abstract[a]	*General Land Office FY 1853 Report*[b]	*State Soil Geographic Database*[c]
Ohio	26,222,000	25,576,960	25,816,933
Indiana	23,158,000	21,637,760	22,662,848
Illinois	35,795,000	35,462,389	35,271,513
Michigan	36,492,000	35,995,520	36,424,662
Wisconsin	35,011,000	34,511,360	35,130,381

a. Statistical Abstract of the United States, 2000 *(Government Printing Office, 2000), 228.*
b. Annual Report of Commissioner of General Land Office, S.exdoc 1 (33–1) *and* (33–2).
c. Provided the author by Sharon W. Waltman, Soil Scientist-Soil Geography, USDA-NRCS. National Soil Survey Center, Lincoln, Nebraska.

A Proliferation of Laws and Implementing Authorities

The Public Land Commission in 1880 found that Congress had adopted approximately 3,500 laws dealing with public lands between 1785 and 1880.[19] Two laws in particular accounted for a large proportion of land patented in the Old Northwest: (1) The Act of 1820 that replaced credit sales with a requirement for full cash (specie) payment of $1.25 per acre, and (2) a series of Military Bounty (scrip warrant) Acts (1812, 1842, 1850, 1852) that provided men who were separated from service with rights to a certain number of acres. These warrants were eventually assignable so they could and were nationally bought and sold freely. Other laws will be mentioned later with regard to swamplands and various grants to states.[20] The focus here is on the land in general, not on the soils and vegetation on the land. Information based on modern soil maps for each state will be introduced later. That is, not all the listed acres in Michigan and the other states had investment-friendly soils. Information on inter-state endowments of soils and the rates at which these soils were privatized provide clues on how to answer Kuhn's two questions.

Several federal departments administered these laws until the General Land Office (GLO) was created in 1812 and placed under the Secretary of the Treasury before being transferred to the newly created Department of the Interior in 1849. This office was staffed by its Commissioner, Surveyor General, registers and receivers, superintendents of public sale and various support staffs in Washington and in an ever-growing number of local land offices dealing with speculators, settlers, land agents, land lookers, timber cruisers, lawyers, and dealers in land warrants, scrip and tax titles. Disposing of nearly 240,000 square miles in five states, as well as land in other public domain states, was a major operation and an industry in itself.[21]

Individual states created their own laws and institutions for the disposal of lands granted to them by the federal government. Later chapters cover the state of Michigan's land-disposal legal and implementation infrastructure.

Closing the Frontier

Each of the five states of the Old Northwest had potentially fertile soils that new farmers could profitably cultivate. And in fact, there was a steady stream of new arrivals and lands that were privatized. By 1860, the territory was home to nearly 29 percent of the nation's farms and 37 percent of all new farms created nationally in the 1850s. *The five states accounted for one-fourth of the nation's population growth from 1790 to 1860.*

There were multiple American frontiers that were being closed. The history of the five states covered in the present study may not have the exact same history as those elsewhere in the expanding national borders. Although there may be multiple histories, they all share a common concern with how public lands were privatized in imperfect markets. One of the central foci of the present study.

Based on standard census reports and the Integrated Public Use Microdata Series, Hall and Ruggles concluded that (1) the first half of the nineteenth century was a high point of U.S. inter-state migration, characterized by long-distance moves westward from east-coast states to the north-central region, (2) *nine out of ten white migrants moved to rural areas* (that is, they were primarily farmers or farm laborers), and (3) these new farmers were motivated by the desire to improve their economic well-being (an assumption awaiting documentation).[22]

An estimated nine out of every ten new white inter-state migrants during the first half of the nineteenth century were primarily farmers or farm laborers on the way to owning and tilling their own patch of land.[23] (Again, the present study is limited primarily to pre–Civil War years only.) Whatever forces drove those settlers from their old homes, the magnet of soils and vegetation pulled millions of them to close the Old Northwest Territory's frontier.

The combined "enumerated" population of the Territory's five states increased from 51,006 in 1800 to nearly seven million by 1860. The yet-to-be enumerated Michigan's 1800 population grew to nearly 750,000 by 1860. The entire region was exploding with new investors. These numbers, however, do not answer Kuhn's questions on whether farmer-settlers in Michigan would have been better off by investing in other states.

While soil maps would have remained fairly constant (some soils were degraded over time), the maps of those who cultivated the soils were constantly changing. As suggested earlier, one might expect that if there was perfect information about soils, then new farmer-settlers would only invest in the most productive soils still available on the markets for land. If there were accurate maps of soils, then we could predict the most likely distribution of settlers who were investing in farming these soils. But, of course, the market for land was largely (but not entirely) vacant of science-based information on soils and vegetation.

Politically-drawn state borders do not define soil and vegetation zones that differ in their potential for cultivating crops that drew settlers to a state. As will be noted later, there were both interstate and intrastate differences in the potential fertility of soils. Heterogeneity existed even within small areas—such as a 40-acre plot (the back 40).

At least some of a settler's success in farming depended on the wisdom (or luck) of the new farmer's choice of land. The very newness of the Old Northwest, the limited information on its soils, the state of agricultural science, and the arrangements for acquiring land: all added to the difficulty of making wise choices. The same lack of reliable locational information existed for forest vegetation of interest to lumbermen.

Some Earlier Soils-Related Research on Closing-the-Frontier

The present analysis is not the first to explore how soils affected early American migration patterns, nor is it the first to link soils with economic welfare. In his "Soil and Southern History," Douglas Helms argued that soils (for example, "base-rich soils with titled alfisols") affected the movement of early migrants from the east coast.[24] Although these settlers did not have the technical language of soil science, they apparently were aware of what soils could be most profitably cultivated.

Helms recognized that researchers cannot assume that "soils of broad geographical regions are unvarying." Since little reliable information was available on which soils were better than others, this suggests that some migrant farmers did better than others in the soils they selected to cultivate. Helms saw that using digital and other soil maps would allow later historians to better identify patterns of land use, but his own research was not at the time able to explore this possibility. The present study attempts to meet the challenge that Helms and others set for social and economic historians. This requires rather extended coverage of sources of evidence and how this evidence can be used for historical analytical purposes.

Several outstanding agricultural economists also explored the links between the welfare of farmers and the soils they cultivated. Jeremy Atack and Fred Bateman, for example, suggested that a farm's profitability was "influenced" by soil type because some had higher potential yields than others.[25] That seems rather obvious. These authors, however, warned that their county and state-level results, which were based on eleven soil types, "should not command much attention" because purely local factors, besides soil, might have influenced the measures of profitability these two authors used.

Atack and Bateman did not explore how soils might have influenced settlement patterns over time, one of the challenges covered in the present study that explores relationships between physical and human geographies.

Other authors to be referenced later wrote on how culture affected farmers' agricultural practices, the links between farming practices and soil depletion, and an array of other farming-related topics—but not settlement patterns and the role that soils played in the continuing migration process that closed the American frontier.

Farmer settlers who made unwise choices of land to begin farming were not anchored to their private property. They could move on, as many did. Examining the soils that movers abandoned provides clues to why soil and population maps did not overlap one another during one pre-soil sciences period in the nation's settlement history. Physical and human geographies today might be in better sink with one another because the market for land (soils) became much better informed and transparent over time—but not in the mid–1800s.

The summary chapter to this study will refer to other earlier contributions to our understanding of the closing of the American frontier.

Numerical Evidence and How It Will Be Analyzed

Evidence used in the present research comes from published statistics, largely untapped archival resources, tabulations based on data from original census and other sources aggregated for different geographical levels (units), and both information and analyses from other to-be-referenced publications.

Evidence on *lands* and their *soils* is drawn from:

- Published soil classifications and maps at the statewide, county and intra-county levels.
- Patent information taken directly from the tract books compiled for one multi-soils county by the General Land Office, as well as patent information found in various published studies.
- Deed records for the same county taken primarily from microfilm copies of the original volumes recorded by the county.[26]
- Tax assessment information taken from the original lists compiled by the county's tax assessor.

Farming and *agricultural information* comes from:

- Tabulations based on copies of the original enumerator sheets from the 1860 population and agricultural censuses for one multi-soils county.
- Official census publications and information in other published studies.
- *Population, manpower* and *wealth* information was taken from the same sources noted for farming and agriculture, as well as from Civil War pension files of veterans provided by the case-study county during the Civil War from 1861 through 1865.

Most of these sources suffer in one way or another. For example, the criteria that the Eighth Census used to include a farm in the 1860 agricultural census excluded a number of smaller farms as well as farmers in the initial stages of farm-making. Because the census reported populations as of June 1, farm laborers who might have been employed only during planting and harvesting seasons may not have had their primary occupations correctly noted. Estimates of the value of real estate and personal property are self-reported approximations at best.

The case-study county began recording deeds nearly twenty years after the first patent was issued for the county, and few of these early patents are entered as deeds in the official deed volumes. Moreover, the population census missed some even prominent residents,[27] and census officials occasionally edited the returns recorded by the local census enumerators.

These and other shortcomings will be discussed when particular data sets are first introduced. Suffice it to note that some of my "findings" are less precise than I would prefer. The data categories used, however, were considered important to the government at the time they were formulated. I am not imposing my own definitions—for example, on the difference between improved and unimproved acres, as well as the meanings attached to real estate and personal property.

Investigators are able to draw on various *technologies* to organize their evidence and relate sub-sets of them to one another. The statisticians' use of the term *explain* (as in the proportion of variance in a dependent variable that is accounted for by changes in independent variables) should not be confused with statements about causes of specific effects. The term *explain* has several meanings. Cause-effect statements are based on *methodologies,* not statistical formulae and models.

When the present book attempts to link time-series information to changes in government policies or the economy, I may unconsciously let myself slip into cause-effect assumptions that a more methodologically-adept analyst would argue are not justified by the evidence or by accepted standards of logical proof. To avoid the impression of precision in explaining variance, I rely primarily on simple time series and cross tabulations (tables) to suggest "relationships" between and among data sets.[28]

Because farming is a soil-based vocation, it will be necessary to distinguish between more and less productive soils. We must move beyond Stoll's poetic reference to soil as "the tablecloth under the banquet of civilization: no matter what people build on it, when it moves all the food and finery go with it."[29]

The quality of the topsoil is central to the value of the land. Its finery includes the vegetation that sits on top of the tablecloth. That does not mean that other important influences were not at play as well. Some of them have already been mentioned. Others will be explored later including how imperfect laws, institutions and transfer arrangements influenced America's settlement history as well as the physical and human geographies of post–Revolutionary America.

The following chapters move down a series of geographical (spatial) units of analysis beginning with five individual states followed one spatial step lower to a brief overview of the sixty-eight counties in Michigan's Lower Peninsula.

Multiple counties involve more numbers than a solo investigator can reasonably handle, so the present research drops an additional step lower in the spatial hierarchy to the 528 cartographic sections ("survey sections") within a single multi-soils mid–Michigan County: Midland. I recorded this county's 1860 within-section information on land patents, soils, vegetation, population, farming and lumbering as a way to assess the relative drawing powers and effects of different types of soils and vegetation relevant to farming and forestry. These drawing powers are reflected in human population maps and reports. The information from analyzing the relationships between soils and farms helps provide answers to Kuhn's two questions.

It is possible that the influences attributable to soils could vary within Michigan as well as within the larger Northwest Territory and elsewhere. For example, access to outside markets can be important at different times in an area's settlement history. Much of early Michigan and certainly its Midland County was on the periphery of marketing systems that were integrated into the larger economy. A farmer could have high crop yields but limited ways to market them.

There are, of course, alternative ways to explore some of the issues covered in this book. For example, an intellectual historian might trace how ideas about individual property rights and the role of the state shaped the settlement process. (You will find some of this in different chapters.) Other historians might prefer that greater attention be given to historical geography (there is certainly much of that in the following chapters), and still others might place the settlement process in some teleological perspective on the American search for order.[30] You certainly won't find that in this book.

The summary chapter links the present book to some of these other traditions in ways that will hopefully resonate with some readers.

At the end of this study we should be able to offer some answers to Kuhn's question: "Why was the restless pioneer [who bypassed Michigan in the second decade of the nineteenth century] so reluctant to settle there?" and his follow-on question "Would they then be as well off as Ohio or Kentucky farmers?" We will have some suggested answers to these and other questions as they shed light on the relationships between two geographies, maps of soils and maps of those who farmed these soils.

Before moving on to the role that soils had in closing the American frontier, it is reasonable to question whether a single county in one state only has man-land relationships that are shared throughout the Old Northwest and the nation as a whole. Historians, as seen earlier, seem to differ in their views of how representative a single county or settlement can be of a country's larger population and environment. Some have suggested that if you have seen one American frontier county you have seen all such places. These counties, it might be claimed, differ only in their transitional status on Frederick Jackson Turner's simplified five waves of the frontier settlement process: trapper, trader, surveyor, land-clearer, and rancher or farmer.

Another claim is that if you have seen one frontier county, you have seen one frontier county only. In support of this argument is a review of "twenty-five studies of colonial New England towns and each has produced a different model of what a typical New England local community might look like!"[31]

Suffice it to note that frontier counties differed from one another in a number of ways. For example, farm-making and farming will differ among prairie, forested and thin-soil rocky counties. Soil type, drainage, rainfall, ease and cost of access to markets, the population of nearby areas, type and adequacy of the infrastructure, the availability of credit, legal and governance institutions, the decade and year, and many other factors can differentiate among counties and within them as well. There were many frontiers that were being closed in antebellum America.

I certainly make no claim that Midland County is representative of all counties in Michigan's Lower Peninsula. Still, an analysis of the links between individual patents, deeds, soils and vegetation (commercially valuable pine forests) within a single multi-soils county should have generic relevance to the same kinds of linkages in other counties and states.

Geographic Level 2: The Old Northwest Territory

2

The Five States of the Old Northwest

"Land" on the frontier is a non-technical term. This technical-heavy chapter introduces readers to how our contemporary soil scientists classify potential farmland. We will see that antebellum markets for land did not adequately adjust prices to what specific soils could yield if properly managed.

The "findings" and interpretations in this new social and economic history rely on soil classifications, population and market trends as well as statistical summaries of crop yields from cultivating different quality soils. Number-heavy chapters using scientific terms and statistical trends can be a challenge both for the analyst and the reader. One way to begin this and other number-heavy chapters is with the summary.

The State As a Questionable Unit of Analysis

Each of the five states carved out of the Old Northwest Territory[1] was richly endowed with potentially productive soils awaiting the investments of farmer-settlers. This chapter takes the state as the spatial unit of analysis for understanding the contributions that the investors in these states made in closing the American frontier.

Although the state is a socially invented unit of analysis, that unit was responsible for creating and marketing land that the federal government granted to the state for its own growth-management and revenue-raising purposes.

There were multiple imperfect markets for antebellum land: federal, state, and private after-privatization markets. The American frontiers were closed under different marketing systems.

There was no magic behind the number five nor the boundaries that were drawn. After all, there are some smaller eastern states such as Delaware and Rhode Island that together could fit inside one of the larger new states in the Old Northwest. However, states do have an established place in American history although not necessarily for the history of farming and settlements. Demonstrating that relevance can be a tedious challenge for both analysts and readers.

This chapter introduces *soil classifications* that will be used later to explore the economic welfare of individual farmers in the single case-study county. One widely accepted classification of soils is based on their potential to be cultivated profitably. We will see that states indeed differ from one another in their endowments of productive soils. These differences are reflected in migration patterns that are relevant to the Kuhn's two questions.

State-by-state soil profiles suggest that a farmer-settler in the mid–1800s would have been advised to invest in Illinois rather than in Michigan. And a later chapter using the same classification of soils will suggest that new settlers would have been advised to invest in some counties within Michigan rather than in others. And still later, we will draw on farm-level evidence to document how soils contributed to a farmer's economic welfare and residential stability.

Note the multiple references to "advise," a term associated with our contemporary investment sector. Advisors work with information, a resource sorely absent in antebellum markets for lands on the expanding frontiers. As will be repeatedly noted, antebellum investors had little reliable information on inter and intra-state soil profiles. This and later chapters will document the questionable and often erroneous information on which soils and acres offered the most promising returns on settler investments.

Prudent investors in nineteenth century America did have access to the questionable field notes prepared by the contractors who surveyed the individual states. The present chapter draws on much later soil science classifications to display inter-state differences in their endowments of more and less promising soils, crucial information not available to antebellum investors and settlers. We see not only significant inter-state differences in the availability of promising soils but intra-state differences as well. These differences are reflected in the harvest returns farmers realized from cultivating different classes of soils. Although this evidence is not perfect, it seems likely that the overall patterns reported in this chapter suggest answers to Kuhn's two questions.

Pre-Soil Science Indicators of Favorable Soils

Before the advent of soil science and the soil classifications, farmer-investors had to rely on available commonsense criteria including rules of thumb on the feel and color of soil as well as to the vegetation that grew on it. One speculator who traveled in Michigan looking for land to buy in 1836 wrote in his diary about land with a large amount of clay, to "too large a dose of sand," to land that contained more Lime, and to soil that "was as black, as light & mellow, as an old asparagus bed." This speculator used the feel criterion to estimate "the quantity of vegetable matter & ashes ... and a due proportion of Silex and clay ... a deep & rich loam which will grease your finger, and feels in the hand like a finely granulated sugar."[2] Even today, farmers and soil scientists estimate the amount of sand in a soil from the feel when rubbing a sample of the soil between their fingers.[3] Color was both an early and present-day technique to classify soils.[4] Black-colored chernozem soils, for example, are known for their humus, phosphoric acids as well as phosphorus and ammonia.

For some patentees, vegetation was a key indicator of the potential productivity of soils. John Gordon wrote in 1836 that Jackson County, Michigan had a six-mile stretch of soil with "a very black appearance and appears to be inexhaustibly rich ... [and] covered chiefly with a thin growth of Burr oak openings, which, as before stated indicate infallibly the most fertile soils"[5] Gordon's journals included numerous references to soil and vegetation. Kenneth Lewis also references early Americans' preferences for forestlands because of the "assumed association between vegetation and soil quality." The "'deep vegetable mold' that accumulated on the forest floor was thought to indicate especially fertile soils."[6]

In colonial Pennsylvania, hickory trees were an indicator of good soil.[7] In Genesee, New York, coverage of hemlock trees lured potential buyers not because of the soil supporting the trees but because of the commercial value of the tree's bark. That is, some settlers were interested in exploiting what was on the land perhaps more than what farm crops the cleared acres could support.[8]

Hulbert claimed that "important soils came early to bear definite reputations, however little their chemical composition was understood" and "while soil colors were not ignored, soils came to bear definite reputations from the trees which grew on them, and are still so known"—for example, piney soil and hickory bottoms.[9] If the classifications and reputations were widely known and were approximately accurate indicators of the fertility of soil (that is, if there was perfect information), then settlers would never have selected poor soils to farm.

There were certainly organized efforts to make existing and would-be farmers aware of the best and latest information on soils and how to manage them. Publications from the Commissioner of Patents included agricultural information. Massachusetts' 1830 initiative in creating a geological bureau responsible for surveying soils and other natural resources was followed by eighteen other states, including Michigan,[10] and by 1856 there were 912 state and local agricultural societies nationwide. Beginning in 1819, agricultural publications disseminated a "growing body of folk wisdom and scientific knowledge" to American farmers.[11] Of more immediate use (or perhaps mis-use through misleading information) to buyers of land were the earlier-noted classifications that surveyors were required to make regarding land as being either first, second or third rate for agricultural purposes. These notes were made available to the buying public.[12]

Congress was aware of the importance of good agricultural land, although it was not possible to define it. We saw earlier that the bounty land to be made available to the veterans of the War of 1812 was to be "fit for cultivation, not otherwise appropriated."[13] Two million such acres were to be made available in Michigan, but the surveyors working in the state reported in 1815 that they found wet land, many swamps and marshes, scrubby oaks, poor barren soil "where not one acre in a hundred was fit for cultivation."[14] As a result, Michigan's bounty land quota was shifted to Illinois and Missouri.

Non-wetland considerations were used in Illinois to classify as unfit for cultivation "much land described as first rate soil but which is prairie and distant from timber."[15] However, for the most part, wetlands were considered central to the designation as unfit for cultivation.

This criterion was the basis for several swampland laws beginning with the 1849 and 1850 Acts and their imprecise terms "swamp and overflowed lands unfit for cultivation" that were to be granted to individual states for their own disposal to private buyers. (These lands will be re-visited again later.) Michigan and Wisconsin drew on the original surveyors' field notes in making selections, whereas Ohio, Indiana and Illinois based their selections on their own surveys.

Michigan selected 7,273,724 swamp acres, more than twice what Wisconsin and Illinois claimed and five times the amount by Indiana. But as a large proportion of these acres was patented over time, it seems likely that the land, after drainage (as anticipated in the Acts but apparently not followed in Michigan) was used for agricultural purposes.[16]

My reading of the surveyors' notes for Michigan's Midland County indicates that townships and their sections had mixtures of wet and well-drained lands. Even the smallest units (typically 40 acres) were heterogeneous with regard to type (fertility) of soil, vegetation and water or drainage. In the absence of detailed soil and land surveys based on modern procedures, large areas of land could be incorrectly classified until quite late in the nineteenth century. This is seen in a study of northern Macomb County in the southeast of Michigan bordering Lake St. Clair. Somewhat poorly drained lake plain considered unattractive by early farmers was, according to more recent surveys, some of the best in the county for crops.[17] Later chapters go into greater depth on Michigan's soils and the farming of them.

Legislative acts that created the market for land referred to swamps, not soils. "Swamp lands" are a part of the legislative history on the closing of the American frontier.

Swamps

An emphasis on swamps rather than on soils might have influenced some settlers to bypass Michigan. But this state was not alone in being relatively late in drawing farmer-settlers to it. "[T]he whole Great Lakes region was settled tardily. Buffalo lagged behind Pittsburgh; Cleveland was a raw village when Cincinnati was a thriving city. In 1820, five-sixths of Indiana's people lived in the south and one-sixth in the center; its north was about as vacant as the adjoining part of Michigan. Chicago's population reached a hundred after Peoria's and, for that matter, after Pontiac's and Ann Arbor's."[18]

Northeastern Ohio's Black Swamp south of the Maumee River was a barrier to movement throughout the year, even after the government pushed a road through it in 1812.[19] And based on his expedition into northern Indiana in 1823, Major Stephen Long wrote that "The country is so wet that we scarcely saw an acre of land upon which a settlement could be made."[20] Hugh Prince quotes a number of similar negative observations about antebellum Ohio, Indiana, Illinois and Michigan. General William Henry Harrison wrote in 1812 that the country north of the Bloomington, Indiana moraine "is almost continued swamp to the Lakes."[21] Looking south, southern Illinois was called "Egypt," a poor, unhealthy area, a "land of darkness."[22]

Modern Soil Science

Soil, according to Stoll as referenced earlier, "is the tablecloth under the banquet of civilization: no matter what people build on it, when it moves all the food and finery go with it."[23] Earlier civilizations realized the economic importance of different soils. For example, Thucydides wrote that fertile soil made for an unequal distribution of wealth, whereas Strabo argued that the fertility of the soil made populations prosperous and peaceful. In 1925, Franklin Thomas placed these writers in the larger context of the environmental basis of society.

By 1993 there was a sizeable literature on the geography of America's own past, including studies on the importance of soil. Douglas Helms' previously referenced "Soil and Southern History" examined the role of soils in that region. At least one study of German settlers in America found that soil was more important than culture in influencing agricultural systems. Steven Stoll's *Larding the Lean Earth* and Archer Hulbert's *Soil: Its Influence on the History of the United States* cover similar topics.[24] But "soil" is too general a term, one that invites science-based classifications that will allow inter-state comparisons in soil endowments that in turn suggest answers to Kuhn's questions on the wisdom of the locational decisions made by Michigan's pioneer settlers.

Over the years, soil scientists developed a variety of classification schemes with technical details well beyond the scope of the present study. The U.S. Department of Agriculture's *The Yearbook of Agriculture 1957, Soil* provides several overview chapters on the history of soil science and the status of the components of soil fertility, soil management, cropping systems, classifications and surveys, and the use of soil maps.[25]

Current soil classifications do not capture all the sixteen elements considered necessary for the growth of green plants.[26] These classifications follow two general concepts. The first is the *capacity of the soil to function*. It "refers to the inherent properties of soil formation," including climate, topography, vegetation and parent material. Soil surveys include these features through analyses of texture, slopes, structure, and soil color.

The second concept refers to *fitness for use* or soil health and use. Measures of fitness or quality are based on "land capability" and "prime farmland" measures taken from actual crop production statistics. These figures are assumed "to reflect the inherent properties of soils."[27]

Even these general concepts are too narrow for some experts. The National Academy of Sciences, for example, defines "soil quality as the ability of a soil to perform its three primary functions: to function as a primary input to crop production; to partition and regulate water flow, and to act as an environmental filter."[28]

In practical terms, soil surveys use various observations (such as soil horizons) and laboratory analyses to label *soil series*. These are soils that "because of their similar origins, chemical, and physical properties cause the soils to 'behave' similarly for land use purposes." The series are typically named after the town or area where a series was first recognized. The members of the series have up to three common horizons: surface, subsoil and substratum.[29] While it might appear that members of a series remain fairly constant over time, in fact they can change due to erosion, runoff, wetness and drainage, climatic limitations and both root zone and tillage limitations.

Further complicating these classifications of productivity and fitness for use are the ways that different crops respond to the same soils. For example, oats are a cool season crop; corn is better adapted than wheat or oats to poorly drained soils, whereas forage crops are better suited than corn to well-drained, steep or easily eroded soils.[30] The management and technical skills of farmers are also very important with regard to cropping systems (the kind and sequence of crops grown) and soil-management systems (use of fertilizers and drainage practices along with cropping systems).[31]

Congress early on recognized that land in the public domain differed in its suitability for farming. The simple inadequate dichotomy of suitable or not suitable was incorporated in the Scrip-Warrant Act of 1812 that awarded "bounty land" to veterans of the war of that year. Only land "fit for cultivation, not otherwise appropriated" was to be selected. Thirty-eight years later the same terminology was included in the Swamp Land Act of 1850. It granted to states "swamp and overflowed lands unfit for cultivation." *Fit* and *unfit* were subjective terms that focused on land and cultivation (as well as drainage), not soil and its fertility.

Soil classification systems are not the only way to describe the farming potential of a discrete area. The number of frost-free days is important as well. For example, northern Illinois has less than 160 of these days, whereas the southern part of the state has more than 200 of them.[32] In Michigan, grain-based agriculture is supposedly not viable north of a convex line stretching from today's Saginaw to Muskegon.[33]

Early settlers and elected officials who created legal markets for land did not have these modern classifications and measurements. Pre-soil science buyers could, as earlier noted, draw on surrogate classifications that included the vegetation growing on the soils. In line with an earlier belief about soils, one source reported that vegetation was "a truer guide than color, for the reason that the latter remained much the same at various altitudes and along the various lines of precipitation, whereas the natural growths showed not only just what the soils produced but what the same soil produced in different positions with respect to the sun, at different altitudes and in different isothermal zones ... soils came to bear definite reputations from the trees which grew on them."[34]

Current soil classifications are state-specific. As noted, a series is named after the location where it was first identified. Illinois recognizes approximately 800 soil types with about 430 of them grouped in 50 soil associations.[35] A 1955 Wisconsin study reported 22 "major soil associations,"[36] and a Michigan soil survey a year later grouped 43 major soil associations into 26 divisions.[37] Ohio and Indiana have analogously unique classifications.

State agricultural experiment stations, in cooperation with the U.S. Department of Agriculture (USDA), have been making and publishing soil surveys since 1899. The Natural Resources Conservation Service (NRCS) provides an online list of hundreds of county-level surveys for the five states in the Old Northwest.[38] Some of the surveys conducted since 1957 include estimated yields of common agricultural crops under what are called "defined levels of management." Because this information is not available statewide in detailed form, inter-state soil-productivity comparisons are not possible. It is necessary to rely on two surrogate measures.

The USDA's Soil Conservation Service (later known as the National Resources and Conservation Service) provides the first such measure, an 8-category classification of soils based on their "limitations" for crop production. Classes 1 and 2 have few or only moderate limitations that would reduce the choices of plants that (as of 1992) might be grown on these soils. Subclasses within the broader classes indicate special limitations, such as excess wetness. And "capability units" within the subclasses in turn "give some prediction of expected agricultural yields and indicate treatment needs."[39] However, land in the two top capability classes do not necessarily have the highest value of crop production per acre. That is, these are not perfect indicators of soil productivity and potential profitability for a farmer.[40]

Our contemporary buyers and sellers of land trade in an information-rich market in contrast to the information-poor markets of the 1800s.

Sharon W. Waltman of the National Soil Survey Center in Lincoln, Nebraska provided me a classification of soil types that included *Alfisol* and *Mollisol*, both considered the most productive of the twelve that were listed. Table 2.1 gives the state totals for each of these two classifications ranked by state according to the proportion of their soils categorized as most suitable to agriculture. Again, this kind of information was not available to nineteenth-century potential farmer-settlers.

These classifications are only general indicators of the agricultural potential of soils, the component of physical geography covered in the present study. But the two separate classifications provide similar rankings that place Michigan as the least promising state for a new settler to begin farming. It should be emphasized, however, that the biasing effects of including the Upper Peninsula and the northern part of the Lower Peninsula somewhat mask the estimated proportionate supply of alfisol and mollisol soils statewide. Still, Michigan has the fewest number of such acres, whereas Illinois has nearly 2.3 times more of them.

The estimates in Table 2.1 indicate that Illinois is the highest soil-endowed state among the five members of the Old Northwest Territory. Michigan's relative endowment of alifsol and mollisol soils was half that of Illinois. Just on a probability basis, a new settler blindly selecting land would have had a great probability of economic success by moving to Illinois rather than to Michigan, although Michigan did have nearly fourteen million of these same promising soils.

Table 2.1: Two State-Level Soil Classifications

	Few or Only Some Limitations for Cultivation[a]	*Alifsol and Mollisol*[b]	*Acres of Alifsol and Mollisol*[c]
	Percent Statewide		
Indiana	64%	82%	18,606,198
Illinois	63%	90%	31,871,339
Ohio	50%	78%	20,163,024
Wisconsin	35%	55%	19,391,970
Michigan	31%	38%	13,954,288

a. *Land Capability Class, by State, 1997 available online at http://www.nrcs.usda.gov/technical/land/meta/m6175.html.*
b. *Soil Survey Staff, 1994. State Soil Geographic Data for U.S. States and Territory of Puerto Rico. USDA-Natural Resources Conservation Service (formerly Soil Conservation Service), National Soil Survey Center, Lincoln, Nebraska. Digital soil maps and attribute tables—9/94 CD-ROM media. http://soils.usda.gov. Soil Survey Staff. 1999.* Soil Taxonomy: A Basic System of Soil Classification for Making and Interpreting Soil Surveys. *2nd edition. Natural Resources Conservation Service. U.S. Department of Agriculture Handbook 436.*
c. *Based on the number of acres surveyed in the tables referenced above in footnotes a and b.*

Quite aside from the importance that soils had for those who cultivated them, some governments in the past levied higher taxes on supposedly more productive than on less productive soils. Being a major source of tax revenue in many countries, including state and local governments in the United States, it is not surprising that a government would attempt to assess land according to its value. After the War for Independence, South Carolina in 1784 assessed land according to "quality and yield."[41] The third-century Roman Emperor Diocletian assessed land "according to its productivity and a fixed sum (renewed every five years) was levied on it."[42] At least one Chinese dynasty imposed higher taxes on land that was advantaged by its proximity to urban markets.[43]

In its efforts to prevent Hungarian and Bohemian nobles from further pauperizing their peasants, the Habsburg Monarchy classified some arable land into nine discrete categories according to fertility, with appropriate tax assessments for each plot of rustical (rather than dominical) land.[44] In the late 1940s, American experts rediscovered that a soil classification could be used to determine tax assessments.[45]

That is, governments (if not investor-settlers in the mid–1800s) recognized that soils differ in their productivity, their yields and their value. The more productive soils attracted higher taxes. However, in America *none of these classifications were used to price federally-owned land* to be individually privatized or granted to states—with swampland and other exceptions to be introduced later. Potential settler-investors had little reliable information on what was being trucked and traded in the markets for land.

As will be seen in a later chapter, "soil rental rates" are assigned individual soil types under the Conservation Reserve Program administered by the U.S. Department of Agriculture's Farm Service Agency. (The titles of these governmental units sometimes change over time.) This kind of information seems only available at the individual county level or on a sample of all farms in a state. For example, Illinois has a soil productivity rating index that ranks soil types according to the soil's productive capacity on a statewide but not on a county-level basis.[46]

But how useful or reliable are these classifications? Unlike many narrative historians, it is essential in the present analysis to dip into some technical language not normally found in general histories.

A measure or classification has high *reliability* if it yields the same or very similar results after repeated tests or applications. High *validity* means that our two measures of interstate differences in quality of soils actually measure differences in potential fertility and productivity.

We do not have details on the protocols that soil scientists used to check the accuracy of their field and chemical analyses. Nor do we know if the soil scientists made repeated independent analyses in the field and in the labs. (They probably did so.) But the fact that two different classifications taken at different times with different components and personnel produced almost the same exact rankings among states suggests that these classifications have analytical value although they may not be 100 percent accurate. (The chapter on the case-study county of Midland, Michigan will use recent soil survey classifications to assess the economic benefits that 1860 farmer settlers realized from working different classes of soils.)

"Validity" is a more significant consideration. If the two classifications adequately measure gross differences in productivity, then the results based on the classifications are probably acceptable as well.

Economic historians Atack and Bateman at least partially tested the validity of standard soil classifications. Their research is essential reading for other researchers.

The Atack and Bateman study of agriculture in the antebellum North found that a farm's profitability was "influenced by soil type, which affected yields and influenced what crops the farmer could best grow." However, the authors warned that their results based on eleven soil types "should not command much attention" because purely local factors, besides soil, might have influenced their measures of profitability. These authors also found systematic crop-specific yield differences related to soil type.[47] (Atack and Bateman did not give much attention to the overlap between physical and human geographies. Their concerns focused on agricultural economics, not the wisdom of the investments made by farmers and how soils influenced the closing of the American frontier.)

Richard Easterlin's statewide estimates of 1840 farm productivity levels in Michigan and Wisconsin were lower than estimated regional and national levels and not much different from older states along the eastern seaboard. He suggested that relatively low productivity and income levels for new states, such as Michigan, may be partially attributable to the heavy labor investments required in clearing land and in adjusting old farming technologies to new environments.[48] (Remember that our time periods were before the arrival of the soil and agricultural sciences.) That is, one might expect differences over time in the congruence between physical and human geographies as represented by population and soil maps. There is no reason to expect that the relationship between these two maps would remain constant over time.

Linking soil types to what was grown on them was covered in other studies that identified some of the perils of statistical analyses such as those reflected in discrepancies among medians, means and ranges of productivity for corn and wheat from 1843 to 1856 (medians and ranges) and later to 1859–60 (means). The Commissioner of Patents provided the earlier estimates; Atack and Bateman estimated the 1859–60 means.

The ranges are fairly sizeable, suggesting considerable differences among farms in the same state, as well as possible increases in productivity over time. But we do not know how these crop estimates were related to soils. And it is not known whether new settlers in these decades were aware of these variations when making their own land and agricultural investments. If they had known, then there might have been a different spatial pattern in the closing of the antebellum American frontier.

These earlier studies should remind the reader of the present chapter's use of state-level aggregated evidence. Later chapters limit our focus to farmers working specified soils in one mid–Michigan county.

Information is available on statewide estimates of corn and wheat yields. According to the Commissioner of Patents (of the U.S. Patent Office), Michigan, but not Wisconsin, had the lowest *median* productivity of corn for the period 1843–1858, but its median productivity (bushels per acre) of wheat was the highest of the five states in the Old Northwest. If statistical means are the measure, then by 1859–60, these 1840 interstate differences seem to have disappeared for reasons not yet studied.[49]

The range of corn and wheat yields suggests wide inter and intra-state variations among farmers, as seen in Table 2.2. It ranks states from high to low with regard to the low end of their corn productivity measures. Current production statistics reveal similar intra-state variations. For example, in Illinois the "areas of highest soil productivity, regardless of management level, are in the east-central and north-central counties."[50] In Wisconsin, both corn and wheat yields per acre from 1996 through 2000 were somewhat higher in the state's southern than in its northern counties.[51]

Modern farmers presumably have fairly good information on which crops will do best on which soils. Pioneer farmers were not as fortunate. They not only had to select a state but also a county that had the most promising soils. Statewide statistics can mask how soils influenced yields at the level of individual farms, a focus of later chapters. The present one is limited to the statewide information that "might" have been available to potential farmer-investors in the mid-nineteenth century.

Table 2.2: Range of Per-Acre Corn and Wheat Yields, 1843–1856

	Corn	*Wheat*
Illinois	40–50	10–20
Indiana	30–60	9–25
Ohio	25–60	10–35
Wisconsin	25–50	12–40
Michigan	15–40	12–30

William Parker and Judith Klein, "Productivity Growth in Grain Production in the United States, 1840–1860 and 1910," in Output, Employment, and Productivity in the United States after 1800 *(Princeton Studies in Income and Wealth 30, 1966), Table B, 1, p. 500 as reported in Atack and Bateman* To Their Own Soil, *164.*

Chapter 4 will examine in greater depth the inter-county differences in productivity within Michigan followed by later chapters that focus on a single Michigan county with intra-county variations that mirror those in all five states of the Old Northwest. This intercounty analysis confirms some of what we discovered based on inter-state comparisons. Suffice it to note that a settler wishing to begin farming not only had to select a state but also a county within it and an exact parcel of land within one of the county's (normally) sixteen townships. Table 2.2 on ranges of corn and wheat yields per acre suggest that many unwise decisions were made.

Those who choose wisely were rewarded. Easterlin's estimates of agricultural income per worker for 1840 suggest, again, that farming in Michigan was not the wisest choice a farmer-investor could make. Ohio's annual "agricultural income per worker" was highest at $157, followed by Illinois ($154), Indiana ($137), Wisconsin ($132) and, finally, Michigan at $116.[52] These numbers provide a partial answer to Kuhn's questions. However, these state-wide totals can be misleading, as each state had its own inter-county differences in soil endowments and yields from them.

Atack and Bateman's estimates of per-capita income of owner-occupiers and tenants for 1859–1860 also place Michigan owner-occupiers at the bottom of the five-state ranking at only $85. Illinois owner-occupiers earned twice as much on a per-capita basis at $165, followed by Ohio ($146), Indiana ($113) and Wisconsin ($96). On the other hand, Michigan tenant farmers had the third highest per-capita incomes among the five states, although in all instances, tenants fared less well than owner-occupiers.[53]

Not only were Michigan farm incomes the lowest in the region, farmers in the state had the lowest rates of return on the investments they made in their farms, a finding we will re-visit in a later chapter. In fact, farmers who did not sell some of their land had a negative rate of return in 1860 (Table 2.3).

Assuming that a Michigan settler was acting on accurate information about what could be earned from farming, this settler "must have viewed starting a farm as an investment whose payoff lay well into the future."[54] Of course, farm families had to live in the present; they had to feed and house their families. That this was a major challenge is seen in the food "deficits" reported for farmers in six of the nine Michigan counties sampled by Atack and Bateman.[55] The survival of these farmers depended on non-farm income or living off the capital the settlers brought with them to their new homes. The reported space-based patterns again reveal a divergence between physical and human geographies as represented by soil and population maps.

Table 2.3: Rate of Return on Farm Investments, 1860

	Without Capital Gains[a]	*With Captial Gains*[a]	*Mean Profitability of Owner-Occupied Farms*[b]
Illinois	10.8	19.1	0.185
Ohio	8.3	13.3	0.120
Wisconsin	6.6	11.4	0.077
Indiana	3.8	10.4	0.061
Michigan	-0.5	5.8	–0.128

a. *Atack, Bateman and Parker, "The Farm, the Farmer, the Market," Table 64. Atack and Bateman,* To Their Own Soil, *255.*
b. *Atack and Bateman,* To Their Own Soil, *257.*

Several qualifications are in order regarding the relative unattractiveness of Michigan as a state for new settlers to begin farming.

First, only three of the nine Michigan counties (each represented by a single township) in the study by Atack and Bateman were in the two lowest tiers of the state's counties. As will be seen in later chapters, these counties had a higher proportion of better farmland than did counties elsewhere in the state. Two of Atack and Bateman's other counties were in the far north of the state's Lower Peninsula. Samples matter. Not all counties were of equal size or with equal soils.

Second, as Atack and Bateman note, farmers "invested in farms, not farming." Farmers who could afford more acres were able to reap higher returns, so that "where the average 'loss' for a [Michigan] farm under 40 acres was –21.6 per cent, the farmer who could afford to buy a farm of 160 acres or larger could expect an average return of 11.5 percent."[56] (The distinction between horizontal versus vertical expansion and investments is relevant here.)

Third, these researchers relied on a farm's total acres, not those that were "improved" and cultivated. The number of improved acres depended on the speed that a farmer was able to clear his land of trees. As Michigan was settled later than three of its neighboring states, it might be expected to have had farms with perhaps the same number of total acres but fewer improved ones and thereby lower total harvests during the early land-clearing process. That however does not explain differences in harvests per acre.

Finally, there are different quantitative techniques available to estimate rates of return with and without capital gains. Other approaches might have yielded results at odds with those of Atack and Bateman.[57]

Perhaps Michigan farmers as a whole were not all that worse off than farmers in other states in 1860, but the existing evidence suggests that many Michigan settlers made some unwise investment decisions: there were settlers attempting to farm land in the far north of the Lower Peninsula; the state had relatively fewer acres of good soil to begin farming; and there were many farmers who would have been better off if they had settled in a neighboring state. As Michigan soil scientist J. O. Veatch noted in 1941, it was "a waste of human effort to attempt to use any poor land for the production of farm crops,"[58] yet many kamikaze farmers throughout the Old Northwest (not just in Michigan) did exactly that. Irrational investors continued to be irrational farmers (but not forever, as will be documented in a later chapter).

Two maps, one of good soils available for cultivation and the other for where farmers were farming, reveal that many farmers were working poor soils. There is some statistical support showing that these unwise soil-selectors had to leave their land between 1860 and 1870. (Other farmers also moved but not in the same high proportions.)

Poor selections of soils can be attributed both to incomplete and to deliberately false descriptions of soils and the potential for farmers to benefit from buying and cultivating certain questionable soils. The market for soils (lands) was far from perfect for reasons suggested earlier and to be elaborated further later. This imperfection not only wasted individual investments but the nation's aggregated resources as well.

States Where New Farmers Settled in the 1850s

Michigan began 1850 with both advantages and disadvantages in attracting new settlers and farmers. On the negative side were the relatively low returns on farm labor and investment, as well as the lowest supply of better-quality land, as seen in Table 2.2. But on the positive side, the low rate of pre–1850 farm formation meant that the state began the decade with a relatively large supply of high-quality unfarmed land.

Before exploring relative rates of farm growth in the 1850s, an important evidentiary caveat is needed, as we are working with incomplete and often mislabeled statistics. The first national census of agriculture was taken in 1840 but detailed information on land, production and monetary values was not collected until 1850. And regardless of the size of a farm and the acres cultivated, a farm needed $100 of agricultural goods produced for home use or sale in order to be included in the two agricultural censuses of 1850 and 1860.[59] The actual written instructions to the census enumerators in 1860 simply stated that "the produce of which amounts to one hundred dollars in value" without specifying home use or market sales.[60] (In the year 1860 $100 is equivalent to $2,817 in 2017.) These were estimated values, as was the other information collected by the enumerators.[61] The $100 threshold meant that settlers in the initial stages of "farm making" were not enumerated. That there were serious undercounts of actual farmers is seen in the population censuses for these two years. That is, we do not have accurate maps of human settlements (human geography).

Census enumerators in 1860 were to distinguish between farmers and farm laborers for each person over fifteen years of age.[62] There were many more farmers than farms, with the discrepancy explained by start-ups that did not meet the $100 threshold, sons in farm families, and various tenancy arrangements.

The combination of agricultural and population census information allows for a variety of farmer-related classifications—for example, farmers without farms, yeoman farms, tenants in part, tenants in whole and, in combination with other information, farms without farmers.[63]

The size of the potential undercount of farms is suggested in Yang's calculation that 34 percent of the Michigan farmers who in the 1860 population census reported they owned real estate were not listed in the agricultural census of that year. Michigan's four neighboring states had fewer than fourteen percent of these farmers without farms.[64]

We will explore some of these ambiguities in later chapters. For the present, we can only admit that the published farm-related statistics are best estimates, incomplete, and perhaps biased differently in each of the five states of the Old Northwest. Our recent soils maps were not available to antebellum settlers who closed farm frontiers.

All five of these states added rural residents, farms and farm acres from 1850 to 1860. The components of these increases differed among the states. Although Ohio, the earliest settled of the five, had a negative population migration rate as early as the 1840–1849 decade, the state's natural population increase more than compensated for these losses both in the 1840s and the 1850s. (That is, the resident population produced more children than the number of residents who left the state.) Indiana, the second state to be more heavily settled, displayed a similar negative migration rate during the 1850s but a compensatory natural increase in population. Illinois (65 percent), Michigan (60 percent) and Wisconsin (120 percent) had more immigrants than emigrants during this same decade.[65]

Rural areas housed most of these five states' populations and growth. Over 80 percent of each state's 1860 population was classified as rural, but the absolute numbers indicate that Michigan had the smallest rural population in 1860, and it was second to last in the number of rural residents added during the 1850s. However, growth rates and rural-urban balances can hide the absolute size of changes and their end points.[66] This is especially clear for trends in the number of farms and their size.

The number of Michigan farms increased by 83 percent from 1850 to 1860, representing an additional 28,330 farms, the lowest of the five states. For every 1,000 new Michigan farms, the other states added 6,700 new ones. (Table 2.4) Even though Michigan's farm growth rate was over three times that of Ohio's, the latter added 7,749 more farms. Every other state also added more improved acres—that is, "cleared land used for grazing, grass, or tillage, or which is now fallow..."[67]

Table 2.4: New Farms Added, 1850–1860

	Farms in 1850	*Farms in 1860*	*Increase from 1850 to 1860*	*Percentage Increase from 1850 to 1860a*
Ohio	143,807	179,889	36,082	25%
Indiana	93,896	131,826	37,930	40%
Illinois	76,208	143,310	67,102	88%
Michigan	34,089	62,422	28,333	83%
Wisconsin	20,177	69,270	49,093	243%

Kennedy, Agriculture of the United States, *222.*

There are at least two culturally relevant explanations of the statistical growth patterns displayed in Table 2.4. First, antebellum settlers had little knowledge of soils, and/or soils were less important than other considerations. Second, although there was some understanding of soils, there was wide misinformation on what Michigan had to offer settler-farmers.

No statistical information is available on what settlers knew about soils. However, one study of Ohio and Indiana household heads in 1860 found that 22 percent of them (both farm and non-farm) lived in a "poor soil area (terminal moraine)," while less than six percent of Illinois household heads lived in similar areas.

Since only 45 percent of the Ohio sample listed farming as an occupation (in contrast to 62 percent for Indiana and 56 percent for Illinois), it is unclear how many farmers made unwise soil decisions in information-poor markets for land. The authors of the study suggested "that migrants tended to avoid those 'geologically disadvantaged' counties with poor quality—counties in the Southern portion of the three states."

Furthermore, there was "no statistically significant relationship between land availability and migration." As might be expected in a rational market, the quality of the land was apparently more important than its quantity.[68] However, we are reminded that although the antebellum economy was agriculturally based, farmer-investors were not the only ones closing the American frontier.

Analysts often use the word "tend," an imprecise term. The historical record qualifies tendencies, as some settlers did take up farming on poor soils, even well after the Civil War. Rose Moore's study of Michigan homesteaders from 1878 to 1890 in the northern county of Oscoda in Michigan's Lower Peninsula found that farmers on "the Grayling sand outwash plains would have been hard pressed to find another area east of the Mississippi so completely unsuited for agriculture." Americans were not the only unwise settlers, for homesteaders made the same mistake trying to farm the Canadian Shield in Ontario.[69] Canada's land market was as opaque as the one in the United States.

There are also examples of the wise choice of soils in early America,[70] and there were American farmers who adopted good soil management practices. That large numbers did not follow good practices is seen in the widespread abandonment of lands that were exhausted or eroded in states east of the Appalachians.[71] According to one farmer who left his native Vermont, the older cultivated lands in that state had by the middle of the 1850s either "lost much of their topsoil by erosion" or "had been exhausted by continued wheat cropping."[72]

As suggested earlier, the relatively greater amount of unimproved land in Michigan and Wisconsin suggests that farmers in these two more recently settled states were still at the beginning of making or establishing their farms. Table 2.5 reports the number of new farms acres added (not the number of farms).

Table 2.5: Net Changes in Farm Acres, 1850–1860

	Total Acres Added	*Improved Acres Added*	*Unimproved Acres Added*
Ohio	2,475	2,774	-299
Indiana	3,596	3,196	399
Illinois	8,875	8,057	818
Michigan	2,647	1,547	1,100
Wisconsin	4,917	2,701	2,216

Joseph Kennedy, Agriculture of the United States in 1860; Compiled from the Original Returns of the Eighth Census *(Government Printing Office, 1864), 222.*

Except for the labor, time and investments required to clear land and begin farming, Michigan's supply of higher quality land should (in a world of perfect information) have been a magnet drawing wise farmers to the state.

Instead of the magnet concept, the trend data are more supportive of a population gravity model. Earlier-arrived farmers had a greater attractive power than did the supply of unfarmed more productive soils. Settlers moved to where most others had already invested in farming.

A good prediction of where farmers settled in 1860 was the geographic distribution of 1850 farmers.

An assumption of rationality is at odds with the apparent irrational (unwise) decisions that some farmers made in selecting the land they were to farm. The rational assumption is that pre–1850 farmers settled primarily on land with such soils as alfisol and mollisol (see Table 2.1). If the numbers of farm acres reported for 1850 are subtracted from the total acres with these two soil types, we have the supply of high-quality land available to new farms beginning in 1850.

Table 2.6 juxtaposes these 1850 totals with the number of new farm acres added in each state from 1850 to 1860. The final column in this table indicates that Ohio farmers theoretically would have exhausted the supply of high-quality land in that state before 1860. New farmers in Ohio, under these assumptions, chose to be close to existing farmers rather than to settle in a neighboring state where better farming soil was still available.[73] This suggests that Kuhn could have asked his Michigan questions for Ohio settlers during different decades within the nineteenth century. Many of these Ohio farmer-settlers made unwise investment decisions.

Table 2.6: Going Where Others Had Already Gone

	Quality Land (alfisol, mollisol) Available in 1850[a]	*New Farm Acres Added 1850–60*[b]	*Percent of Quality Land Taken by 1860*
Ohio	2,166	2,475	114%
Indiana	5,813	3,595	62%
Illinois	19,834	8,875	45%
Michigan	9,570	2,684	28%
Wisconsin	16,415	4,517	28%

a. *In 1,000s of acres. The number of acres reported in the USDA's soil tables (see Table 1.1) are multiplied by the percent of each state's alfisol and mollisol soils, also Table 1.2. There are several different estimates of each state's total acres. For other totals, see the* Statistical Abstract of the United States: 2000 *(Government Printing Office, 2000), 228; also* Historical Statistics of the United States 339.

b. *In 1,000s of acres. Kennedy,* Agriculture of the United States in 1860, *222.*

These hypothetical numbers suggest that many Michigan farmer-settlers were wise in their selection of land despite the earlier reference to incomes, rates of return on investments, and food deficits. Although aggregate totals ignore intra-state variations, they indicate that some Michigan farmers settled in northern counties that were the least favorable, if not very unfavorable, to agriculture (as Atack and Bateman reported). Farmers in other parts of Michigan did not have the same experiences. In an information-poor market, some northern Michigan farmers were making unwise investments.

We are unfortunately again dealing with definitional and aggregation problems that can lead to tautologies and confusing results. And by definition, farms that produced less than $100 in market or home-use value were not included in the agricultural censuses. These excluded large numbers of Michigan farmers—perhaps up to the 34 percent estimated by Yang. It is no wonder that population maps differed from soil maps.

Farmers in Michigan during the 1850s added many more acres than reported in the official census for 1860. By excluding farms below the $100 level, only financially more viable operations are included in the statistics analyzed by scholars. Relative success is assumed from the beginning. But this appears to be a failed tautology, for the Michigan farmers who were included in the agricultural censuses were still worse off than farmers in other states, as seen earlier in Table 2.3. Again, according to Atack and Bateman, the only economically viable Michigan farms had 160 acres or more.[74] And according to other analyses, the state had a disproportionately large number of farms with 20 acres or less of the combined improved and unimproved land (Table 2.7).

Table 2.7: Acres Per Farm, 1860

	Improved Acres Per Farm	*Number of Farms Under 20 Acres*	*Percent of Farms Under 20 Acres*
Ohio	70.2	13,381	7%
Indiana	62.5	12,183	9%
Illinois	91.4	8,414	6%
Michigan	55.7	8,157	13%
Wisconsin	54.0	11,028	9%

Based on Kennedy, Agriculture of the United States, *222.*

It is possible that Michigan's farming disadvantages were attributable in part to the size of farms, not (just) to the soil being farmed or to the growing conditions. We need more information on farming as an industry in order to better understand the congruence between physical and human geographies. This challenge will be addressed in a separate chapter on one Michigan county only.

There is no clear explanation for why relatively more farmers in Michigan than farmers elsewhere worked on smaller farms (other than failing to distinguish between total acres and those being cultivated). This could be a statistical anomaly resulting from a loose definition of terms or the application of them. An annex table provides tenancy and related statistics for the five different states in 1860.

The 1860 published agricultural census is unclear as to the category of land used in tables reporting the size distribution of farms. Calculations that multiply the number of Michigan farms in a size category by the mid-point in each category yields 1,760,544 more acres than the state's total of improved acres but 1,793,984 fewer acres that the total of improved and unimproved acres!

Based on comparisons between analyses based on published census reports and their own work based on information recorded from the original census forms, Atack and Bateman found enough errors to warn others that "comparisons of the original data with the published summaries would provide sufficient evidence to impeach any work based on those published figures."[75] The markets for land were information-poor and the statistics reporting on markets were questionable as well.

Michigan was not the only state with small farms, although it appears from Atack and Bateman's research that small farms in other states were financially more rewarding than those in Michigan. And certainly, farmers in all five states made unwise choices in cultivating poorly endowed soils. But, of course, land had value beyond the agricultural potential of the soil. Certain tree species (especially varieties of white pine) gave worth to the land. The owners of land with commercially valuable trees neither planted nor cultivated the flora; owners only harvested it.

Logging companies and individuals also had to make wise decisions in selecting land they bought for the vegetation on it. I covered some of these considerations in a separate article.[76] We focus here on farms, farmers and soils, ingredients for both physical and human geographies. But first, some other possible reasons why the two maps, one on the physical geography of soils and the other on the human geography of farmer-settlers, differed from one another.

With a large supply of high-quality soils in Michigan and a dwindling supply of the same in other states, especially in Ohio, why wouldn't a large majority of prudent settlers choose Michigan to begin farming? Many, of course, did, but fewer than those who moved to each of the neighboring states during the 1850s. (Table 2.4) Moreover, Michigan during the 1850s attracted only 2,000 more new farms than were newly established during the same decade in the state of New York, a major home state for migrants to Michigan. (New York added 26,378 new farms while Michigan added 28,333.)

These growth trends suggest that migrants were probably attracted both by the available supplies of farmable land and by the number of earlier farmers already on the land (again, an example of how the wisdom of crowds operated).

Back to Questionable Statistics' on Land

I have not been able to identify complete state-level statistics on how farmer-settlers obtained their land and the evidence on which investment decisions were made. Statistics that the General Land Office published in its annual reports are incomplete because they refer to land patented by that office, not the land that was granted to states for their own sale to private buyers.[77] And neither state nor federal patents indicate how privately-owned land was used.

In 1935, the U.S. Department of Agriculture prepared a chart showing the number of patented acres issued from 1800 to 1934 along with notations on the chart indicating the start of major new laws on the public domain—including the 1800 credit system, repeal of this system in 1820, the General Preemption Act of 1841, the 1847 Military Bounty Act, the 1854 Graduation Act, the 1855 Military Bounty Act, and laws subsequent to 1860. Grants to states and railroads were not included as land entries covered in this graph and related statistics,[78] but the chart clearly indicates a significant increase in patents following the adoption of more liberal terms for acquiring land. Investors were sensitive to prices but not necessarily to soils that farmers would cultivate.

Arthur H. Cole's classic 1927 study of national and inter-state variations in the sale of public lands from 1816 to 1860 analyzed the annual "dollar receipts" from the sale of public lands. His substitution of dollars for acres not only missed grants to states but also the approximately sixty million acres of military land warrants provided under several congressional acts.[79] Moreover, Cole's dollar figures included differently priced land resulting from the Graduation Act passed in 1854. This law lowered the price per acre according to how long the land had been on the market and not patented.[80] Despite these limitations, the large orders of magnitude revealed in the sales trends suggest that new, more liberal laws propelled sales and that "the speculative fever so widely prevalent in the United States during these decades was chiefly responsible for variations in the movement of sales," *with less significance attributable to immigration and transportation improvements.* America's land craze was somewhat analogous to Holland's seventeenth century tulip mania. It was a speculative market that also included farmer-investors who were closing the American frontier.

States differed in their sales trends,[81] but speculators played a significant role in all of them. Gates reported that speculators, not farmer-settlers, acquired 29 of the 38 million acres of public land sold between 1835 and 1837.[82] In the 1850s, 112 individuals and groups bought or directly entered 2,045,000 acres in Illinois. Seventy parties entered 955,000 acres in Michigan.[83] Speculators of course had an interest in marketing land that few of them had independently and "scientifically" assessed. Soil science entered the market much later.

Speculators did not buy land to hold but instead to sell it to farmers, lumbermen and others. As we will see later, most of the small number of farmers in antebellum Midland, Michigan bought their land from others, not from the federal government. Their names are not in the tract books listing the initial patents for land in this county. Researchers necessarily must mine local deed books as well the land patent records.

Lumber interests also bought land for the timber on it, although such land would be available for re-sale once it was stripped of its commercially valuable trees. In 1850, speculators and lumber interests owned slightly more than half (52 percent) of all federal-patented land up to that date in Michigan. The comparable percentages in the other states were Indiana 19 percent, Illinois 22 percent, and Wisconsin 39 percent. Information is not available for Ohio.[84]

By definition, speculators bought in order to sell. Their choices were subject to the same criteria of wisdom applicable to farmer-settlers, with the important caveat that the selection criteria for lumbermen included the commercial value of timber on the land they purchased. The government-created markets for land were absent reliable information on either soils or vegetation.

A Focus on Michigan

Just as many early observations on land and soils were inaccurate or exaggerated, there were also many positive statements by early explorers and settlers. Madison Kuhn demonstrated the skills of a careful professional historian and bibliographer in identifying how widespread these early negative and positive statements about Michigan were. He could not verify claims of harm attributable to the 1812 Military Bounty Land report and to President Madison's 1816 message that Michigan was "covered with swamp or lakes or otherwise unfit for cultivation." There were few if any public references to this message; statements made by surveyors did not make it into the papers; maps that supposedly printed "interminable swamps" across the state were a fiction. In fact, Kuhn found so many positive statements about Michigan that he suggested the state's eastern reputation was too good.[85]

Geographers and others might characterize these early beliefs as human perceptions of the environment rather than actual knowledge. But they were both, and both had elements of truth and fiction. Thanks to scholars such as Kuhn, Prince and others, we now have a better appreciation of the ambiguity surrounding knowledge and attitudes affecting farm settlement if not farming practices. This cultural overlay should not, however, deflect attention from the underlying forces of the physical or material world of soils, vegetation and drainage, as well as the demographic and economic forces that both describe and help explain early settlement patterns and settlers.

Of course, farmers and settlers were clearly not the only people who bought land from the federal government, for as will be seen in the later analyses of patents and farmers in one Michigan county, farmers were more likely to have bought their land from private speculators and owners than to have acquired land through a patent directly obtained from the General Land Office or from the State of Michigan. Future researchers will hopefully be able to provide information on how different speculators priced and marketed their holdings.

Summary

This state-by-state overview suggests that the history of those who privatized the public lands within the five states of the Old Northwest Territory is different from a history of the farmers who invested in soils to cultivate in these states. Speculators were major market players in all states playing a middle-man role in transferring public lands to those who would cultivate them.

Some governments in other countries recognized the economic value of different classes of soils. Taxes were adjusted to soils but doing so in America required information on the promises of different classes of soils. That information was absent, one of the reasons why so many farmer-settlers made unwise investments.

Both the animate and inanimate environments influenced individual farmers' decision-making as expressed by the rate and pattern of the privatization of land followed by the settlement of Michigan and its four neighboring states. On the animate side, the Land Ordinance of 1785 and the Northwest Ordinance of 1787 preceded a lengthy series of laws that created the legal, institutional and organizational structures and procedures regulating how land was to be mapped, described, privatized, protected and taxed. These laws and the institutional structure were consciously intended to influence the larger population's decision-making on what land to buy, where to buy it, and where farmers might settle. But the markets that were man-made were devoid of accurate information.

Early Congresses recognized that not all land was equally fit for farming. Some unfit land became associated with swampy terrain. With the later arrival of soil science and both drainage and farming technologies, some of these lands could support marketable crops. The fit between physical and human geographies could and probably did change over time. The market for agricultural lands today is vastly different from the same markets in the 1800s.

There were rules of thumb used to identify better soils, a key component of the inanimate environment for agriculture. These rules included the color and feel of the soil, as well as the vegetation that grew on it. By the early nineteenth century, soil scientists were developing standards and procedures to classify soils according to their chemical and other properties. Each state adopted its own detailed classifications that prevented accurate inter-state comparisons of the supply of soils differing in their potential productivity.

The two soil-productivity measures introduced in this chapter, together with studies based on other classifications, demonstrate that more fertile soils are apparently just that—they seem to produce higher per-acre yields of selected crops.[86]

Not all states are equally endowed with fertile soil. Although Michigan had a large supply of this essential resource, the state was among the least endowed of the five that were carved out of the Old Northwest Territory. Antebellum settlers who began farming in Michigan could expect relatively lower incomes and lower rates of return on their investments in farming. These statistics suggest that many Michigan settlers made unwise decisions in coming to the state and then in their selection of land to farm. Maps of the most productive soils were not the same as maps of soils that farmers were actually cultivating.

In a world with perfect information, farmers, speculators and lumbermen would only buy the most fertile land or land densely covered with high-value trees. The relative supply of fertile soils should, in a world with perfect information, have acted as a magnet drawing new farmer-settlers. Many migrants were no doubt drawn by the prospects of good farming lands, but other migrants were drawn to where earlier settlers had already established their farms. The pull of existing populations (as in a gravity model) counteracted the magnet of still-available high-quality soil. These forces seem to have affected individual decision-making that collectively shaped the choices of land and settlement patterns. Many decisions proved to be unwise.

Michigan did not have a monopoly of farmers who made unwise choices in the antebellum world of imperfect information. Unwise choices were made in every state, as suggested by the range of corn and wheat productivity figures.

We move now to an examination of within-Michigan inter-county differences in the wisdom of choices of land made by antebellum farmers. This again allows us to compare soil and farmer-settler population maps. While the focus in the following chapters is on one state only, it is very likely that Michigan's spatial settlement history fits a pattern common to all five states of the Old Northwest Territory. The present case study should travel well.

Annex Table 1: Growth and Size of Rural Populations

	State Population 1860	*Rural Population 1860*	*Percent Rural in 1860*	*Rural Population Growth 1840–1860*	*Rural Population Growth 1850–1860*
Ohio	2,349,502	1,939	83%	302	201
Indiana	1,350,428	1,235	91%	269	291
Illinois	1,711,951	1,466	86%	320	679
Michigan	749,113	646	86%	166	277
Wisconsin	775,881	664	86%	246	387

State populations taken from Jos. Kennedy, Preliminary Report of The Eighth Census, 1860 *(Washington: Government Printing Office, 1862), 2. Rural population numbers taken from* Historical Statistics of the United States: *Series 195–201.*

Annex Table 2: Farms, Farm Populations, Tenancy

	Farms[a]	*Farmers*[a]	*Farm Laborers*[a]	*Total Farm Population*[a]	*Workers per Farm*	*Tenancy Rate per 1,000*[b]	*Farmers with Real Estate but not Listed in the Agricultural Census*[c]
Ohio	179,889	223,485	76,484	299,969	1.67	137	11.6
Indiana	131,826	158,714	40,827	199,541	1.51	210	8.2
Illinois	143,310	153,646	47,216	200,862	1.4	179	13.4
Michigan	64,422	88,657	35,884	124,541	2.0	71	34.3
Wisconsin	69,270	99,859	31,472	131,331	1.9	114	12.2

a. *Gates,* The Farmer's Age, *273. With few exceptions relating to widows, these refer to male farmers and laborers. An unknown proportion of farmers are sons living at home and working on their fathers' farms.*
b. *Atack and Bateman,* To Their Own Soil, *111.*
c. *Yang,* Aspects of United States Agriculture, *14.*

Geographic Level 3: Michigan's Lower Peninsula

3

The Privization of Land in the State of Michigan

A Case Study

After the Northwest Territory became part of the new United States of America that new national government passed laws and created agencies to privatize the lands in the Territory's five-to-be new states. The market was a national one with several major players: (1) Washington and its state and local implementing offices, (2) individual states themselves, and (3) the private sector working both within and across states.

These new states were already occupied by Native Americans (Amerindians). That is where this chapter begins.

The following long section covers the multiple innovations that the federal government introduced to create a national market for privatizing public lands that England ceded to the new United States of America. England had already largely abrogated native American claims to their collective property. We close with an overview of the illustrative State of Michigan's own responsibilities for privatizing lands that the national government granted to the state. Other states had analogous implementation histories.

A number of outstanding historians already covered some of what is included in the present chapter. Paul W. Gates, the dean of researchers on the federal land-disposal system, gave particular attention to how American land policy malfunctioned and made life more difficult for potential settlers by interposing speculators between settlers and farmers. That assessment overlooks that some speculators offered credit missing in the financial system that America had at the time.

According to Gates, America had "an incongruous land system,"[1] certainly an imperfect one as seen in the thousands of settlers who wasted their investments in land with unpromising soils, the very source of income to support a family and repay the investments made in closing the American frontier.

We are less endowed with Gates-quality studies of Michigan's own land disposal system. Eight years after one of Gates's students, Dallas Lee Jones, finished his Master's thesis on "The Survey and Sale of the Public Land in Michigan, 1815–1862,"[2] Gates wrote that "a great deal of intensive research in the entry volumes of various land offices needs to be done preparatory to the history of disposal in states like Michigan."[3] Jones's research is an important contribution, although it was never published.

More recent contributions include Kenneth Lewis's *West to Far Michigan* in which he "reconstructs the history of southern Lower Michigan by investigating how frontier settlement created its historical landscape." To Lewis, the "dominant aspect of a landscape is the patterning of its settlement."[4] Contemporary investigators also are beneficiaries of Susan Gray's *The Yankee West*, a "story of three townships on the antebellum southwestern Michigan frontier." She gives particular attention to cultural influences on settlement and settlers.[5] And all researchers on Michigan's past are indebted to Willis Dunbar and George May's general history *Michigan, A History of the Wolverine State*. The *Michigan Historical Review* is another invaluable resource for those researching the state's past.

Most states have their own historical journals and public colleges that offer courses on their own state's history. Central Michigan University is the home for the *Michigan Historical Review* as well as a valuable archive of the state's past. The State Archives in Lansing, the Bentley Library at the University of Michigan as well as local historical societies all provide relevant materials on how the state was settled.

We also benefit from those who have written on antebellum agricultural, especially the previously referenced publications by Atack, Bateman and many others. These studies remind us that a farmer had to make many decisions, including whether to acquire land (through purchase or as a renter or tenant), where to locate, what kind of soil to select, the vegetation on the soil, how many acres to acquire, and how to finance the acquisition. A wise choice of land could be wasted later by unwise decisions on how to farm the land. And a farmer who made an unwise choice of land could still improve the family's fortunes by improved soil and farm-management choices. Decision-making was an ongoing process with individual steps that can be viewed as wise or unwise in their consequences.[6]

Replacing Michigan's Original Inhabitants and Cancelling Their Land Rights

The area stretching from the Blue Ridge to the Great Plains was not an imaginary uninhabited pathless wilderness. In fact, there were both people and a "marvelous network of thoroughfares,"[7] trails that stretched both north and south, as well as east and west in Michigan's Lower Peninsula.[8] It is likely that many subsequent wagon roads followed these paths. River transport in a state with approximately 16,000 miles of waterways on thirty primary rivers and streams was also a significant mode of travel both for the Amerindians and the settlers who replaced them.[9] Waterways not only influenced the geography of native population settlements but of those who replaced them as well.

Michigan's native peoples were on the move well before there was a Michigan Territory and the subsequent twenty-sixth state. Inter-group warfare forced geographical movements.[10]

The state's Amerindians were not organized into large lineages and tribes. Instead, they were acephalous (without a head) bands[11] whose customary vague geographical boundaries gave them implied rights to the resources within these loosely defined areas.[12]

Many of the woodland Amerindians, including the Hurons, "were able to keep extensive cornfields productive for a dozen years or more without resorting to what modern farmers depend upon..."[13] We will see in a later chapter that federal surveyors reported Amerindian farm fields in Midland County, Michigan.[14] They were not on the county's most promising soils. This suggests that farming and settlement patterns were shaped by physical features (rivers) other than soils.

Amerindians in Michigan and elsewhere were regarded as a geographical and physical obstacle to settling by the white population.[15] In fact, unrest among these native peoples in 1815 threatened to delay land surveyors working in both Michigan and Illinois.[16]

Surveys had to be completed before land could be put on the market. But more was required. Because the federal government recognized the claims that Amerindians had to their vaguely demarcated domains, these claims had to be quieted. This was done in Michigan by six major treaties, not by congressionally enacted statutes. That is, Michigan's scattered acephalous bands were treated by Washington as foreign governments that could sign treaties involving the transfer of property rights that were not part of the Amerindians' unwritten legal systems that seemed to recognize rights of use but not sole ownership nor land demarcated by clear boundaries. Other states had similar histories of dispossessing their original residents of their lands and forcefully relocating the inhabitants. This history is part of the history of how land became publicly owned before it was trucked and traded as a market commodity.

The first Indian cession in Michigan was in November 1807, followed by other cessions in 1817, 1819, 1821, and 1828. (Cessions in the Upper Michigan were negotiated in 1836 and 1842.)[17]

It is perhaps not surprising that representatives of the U.S. Government resorted to force, deception and dishonesty to remove claims that Michigan Amerindians might have had to their lands. Under the threat or actual use of force, the native populations were physically removed from the lands covered by these treaties.[18] Physical force altered Michigan's human geography.

Whether or not the native and newly arriving settlers realized that the United States of America was a colonizing power, this seems to be what was actually happening on the ground.

In other colonized areas outside America, local populations had legal-like claims to their land. Amerindians lost their lands, although relatively few individuals were enslaved in the five states of the Old Northwest.

American slaves stolen from Africa did not hold their own land in America. They were the private property of their owners, whereas Amerindians in Michigan were not the private property of white settlers. In theory, the revenues the national and state governments received from the sale of land could have gone to the original owners instead of to federal and state coffers.

The Federal Government's Role in Creating a Market for Land in the Five States of the Old Northwest Territory

In addition to the central government's land-disposal arrangements, states were also granted lands for their own marketing and other uses. This section is limited to how the federal government through its local district offices of the General Land Office directly sold and patented land under an ever-changing system of laws. In Michigan, the Federal government disposed of about two-thirds of all patentable land; the State of Michigan was responsible for the other third.[19] Michigan's neighboring states had their own proportions.

The first federal land sales in Michigan were in 1818. By 1820 only 67,362 acres were sold.[20] The minimum price at that date was $2 per acre, and a buyer had to acquire a minimum of 160 acres (as of 1804). Credit was provided after a buyer made a down payment of one-fifth the cost of the purchased land, with the remaining debt paid in each of the following three years.[21] Except for the credit feature, this was a policy to generate revenues for the federal government.

The high minimum number of acres required, as well as the minimum price of $2 per acre, excluded potential farmer-settlers with modest financial wherewithal. Moreover, the federal government discovered that many buyers were unable to meet their annual loan payments. This situation (exclusion of buyers with modest resources and payment arrears) contributed to the passage of a new law in 1820. The minimum purchase was dropped to 80 acres and the price was lowered to $1.25 an acre, but full payment in specie was required at the time of purchase. In 1832, the required minimum acres were halved again to 40. Nearly all of the land patented in Michigan until 1847 and 1848 (with the implementation of the first of four Military Warrant Acts) was made under the provisions of the 1820 Act, as amended.

By reducing the minimum number of acres in a single patent from the original 640 in 1785 down to 40 in 1832, and by lowering the price per acre from $2 down to $1.25, congress attempted to make it possible for the less affluent to purchase, settle and begin farming. Still, this was a regulated market that focused on acres and prices without regard to differences in soils and access to markets.

A completely free, unfettered market with minimal transaction costs and maximum information on lands available on the market would likely have produced an entirely different settlement history and human geography. For example, the price of an acre of land would vary according to the quality of the soil, the vegetation it supported, and the climate where the land was located (among other considerations). After all, land is not a homogeneous resource. Moreover, one might expect a demand for patents for smaller patented plots such as 10 to 20 acres, not the 40-acre minimum specified by law. As discussed elsewhere in this chapter, smaller plots were sold by speculators (including farmer-speculators) after they had received their own patents or deeds.

There might also have been extremely large landholdings, the creation of an American land-owning aristocracy and "a modified feudalism," one of Horace Greeley's fears.[22]

Numerous agencies were in place to enable non-residents with access to finance to locate, buy, manage and sell land,[23] and there are many examples of individuals who owned thousands of acres of Michigan land as well as land in other states as well. Michigan was a line-item investment among some multi-state land portfolios.

Investors and farmer-settlers didn't invest in Michigan because of some parochial interests. They were buying land that could be re-sold at a handsome profit even if the soils and vegetation on the land were not especially attractive nor known to those who bought and sold the land. Forty acres of poor soils were priced the same as forty acres of highly productive publicly owned soils. There was no price sensitivity, although speculators could vary the prices they demanded for their land holdings.

This was not an ideal twenty-first century transparent market.

Scholars have debated the weak features of American land-disposal laws and how the system that was put in place shaped the decisions made by potential farm-settlers and others. It was not the intention of this system to provide an agricultural policy and, in fact, it might be argued that encouraging farm-settlement could, *ceteris paribus*, have resulted in the over-production of agricultural commodities. Monica Prasad's award-winning *A Land of Too Much* argued that this is what happened decades later.[24] Nor was the American system an integrated settlement strategy such as the Canadians developed over time with the construction of "colonization roads," financial guarantees for railroad companies, and specific searches for land with good agricultural potential.[25] Moreover, the lack of federal credit provisions shifted the responsibility for any such feature to the states and speculators.

Despite the 1820 Act's lowering the barrier to becoming a farmer, a large proportion of Americans were still excluded from following this occupation. This was largely due to the cost of farm-making, not the cost of the land itself. Forty acres of land at $1.25 an acre—or $50—was within the estimated reach of an estimated 90 percent of the population.[26] However, the total cost of land and farm-making to develop and cultivate that land was about $1,200 for a 40-acre Midwest farm, $2,000 for 80 acres, and $3,000 for 160 acres.[27] These numbers suggest that a farmer who bought 40 acres of land under the 1820 $1.25 per-acre provision would have spent $50 for his right to the land. That same average farmer needed another $1,150 to support his family until his crops and cattle could be marketed.

An imperfect market for land and the per-acre cost of land were not the only influences affecting the settlement or non-settlement decisions of aspiring farmers. There was not an adequate national or state financial system in Michigan that would provide credit for new settlers. This gap will be referenced again later.

Many would-be farmers were priced out of this investment and follow-on settlement in Michigan. On the basis of the above costs, 40 percent or more of the population was too poor to participate at the 40-acre level, the "minimal viable size for a family farm that provided the sole source of support." An 80-acre farm was beyond the means of 54 to 74 percent of the population. "Even 'tenancy' on an 80-acre farm lay beyond the means of 5 to 25 percent of the population." Atack and Bateman state that a "midwesterner should have had at least 80 acres" to be profitable.[28] Perhaps more acres were required in Michigan. Those who had more acres also needed more capital to buy land and begin farming it.

These cost estimates suggest that the American agricultural frontiers were closed by relatively more affluent emigrants from eastern states.

These figures also suggest that it is not surprising that millions of acres remained unsold—except for speculators and lumbermen. They were a major part of the market for land with the result that neither the revenue nor the settlement objectives were fully realized. The former became less significant as the national debt incurred during the country's wars was retired. That did not happen until decades later (after the Civil War).[29]

Two new sets of laws were approved unrelated to raising further revenue. First, Congress approved a series of acts awarding military veterans and their survivors with warrants (scrip) that could be used to purchase land or, beginning in 1852, to sell the scrip on the open market. Second, the Graduation Act of 1854 reduced the price of an acre according to how long the land had been on the market unclaimed. Both sets of these laws had significant implications for the human geography of Michigan and other states.

These changes presumably made it possible for those with less access to financial wherewithal to close the American frontier. The "free soil" Homestead Act was not passed until 1862, beyond the 1860 cut-off date for the present study. That act played an important role in the settlement history of land west of the Mississippi River, not the five states of the Old Northwest Territory.

Congress approved Military Bounty Land Grants in 1847, 1850, 1852 and 1855. All four acts provided scrips for 40 and 160 acres; 80 and 120-acre warrants were provided under two of these acts.[30] "Wholesale traffic in military bounties" began in 1852 when Congress made all warrants assignable.[31] Fifty million of the sixty million acres in warrants issued before the Civil War were "taken up by purchasers."[32] In Michigan, warrant sales exceeded cash sales by more than three to one.

The price of warrants was listed by financial news services. Except for the period February 1853 through May 1856, the median monthly warrant price never exceeded a dollar an acre.[33] Oberle estimated that 2,264,000 Michigan acres were patented using these warrants.[34]

The Commissioner of the General Land Office estimated that 90 percent of all military warrants were used for land speculation, not for immediate occupancy and farming. Benson estimated, on the basis of her sample of 147 Michigan townships, that military bounty land warrants in the state were used primarily to acquire pinelands.[35]

Benson concluded that military warrants had minimal impact on farm formation in Michigan. Relatively few potential farm families seem to have based their land decisions on the availability of these warrants. And as noted earlier, the start-up costs of farming loomed larger than the cost of the land itself.

Beginning in 1854, two years after bounty land warrants were made assignable (freely sold on the market), the Graduation Act reduced the price of land according to the number of years it had remained on the market unsold. After ten years, the price of an unsold acre was reduced to $1; after 15 years the price dropped to 75 cents an acre; the price was reduced to 25 cents after twenty years and only12.5 cents after thirty years. As all of Michigan had been surveyed by 1854, this meant that approximately 8,785,890 acres were covered by the Graduation Act. And as there was no limitation on the number of acres that one person could buy, this Act was of particular benefit to lumbering interests and speculators.

We will see that much of the land (especially land with higher quality soil) in lower-tier counties in Michigan was privatized by 1854. The acres not sold in these counties were likely overlooked for good reason: their soils (the physical geography of Michigan) were not particularly favorable for farming purposes. That would presumably have been obvious to farmers who selected land after on-the-ground assessments. However, an unknown amount of land was probably sold unseen by large speculators.

Congress had created multiple land-disposal programs with different regulated prices unrelated to the quality of an acre's soil or the vegetation growing on it. Farmers could lower their development costs by drawing on the Graduation Act and military warrants but, again, land costs were not the major component of the total costs of American farm-making and the closing of the frontier.

Federal Implementing Agencies

Federal and state laws and policies on the disposal of land were not self-executing. Each level of government had its own implementing organizations. Any appreciation of the land disposal system and settlement patterns warrants an overview of the organizations that dealt directly or indirectly with the land-buying public. And in addition to creating the environment in which decisions were made and processed, the organizational context had broader effects on how property ownership and settlements evolved over time.

As noted earlier, GLO had two major responsibilities. The first was a one-time only task of preparing rectangular surveys (although at least

400 Michigan townships northwest of Saginaw had to be resurveyed). The second and more enduring work was to process applications for patents, collect the established fees, and enter the approved sales in tract books.

Most of Michigan's Lower Peninsula was surveyed by the time the Territory became a state in 1837. Over two-million acres were surveyed as early as 1819. This jumped to over eleven million in 1833. From 1837 to 1840, all except 23 townships were surveyed in the lower 68 counties. That is, potential settlers had access to maps that, as will be documented in a later chapter, included questionable observations on both soils and vegetation.

These mapping accomplishments refer primarily to township borders. Laying out of section lines within townships lagged.

In 1837, the Commissioner of the GLO authorized the survey of section lines in all townships south of 30 North that "would command purchasers to a reasonable amount, if brought into market immediately after the survey shall be completed."[36] National land-disposal policies were sensitive to local markets as seen from far-away Washington, D.C. Government officials were aware of and responded to changing market conditions in general, not just to the market for land that had agriculturally more promising soils. With some possible exceptions in the southwestern part of the state, the number of acres proclaimed for patenting was well ahead of sales (demand).

Quite aside from establishing the geographic coordinates that gave legal specificity to land holdings, the surveyors' field notes and maps were made publicly available and thereby lowered the information costs incurred by potential buyers. And as mentioned earlier, surveyors in 1815 were directed to "be careful to note" in their field books the "quality of the soil" relating to potential agricultural use.[37] Lumbermen were beneficiaries of these notes as well, for surveyors were to locate at each corner of a section "witness" or bearing trees, and their size and species were to be noted.[38] Minimal but questionable information was available on the physical geography of all the counties in the State of Michigan.

Michigan surveys and surveyors' notes were hardly fault free. As early as 1830, some Oakland County residents complained in a memorial to Congress that the surveys in their county "were so inaccurate that they were useless."[39] A later chapter provides the limited and questionable information the surveyors recorded for potential investors in the state's Midland County

Surveyors were private contractors, not public employees. They often worked under very difficult conditions—of unbearable mosquitoes, thick underbrush, swampy land, winter snows and cold.

My comparison of notes kept by several surveyors working in

Midland County suggest that even honest workers differed widely in the number of observations they made and probably in the accuracy of them. It is unlikely that there was close professional oversight of local contractors.

Land-buyers had to be aware that some surveys were complete frauds. Deputy Surveyor Austin Burt's remarked in his re-survey of county 13N, R1W (Porter Township in Midland County) that "the old Survey was found to be mostly fraudulent."[40] As early as 1826, the Surveyor General's office located in Chillicothe, Ohio reported that "designing men" or purchasers of public land "with a view to deceive and mislead others" altered the marks and numbers of early surveys. Harvey Parke, a contract surveyor living in Pontiac was dismissed for his misrepresentations.[41] Large-scale fraud was discovered for 400 townships north and west of Saginaw.[42]

Although Congress appropriated funds in 1845 "for extensive re-surveys to correct erroneous and defective surveys" in Michigan and three other states, problems remained as late as 1855. The Commissioner of Michigan's State Land Office noted in his annual report for 1855 that the GLO re-surveys of "considerable tracts of land" forced the State to suspend its sales of a good quantity of swampland.[43] It was not that the surveyors' technical skills were weak. Instead, there was outright dishonesty on the part of some private contractors as well as little governmental oversight of their work.

That is, although it appears that a very large proportion of surveys met the legal specifications set for them, savvy land-buyers had to be wary. Still, field notes and plats (maps) helped reduce the cost and time of identifying good agricultural land and valuable timbered acres. More on this in later chapters.

GLO established local district offices to process the information and patent requests submitted by buyers directly or through their agents. Detroit had the first Michigan office in 1804. New offices were added and district borders redrawn over time. Thirteen offices existed at one time or another.[44]

The Detroit office did not become operational until surveys were completed and land proclaimed available for auction. The first recorded sales were in 1818.

These basic operating units had two officials in charge, a Register and a Receiver (bursar). The latter took the claimant's payment and administrative fees for forwarding to the General Land Office. Someone who wanted to make an "entry" indicated to the Register the desired tract of land. This led to the completion of a series of signed documents, including any monetary receipts required. If a warrant or scrip was used, a certificate of location was required. The completed papers were sent to Washington and, if accepted, were returned to the district office and given to the applicant ("entryman"). The district office had already noted on its plat book that the specific acres were in the entry process. This helped subsequent buyers to identify only the land available for new entries as well as the questionable wisdom these earlier patentees had made (one of several possible indicators of the potential value of land).[45] Again, the Receiver's (bursar) responsibility in this transaction was for collecting the claimant's payment and administrative fees for forwarding to the General Land Office.

Newly proclaimed land was first offered at a public auction that was typically held in the autumn. To allow potential buyers an opportunity to review the information available in the district office and to personally inspect the land to be auctioned, the date of an auction was announced the prior spring. It was the buyer's responsibility, not the government's, to assess the potential value of soils, vegetation and possible returns on investment.

Land not sold at auction was then made available for private entry at the designated minimum price (which was $1.25 an acre for land covered under the 1820 Act; lower prices, as earlier noted earlier, were also established).

Adding new federal district offices was to help spread the workload and accelerate the processing time—to make it more convenient for the buying public. It appears that an eastern buyer had to have a local agent to process a patent application.

There were governmental administrative steps established to deliberately help re-shape America's human geography. The physical geography, of course, remained relatively constant. (It too could change, as happened when soils were not appropriately managed.)

"Michigan entered the Union as a child of the land office business," and demand for GLO services in 1836 exceeded the capabilities of the state's busiest district office, Bronson (now Kalamazoo). Five or six hundred clients queued up for service, and nationally the Washington office of the GLO was said to be three years behind in its work.[46]

With so large a workload and the reported questionable ethical standards of many Americans at the time, it is not surprising that the GLO and the land disbursement system in general came under attack. In Michigan (and in the country in general) "nearly every legislative land action was subjected to some form of mismanagement, inefficiency or fraud. The nature of the abuse varied from poor judgement and management to fraud and corruption of the rankest sort."[47] Similar criticisms made in Ohio could also be said of Michigan—that the disposal of public land in the state was "probably the worst example in the United States of sustained governmental failure either to develop a coherent public policy or to build an administrative structure capable of withstanding pressure from special interests."[48] The market for land not only was largely information-free: the processing of land purchases fell short of high ethical, administrative and legal standards.

There are many specific examples of chicanery, especially relating to illegal logging. Timothy Jerome and George F. Williams were the principals in the "Ísabella Land Swindle" that took advantage of Michigan's Chippewa Indians. While this swindle was tied up in the courts, Jerome and Williams were removing valuable pine trees.[49]

As one historian noted, "Like other early settlers, lumbermen often exhibited a certain disdain for the necessity of buying land. Joseph Smith, for example, supplied his mill from 1832 to 1835 with timber from government land."[50] One lumberman north of Saginaw recalled that "illegal logging was a common practice until the early 1850s." Federal agents who moved against "moonshine lumbering ... met fierce opposition."[51]

GLO did little to police the public domain of lumber-rich or soil-rich lands.[52] Lumbermen were interested in the pine trees on the land, not the land itself. To gain access to these trees, some lumbermen made fraudulent entries under both the federal preemption legislation and Michigan's own primary school lands. The federal preemption laws gave buyers a one-year grace period before a payment had to be made. This was sufficient time to cut the marketable timber before relinquishing the claim.[53]

Gates reported that "it was the small loggers who were most constantly in trouble."[54]

Michigan attracted many large lumber interests. Some lumbermen from Maine and New York began investigating and purchasing Lower Peninsula pinelands as early as 1836.[55] Based on a sample of 147 townships in 49 Lower Peninsula counties, Benson found 320 buyers of 304,811 timbered acres (952 acres per buyer). Some (if not most) of these buyers used military warrants to acquire their land.[56] These large purchases were well ahead of logging operations. And no doubt some purchasers were speculators who hoped to sell their land and trees on it to other lumbermen, or at least to sell the logging rights. In either case, potential new settlers were faced with marked-up land prices offered by private sellers.

The value of timber to timbermen no doubt greatly exceeded the value of the logged-over land.[57] Since the most valuable pineland was in middle and higher-tier counties with a relatively small supply of higher-quality agricultural soil (as we will see in later chapters), the settler who decided to begin farming on pinelands may have made unwise decisions.

Michigan's generous pineland resources and those attracted to them distinguish the state from its neighbors (except for Wisconsin). Large speculators operated in all these states, but in Michigan the interest was both in farming and in pinelands.

There were also speculators who purchased farmable land. According to one study, a speculator was "an individual who purchased large acreages of unimproved lands intending to sell after land values had risen sufficiently to make their sale remunerative and was not interested in working the land as a personal enterprise or in building up a long-term tenant estate."[58] This definition emphasizes both motivation and settlement, presumably by a farm family.

One Canadian study limited the concept of speculation to people or institutions owning at least 400 acres of land and engaged in at least three transactions beyond their immediate family.[59] One might add that plots should be non-contiguous. But these definitions incorrectly exclude farmer-settlers who bought more land than they could farm or anticipated farming. There were large numbers (probably a good majority) of such farmers in Michigan.

Speculators were behind the robust sales in 1836 and in other years. Their buying was fueled by reports of large capital gains already realized and anticipated in the immediate future. John Gordon refers to a number of these gains in the chronicle he kept during his search for Michigan land in 1836. One man expected to make 1,000 percent gain over five years. Another claimed his capital increased from $5,000 to $500,000 prior to 1836. Gordon himself wrote that the state had "great opportunities for making a fortune by investing in Public Lands."[60] This was a widely held opinion, as one source claimed that speculators bought 81 percent of the land sold in the Bronson (Kalamazoo) area from 1834 to 1837.[61] Statewide, seventy parties entered 955,000 acres before 1860, an average of 13,643 acres per buyer.[62] Jones listed six large speculators, one from Massachusetts and the rest from New York. Gates mentioned three speculators from Maryland (Charles and William Carroll and Daniel Fitzhugh), as well as the Wadsworths from Connecticut.[63]

Some large speculators bought land throughout Michigan as well as in other states. Their holdings included pinelands and proven agricultural acres in already settled farming townships in the state's southern tiers of counties.

A few owners attempted to promote new villages by issuing false information—for example, that "It is confidently believed from the great natural and acquired advantages of Allegan that it will ere long rank with the first cities of the west."[64] Promoters of Oscoda County in the northeast part of the state claimed the county had four-foot tall alfalfa and head-high rye.[65] Settlers who relied on these dishonest promotions of farm acres were victims of their own unwise decisions.

Some of the larger speculators and lumbermen did not rely (at least not entirely) on rumors and claims. With one alleged exception, large buyers were said to have either personally examined the sites they bought or contracted the selection (and subsequent management) to experienced land lookers and timber cruisers.[66] According to Benson, "[l]umbermen and speculators seldom, if ever, bought pinelands without careful study."[67] William and Charles Carroll were the exception when in 1836 they purchased unseen all the unsold land in several townships in Monroe County. Jones reported that most of the 40,000 acres involved in this transaction were low and swampy.[68] The surveyors' field notes available to these brothers should have alerted them to how unwise a decision they were making.

Speculators and lumbermen who owned large tracts of land withheld their land from sale until they were offered a price above what they paid GLO and its Michigan analogues. New settlers had the option of paying a higher price for their land or moving to counties with a supply of good soil available at the then private entry-price levels. In either case, one might expect that there would be both negative and positive measurable effects on the subsequent overlap between physical human settlement patterns. The divergence between the two patterns can be partially attributed to the ways that markets for land were organized and operated.

Paying a higher price for soil-poor land was an inefficient use of scarce resources,[69] and withholding land from settlement could result in a dispersion of farms that were distant from one another and lowered the collective effects that thicker settlements would have on property values, local tax revenues, and local economic development. Individual decisions made by settlers, lumbermen and speculators accumulated in ways that one might think would have affected economic and spatial systems.

Research to date is not uniformly supportive of all of these assumed deleterious effects. Some have argued just the opposite. Instead of speculators being the force behind shifts in the number of acres being patented, one economist claimed that land sales in the 1850s reflected "real economic forces rather than purely financial speculative motivations." Rising agricultural prices after 1850 were claimed to be the driving force.[70] Two other economists looking at whether large-scale speculators reduced national income by withholding potential agricultural land from production found virtually no such effects in 1850.[71] Still other researchers have argued that the inequalities of wealth (including land) in neighboring Ohio were not particularly oppressive.[72] And, finally, Allan Bogue and others argued that "speculators did not constitute a distinct class: nearly everyone speculated on one level or another." Moreover, speculators extended credit and thereby became the "means by which cash-poor people bought land and made improvements."[73]

From the perspective of aspiring farmer-settlers, federal land-disposal policies allowed for purchases of 40-acre parcels of land at a minimal cost per acre. Those with modest financial resources could buy additional 40-acre parcels for speculative or farming purposes. But many aspiring buyers could not even afford these minimal prices, and they found that speculators already owned the best farming land. However, unlike the federal government after 1820, many of these speculators offered credit and thereby allowed new settlers to begin their farm-making often on holdings of less than forty acres per farm.

There was not a single market for land or a single seller. Understanding the closing of the American frontier requires an understanding of many different influences well beyond soils and those interested in them.

Still, the decision to buy and begin farming was not necessarily a wise one, for as Gates noted, the "pioneer farmer was well aware that in the end his profits would come largely from rising land values," a conclusion supported by Atack, Bateman and Parker's analysis of rates of return realized by Michigan farmers in 1860. Without capital gains, there was a negative 0.5 return. Capital gains gave a positive 5.8 rate of return.[74] Speculation, according to these authors, was part of if not central to the decisions that farmers made. That conclusion raises questions about Turner's settlers-based frontier hypothesis.

Michigan's Own Land-Disposal Laws and Programs

Each state government formulated its own conditions for the disposal of land granted to them. According to one estimate, the federal government granted Michigan 1,621,164 acres by the end of 1849 and an additional six million acres during the 1850s—for a total of 7,637,852 acres.[75] The major grants for swamp lands were to provide states with funds for primary schools, internal improvements, transportation (railroads, canals and roadways), and especially swamps.[76]

Most programs had dedicated purposes—for example primary and post-secondary education, canals and railroads (where the state acted as a pass-through agency for approved private companies), and public buildings. Other programs related to specific kinds of land—a small number of saline acres (46,080) and, over time, in excess of seven million acres classified as swamp. Another 500,000 acres that were granted to the state in 1841 were to be sold and the proceeds used for internal improvements. Other states in the Old Northwest probably had analogous programs.

That is, land markets were used in a number of states to generate revenue needed by the state for their own-self-identified needs.

Prices and credit arrangements differed by program. Whether the proceeds of sales were earmarked or not, they were an important supplement to the state government's limited budgetary resources. The original Amerindian owners did not receive anything for the lands they were forced to forfeit.

The price that a settler (or lumberman and speculator) had to pay for the land under these different programs is relevant, as this price affected the overall cost of farm-making. Unfortunately, there is little available information on certain grants to the state and the acres that were sold or disbursed. We are dealing with general estimates. However, the order of magnitude for overall grants and disposals provide rough estimates of acres disbursed by both the federal and state governments at the end of each decade from the 1820s through to 1859. These decade estimates can then be juxtaposed with the faulty census totals for farms and farm acres in 1850 and 1860 to suggest how many of these acres were in farms. Later we will also reference the physical geography of these lands as revealed by twentieth-century scientific soil surveys.

Michigan initially incorporated credit features in its own disposal programs. But, as will be noted later, the state's own private sector financial system did not bring acclaim to Michigan nor credit to new settlers. Other states may have had different financial histories and different ways to encourage and assist new settlers, many of whom obviously made poor selections of soils to cultivate. More research on comparative financial arrangements among states could contribute to our understanding of where and how the frontier was closed.

But first, some additional brief remarks on Michigan's own land disposal programs. Again, other states had analogous programs.

In the Enabling Act of June 15, 1836, Congress provided Michigan, upon its entry into the Union (on January 26, 1837) with section 16 of each township. The receipts from the sales of these acres were to be used to support primary schools.[77] Michigan set an initial minimum price of $8 per acre for these sections, halving that to $4 later on.[78] Unlike federal land disposal programs after 1820, the state provided credit ranging from 50 percent to 90 percent during the 1840s.[79]

The price of over one-million state-owned acres was from 3.2 to 6.4 times more expensive than federal land then available. But with ever-more liberal credit terms, a purchaser only had to make a down payment of from 40 to 80 cents an acre, less than three times what federal land required at the time. However, much of section 16 land was located north of the then-current settlement frontier, and the quality of this land might not have been especially attractive (as will be seen in Chapter 4).

Congress added to the 500,000 acres granted to Michigan in 1841 for "roads, railways, canals, improvements of water-courses, and draining of swamps." At least that is how the Commissioner of the General Land Office characterized 1,250,000 Michigan acres in his report to Congress in 1853.[80] Only land not already patented could be selected and sold under these internal improvement programs. Again, there were multiple influences that shaped the human geography of Michigan and other states.

Unlike section 16 land that had definite boundaries, the state could limit its selection to the highest quality soils and timbered land not yet patented at the time. But instead of charging higher prices for these acres, just the opposite was done. Only 30 to 40 cents per acre was charged, making these lands much more attractive (financially) that either section 16 or the federal cash sales act of 1820. The Commissioner of the State Land Office reported that this low price helped explain the decline in the sales of the higher-priced Primary School lands.[81]

The federal Swamp Land Acts of 1849 and 1850 (followed by another Act in 1860 that was relevant to other states, not just Michigan) were the largest sources of pre–Civil War grants made to Michigan for its state government to manage and sell. As previously noted, these were to be "swamp and overflowed lands unfit for cultivation." The state had much land whose soils were not farmer-friendly.

Michigan used the federal surveyors' field notes to identify the land claimed under these Acts. In fact, surveyors only noted wetlands on the border lines they were laying.[82] Furthermore, if a survey was conducted during the winter, the survey team would have missed overflowed land that was frozen. Identification of swampland was open to interpretation.

Michigan prepared its own list of these lands and submitted them to Washington for approval.[83] In 1850, Michigan reported 4,544,189 of these acres and added another 2,719.535 acres over the next decade for a total of 7,273,724 acres in 1860.[84] As with the internal improvement acres, the state could only claim land that had not been patented.

Swampland (and probably other state and federal lands) were to be sold in multiples of 40-acre units.[85] If not sold at auction, they were then made available through private sale (private entry). The buyer dealt directly with the state land office.

When first offered, swampland had a minimum price of 75 cents an acre.[86] This was raised to $1.25 an acre in 1858, the price that most such land was sold, according to the State Land Office. (The State Legislature approved new pricing in 1869, a date beyond the present study's time frame.) As with Primary School lands, the state provided liberal credit terms: 25 percent down and a 10-year payment schedule.

Michigan received other large grants, especially for railroads and the St. Mary's Canal. Acting as a pass-through agency, the state transferred the land to private companies that in turn marketed acres to farmers, lumbermen and speculators. However, it is unlikely that few such sales were transacted prior to the 1860 federal census.

Congress approved concessions to nine railroad companies in 1856. Five of these were in the Lower Peninsula.[87] Other states had analogous transportation-related programs.

The Grand Rapids and Indiana Railroad was eligible for 853,000 acres; a road linking Jackson, Lansing and Saginaw qualified for nearly 744,000, and the Flint & Pere Marquette could claim nearly 513,000.[88] It was intended that the state's own land disposal programs would help shape the larger human geography of Michigan.

A designated company had to complete twenty miles of road in order to receive the odd-numbered sections of land within six miles on either side of the line (but only among land not already patented). Land designated as swamp and overflowed could be claimed. However, few of these acres seem to have been awarded to companies and then subsequently sold to private parties prior to 1860. Railway companies did claim land, and in some counties (including Midland) new federal patents were suspended until the railroads made their selections. Unlike the federal and state programs, prices could be adjusted according to the quality, vegetation and location of the land.

Similar flexibility was provided the company that built the St. Mary's Canal. Approved by Congress on August 26, 1852, the company qualified for 750,000 acres anywhere in the state not already patented or given a special designation, such as mineral lands.[89] The state worked with the company in selecting its land. The first ship passed through the canal on June 18, 1855.

While the St. Mary's Falls Ship Canal Company received much of its land by 1855, little information is available on how many of its acres were actually sold, where the sold land was, who bought it, how the land was used, and how this program influenced Michigan's human geography. Patent records and tract books are of little use for this type of research. Instead, one would have to examine deed books for individual counties—that is, the secondary (or post-patent) market. As will be seen later, this was an active market. Patented land could and did change hands a number of times. Land was a tradable in an often hyper national non-transparent market.

The Canal Company had a flexible pricing policy. Not all land had the same price, but little information on this is available—other than the few comments made later in this chapter. Greffenius's search of Michigan records found that the company's land was not disposed of until after 1860, the cut-off date for the present study.[90]

Potential buyers could obtain land from several federal and state programs that differed in how transactions were conducted, the cost of the land, and credit for purchasers.

The standard histories of land policies by Gates, Hibbard, Donaldson, Billington and Ridge (their *Westward Expansion*) and others at the federal level, as well as studies specific to Michigan (such as by Jones and Greffenius) have tracked yearly changes in purchases and possible influences these changes had. For example, in 1836, one year before the Michigan Territory became the State of Michigan, slightly over four million federal acres were patented. This number dropped off to 772,000 the following year. Financial panics, crop failures in Europe, and wars on the continent seemed to have had conflicting effects on land sales and changes in human settlement maps.

As noted earlier, states had their own laws and organizations to manage and dispose lands granted to them by the federal government. Michigan's institutional and legal environment provided its own incentives and constraints on individual decision-making that were parallel to but also different from the institutional environment established by the federal government. Yes, the State was responsible for much less land than administered by the GLO, and, yes, the permissible uses of some state lands (or at least the use of the revenue raised from selling the land) were defined by congress. Furthermore, many of the speculators, lumbermen and settlers who sought federal lands also bought land from the State of Michigan, and just as the federal system was criticized for fraud and mismanagement, the same charges were leveled against the State.[91] However, the state's institutional environment was not just a shadow of the federal one. In at least two of its grant programs (internal improvements and the St. Mary's canal) the state had a more proactive role in identifying higher quality agricultural and pine timber acres. And unlike the post–1820 federal programs, the state offered credit arrangements to buyers. The state had a role in influencing the human geography of farmer-settlers and others.

From the perspective of buyers (decision-makers) these were positive contributions. On the other hand, decision-makers were hampered by what the state failed to provide. After early major financial missteps, the state had only a minor role in providing infrastructure that would facilitate settlement, and early reckless banking practices left small buyers without ready access to credit. As noted earlier, these wounds were self-inflicted by Michigan's inept public leaders and widespread dishonesty on the part of the private sector. Capitalist markets including markets for land were not what blind ideologists claim was the proud history of America.

Michigan entered the Union with land-disposal responsibilities under the public school provision of the Northwest Ordinance and the congressional act approving statehood. Responsibility for the public school lands was assigned to the Superintendent of Public Instruction, but because of this office's deficient accounting system, as well as additional land grants to the state, a state land office was created in 1843 with an appointed commissioner. In 1850 the commissioner became an elected officer, a politician with responsibility for influencing the state's population map and economy.

As with similar offices in other states, this agency was responsible for selecting "unlocated tracts, to manage, appraise, lease or sell these and other grants [such as section 16]..., to protect them from timber thieves, to make collections if land was sold on credit, to eject squatters, determine boundary disputes, and even to survey where the original lines were defective." Paul Gates goes on to list the responsibilities of state legislatures ("define policies, determine prices ... provide protection against corrupt use of authority..."), courts, and the administrative officers who had to interpret and enforce these new responsibilities.[92] With so many responsibilities and the politicizing of the land office, it is not surprising that it would be criticized for mismanagement, fraud and enabling market imperfections that favored some money interests over others.

In two of its pass-through programs the state was able to help potential land-buyers to locate the choicest acres. Information costs were significantly reduced under the Distribution Act of 1841 that granted Michigan 500,000 acres of federal lands to be sold by the state and the receipts to be used for internal improvements. The state contracted with John Ball, an experienced land looker with knowledge of the Grand River country. It took him a year to select more than 300,000 acres, mostly good agricultural land in the Ionia region of the GLO. By 1844, over 492,000 acres were selected in ten counties in the southwest part of the state, as well as seven in the east, including Saginaw and Shiawassee. The first of these lands were offered for sale in 1843 but instead of the state selling directly to buyers, scrip for the land was issued to contractors as payment for improvement projects. These contractors in turn sold the land free of minimum price levels that the state used for its other programs (such as the public school lands).[93]

Even greater care was used by the Saint Mary's Falls Ship Canal Company for 560,000 acres, primarily pinelands "within a reasonable distance of good streams for floating logs." As noted earlier, with the concurrence of the state, the company employed between 55 and 75 "experienced woodsmen, surveyors and lumbermen" working in 18 to 25 separate parties over an 18-months period in 1853 and 1854. Most of these lands were in 26 counties in the northern part of the Lower Peninsula. The company freely made its maps and field notes available to potential buyers. Given the confidence that the company had in its selections, it varied the prices from 5 to 15 dollars per acre depending on quality and quantity. Credit was also available.[94]

Any benefits that potential buyers enjoyed from these two state programs were offset by two linked major failures. First, the state was constrained in the contributions it could make to transportation and other infrastructure projects that would have improved settler access to land, and, second, the early failure to provide infrastructure, together with weak laws and oversight, ruined the state's credit standing and decimated Michigan's banking community. As a result, there was minimal bank credit for buying land or farming it.

Michigan and other new states did not have the private capital to fund their ambitious improvement projects, including railroads, canals and wagon roads. The state's solution was to borrow the needed funds—which it did through a $5-million bond issue that pledged the state's credit to retire the debt. This borrowing was authorized in Article XII.3 of the State's 1835 constitution (adopted two years prior to statehood). "Internal improvements shall be encouraged by the government of this state; and it shall be the duty of the legislature, as soon as may be, to make provision by law for ascertaining the proper objects of improvement in relation to roads, canals, and navigable waters, and it shall also be their duty to provide by law for an equal, systematic, economical application of the funds which may be appropriated for these objects."[95]

A combination of a banking crisis in 1837, unwise decisions by the state, purchases by land speculators, and wildcat banking contributed to the ruin of the state's credit and its banking system.[96] In response to this history, the state's revised constitution of 1850 limited the state's debt to $50,000 and (in Article XIV, Sec. 9) prohibited the state from becoming a party to or having an interest "in any work of internal improvement" or "in carrying on any work, except in the expenditure of grants to the state of land or other property." The state's ability to influence the population map was somewhat but not entirely constrained. Other states might have had a more favorable marketing history.

With its large grant of swampland, the state should have had some wherewithal to fund infrastructure projects. Congress specifically intended that "all proceeds from the lands ... be applied exclusively, as far as necessary to the purpose of reclaiming such lands by means of levees and drains."[97] The state promoted the sales of these lands, as it promoted immigration.[98] In a flyer dated June 3, 1858, and titled *Great Land Sale, About 5,000,000 Acres of State Land to be Offered at Public Sale,* the State Land Office claimed that these were "not only the best grain and grassland" but also of "the most valuable pine" and other timber. Speculators were encouraged, as "great bargains will be many undoubtedly be made." Land was available in 48 Lower Peninsula counties, with most acres in the middle and northern-tier counties. As with the St. Mary's Ship Canal sale, this swampland promotion was of much greater interest to lumbermen than to settlers, although the latter were offered more attractive credit terms. In fact, an 1868 U.S. House of Representatives committee found that half of all swampland nationally was in the hands of speculators.[99]

Whoever the buyers were, their payments should have gone into draining the land, an effort that could have encouraged settlers to acquire land and begin farming. Michigan, however, worked around congress's intention by asserting "that no other system of drainage for a new county is so effectual as the construction of public highways." The trunk lines that were to open undeveloped counties would meet congress's objectives by ditching, bridging and filling these new roads.[100]

The 1837 crisis that fundamentally altered the state's approach to providing infrastructure that might have encouraged more farmer-settlers also nearly eliminated all banks in the state. Michigan's General Banking Law of March 15, 1837, allowed any twelve landowners to create a banking association by applying to a county clerk or treasurer. The required capital stock of $150,000 was to include thirty percent in specie.

This free banking law was an invitation to dishonest self-serving locals to enhance their own land holdings and investments.[101] One analysis of twelve free banks in 1838 found that 75 percent of their loans went to the directors and stockholders. "Unimproved real estate was the principal collateral for loans and was thus the ultimate backing for the currency they circulated. Banks were frequently organized by lending money to their promoters to complete the purchase of their shares. The promoters then pledged these stocks for the loans they received to buy them."[102] County tax assessors contributed to these hoaxes by overvaluing the unimproved land that borrowers used as collateral for the loans they made to themselves.[103] Michigan, however, was unlikely to have been the only state that experienced phony capitalism.

Michigan's banking system was of minimal assistance to farmer-settlers and to those who needed credit to acquire land. The banking crisis of 1837 that led to the state's bond debacle and the loss of good credit standing also eliminated most of Michigan's banks. Only one of the 67 banks chartered in Michigan between 1835 and 1846 "preserved an untarnished credit record."[104] The U.S. Treasury Department reported only six Michigan banks in 1851 and only four in 1855.[105] Between 1820 and 1860, Michigan had the least bank money per capita of the five states in the Old Northwest.[106] And since private banks, not the state or federal governments, issued paper notes, this meant higher transaction costs and uncertainty in land and other market transactions by farmer-settlers and others.

In 1861, there were 1601 state-chartered banks nationwide. They issued about 10,000 differently designed circulating notes.[107] *Thompson's Bank Note and Commercial Reporter* listed nine state banks (including an insurance company) operating in Michigan in August 1854. Only two of these nine issued notes as large as (but no larger than) $10.[108] Even these were of uncertain value, as bank notes were typically discounted against gold and foreign currencies.

Michigan had to rely primarily on private bank notes issued by out-of-state institutions, and these notes were generally valued at their face value only within a 50 to 100-mile radius of the issuing bank.[109]

Despite this uninviting environment for decision-making, one author writing in 1975 wrote that there was no evidence in the literature "that shortage of credit and currency exerted a restraining influence on the growth process of Michigan."[110] If this was true, where then did yeoman farmers find the funds necessary to buy their land and begin developing it?

We know of five sources but not how many settlers drew on each. First, as already mentioned, the State of Michigan provided credit under its grant programs. Speculators were often the beneficiaries of these programs. For example, the deed books for Midland County show that John Larkin, perhaps the county's wealthiest resident, was the grantee for 40 swampland acres in 1858 and 270 acres in 1859, as well as 160 acres of primary school land. The credit terms for one of these sales read "received therefrom the said purchaser is the sum of one hundred and sixty dollars and that the consideration to be paid for the said purchaser is the sum of four hundred and eighty dollars to be paid at any time hereafter at the option of the purchasee but the interest of seven per centum from the whole amount of principal unpaid to be paid annually on the first day of March or within sixty days thereafter in each and every year...."

Speculators and grantees were a second source of capital. The St. Mary's Ship Canal Company is known to have extended credit.

Third, of course, farmers used the proceeds from the sale of their farms back east (or elsewhere) to finance the purchase of Michigan land and to begin farming it. Fourth, prominent local Michigan men bought and sold mortgages in their own county. John Whitman's name appears in the early Midland County deed books as having funded mortgages and to later have sold them to other investors.[111]

Fifth and finally, there were both informal and formal means by which eastern investors provided mortgage funds for Michigan land-buyers, including farmer-settlers.[112] It is possible that Michigan's usury laws (which every antebellum state except California had) might have discouraged this source of credit. However, the interest rate caps could be evaded by "placing the nominal value of the debt above the actual sum."[113]There was also a national market for bankruptcy and tax-auctioned lands. For example, the Midland deed books record that Frederick Shaw of New Bedford, Massachusetts bought the land of Mathor and Susan Larue when this couple failed to make their mortgage payments. These were typically short-term balloon mortgages.[114]

Financing the purchase of land and then to begin farming it were just two of many decisions a farmer-settler had to make. Lumbermen had other types of vegetation-related decisions to make, and speculators had still others. These decisions taken collectively, especially those by resident farmers, shaped the spatial pattern and pace of settlement of the state, a central concern of the present study on the closing of the American frontier (or more properly, the privatization of lands along the frontier, not their settlement).

Although we are unable to statistically estimate the impact that the larger institutional environment had on locational and soil decisions that were made, it is possible to draw on census and other information to describe the state's geographic settlement pattern, especially for the period 1850 to 1860. Again, readers are reminded that geography refers here to human geography, not a physical one; both are used in this study to document and then explain why the two geographies did not, as might be expected in a market with perfect information, exactly overlap one another.

When census data are combined with soil classifications, it is possible to explore whether soil type had much of a statewide impact on the locational choices of farmer-settlers. We take up this possibility in the following chapters that more narrowly links the physical and human geographies of Michigan.

Time Trend for National and State Land Sales

Further descriptive and analytical studies of the causes and consequences of annual changes in land disposal totals are beyond the present study's scope of concern. Suffice it to note that Arthur H. Coles was among the first if not the first economist to examine the "Cyclical and Sectional Variations in the Sale of Public Lands, 1815–1860."[115] His data are dollar receipts for federally-patented land but do not include land acquired through military warrants or state programs. Coles' figures also mask the significance of lower-priced land introduced by the Graduation Act.

Coles reported the annual "receipts" from the sale of federal lands in Michigan, while Jones (among others) gives comparable "acreage totals" for the state. Other researchers have variously emphasized the influence of poor domestic harvests (as in 1856), similar variations in Europe, along with wars on the continent. Still others have argued for the importance of shifts in commodity prices more generally, the significance of transportation improvements, the central role played by speculators, and the effects that economic downturns had on the availability of money, the bankruptcy of financial institutions, changes in the value of real estate, and auctions of tax-delinquent acres.[116] There were multiple influences on the decisions that individuals made on land they patented (or did not patent). These decisions in turn can be mapped to visualize the closing of the frontier (although I do not provide a moving series of such maps).

I am aware of the limitations of census sources for some mapping purposes. They must be treated with appropriate skepticism for some of the reasons included in the Annex to Chapter 5. Similarly, patent statistics reported by federal and state sources warrant similar skepticism. We are dealing with general orders of magnitude. That is how the estimates given in Table 3.1 below should be considered. Most importantly, as will be seen later, the acreage numbers for pass-through patents are overstated. For example, more than 640 acres are reported to have been patented in a number of sections. Most of these excesses seem to have resulted from conflicting claims by railroads and swampland for the same acres, and railroads themselves seem to have entered more than one patent for the same acres. Acres patented to individuals do not suffer the same problem, although the official records do contain an occasional discrepancy.

These qualifications should be kept in mind when interpreting Table 3.1's estimates of the federal and state land sales from 1819 to 1859.

Table 3.1: Approximate Number of Acres Sold Under Federal and State Programs by Decade

Decade Ending in	*Federal Programs*	*State Programs*	*Total*	*Cumulative Total*
1819	470,529		470,529	470,529
1829	390,904		390,904	861,433
1839	8,320.58	71,593	8,392,173	9,253,606
1849	419,184	498,666	917,850	10,171,256
1859	4,201,171	544,758	4,745,929	14,917,385
TOTAL	13,802,368	1,115,017	14,917,385	

Source: Greffenius, Development of Michigan Public Land Policy, *219.*[117] *These figures are for the entire state, both the Lower and Upper Peninsulas.*

The "Michigan Fever" of the 1830s was followed by a slump in the following decade. Effects that land prices had on buyers' decisions made in the 1840s are seen in the relatively higher state totals compared with federal programs during that decade. Michigan's internal improvement lands (but not others) granted to the state in 1841 were sold at well below the $1.25 charged under the federal program in place since 1820. And as noted above, swamplands were sold at a lower price per acre, while other programs offered favorable credit terms.

Even at the end of 1860, Michigan had ample supplies of patentable land with high quality soils. If patents were only issued for the 68 counties in the Lower Peninsula with their 26-million acres, then 54 percent of the Peninsula's acres were still available. But, of course, land sales and the quality of farmer-friendly soils were not evenly distributed throughout the state, as we will see in later chapters.

Summary

Land is not just a physical resource with certain chemical, physical and biological characteristics. It is also a commodity defined in ways that shape how land is acquired, used and sold. This larger legal context set the parameters for how Michigan's Amerindian land was transferred to the federal government and how that government in turn privatized the land or granted it to states for them to privatize.

The rules of the land game were not set in stone. They evolved over time to create multiple land-disposal programs with different regulated prices and credit arrangements. The sheer number of acres available for privatization represented an unprecedented administrative burden on the federal and state organizations responsible for managing their mix of land-disposal laws. This complexity and the questionable capabilities of the implementing organizations contributed to flaunting these organizations and to the control of large amounts of land by speculators and lumbermen.

Neither Michigan nor the federal government had coherent settlement strategies that went beyond disposing of land to include an adequate supply of investment and working capital for aspiring farmer-settlers or for the infrastructure that would facilitate settlement. Second-best solutions did evolve, as seen in the credit that the state provided, as well as grants of land made to transportation companies to cover the costs of their start-up financial needs. All this evolved in a disjointed and incremental manner.

While some scholars of this diverse mosaic of laws, organizations, credit facilities and implementing organizations have been highly critical of the resulting land ownership and settlement pattern, there were thousands of settlers who were able to navigate themselves onto land and to begin farming it.

Chapter 4 will examine where these farmers settled in Michigan, what soils they selected, and how wise and successful they were in the multiple decisions they made. That is, we can explore the overlap between soil and settlement maps (physical and human geographies). Although the focus is on Michigan, the approach and results of the research covered in Chapter 4 no doubt have near-parallels in other states. What happened in Michigan no doubt was in many respects replicated in other states as well. Again, Michigan is a case study for understanding how an information-poor market for land led to wasted investments during the closing of the American frontier in antebellum America. I use the overlay of two geographies to help document the extent of this wastage. However, there are limits to the numerical evidence aggregated at the state, county and township levels. Later chapters move beyond aggregate statistics to an analysis based on evidence relating to individual farmer-settlers.

4

Soils and Settlements in Michigan's Lower Peninsula Counties

This chapter on closing the American frontier moves from the level of states to counties within a single illustrative state: Michigan. Readers will find another heavy dose of numerical evidence mixed with standard narrative history in the course of exploring some of the locational challenges that antebellum farmer-settlers had in making their investment decisions. "Investments" are more than locational decisions. They also involve possible rates of monetary returns from cultivating different classes of soils.

Both the introduction and summary of this chapter capture the problems being addressed, how to answer the problems and some of the answers to them. The following also heavy-numbered chapter builds on the present one by estimating rates of return on investments made by mid-nineteenth century farmers.

Our focus is on inter-county differences in soils, farms and farming. Although counties in general are an overlooked unit in American history, they were federally mandated governance bodies in addition to being markets for land and soils. Federal and state records also report county-level numerical evidence that economists have used in their historical studies of American agriculture.

County-level soil and farming statistics add to our understanding of how closing the frontier wasted the investments of farmer-settlers and the nation more generally. Evidence is absent, however, on why individual farmers decided to invest in one state or one county rather than in alternatives to them. It is possible, however, to use county-aggregated statistics to explore the relationship between soil profiles, farms cultivating different soils aggregated at the county level and the likely economic returns from farming in counties that differ in their endowments of the most promising soils. That is what the present chapter overs. But county-level evidence can hide variations among individual farmers with regard to the soils they were cultivating. An analysis of that evidence is provided in later chapters that draw on the soils that individual farmers in the case-study county were cultivating as well as the crop yields associated with different soils.

Investors infected with the Michigan Fever's promise of high returns on investments in land and farming the land had a very large diversified market available within two separate peninsulas: the Upper Peninsula and the Lower one with its sixty-eight artificially-created counties differing in their shapes (borders), size, growing seasons and soils. The present chapter is limited to the Lower Peninsula.

Inter-county differences are analogous to inter-states ones, and just as settlers had to decide which state to make their homes, they also had to make the same decision on where in a selected state to begin farming. The market for land was national but investments were local.

National, state and local governments had an interest in privatizing land as it was a revenue source for all three levels. Counties and states depended on property taxes. More settlers, more tax revenues. Speculators also had an interest in inflating the value of their own land awaiting new closers of the frontier.

This chapter begins a series of closing-the-frontier topics based on individual counties in Michigan's Lower Peninsula:

- First, just as states were socially-created units with artificial boundaries so were the counties within a individual states. And just as states differed in their endowments of soils, so did Michigan counties have analogous differences. It would have been a mistake for a settler to focus on one soil-promising county if that county's supply of the most productive soils was already under cultivation. Exploring this line of analysis requires county-by-county soils maps along with acres that were already privatized and presumably farmed as well.
- Second, the county is more than its soils and vegetation. In closing the American frontier, settlers were also creating a governance system that settlers supported by taxes and civic participation. Life on the farm was more than tilling soils. The present chapter takes a thematic detour in covering basic high school civic course lessons on how the west was divided into governmental units that were not based on soils. Later chapters will move beyond counties as the unit of analysis by shifting to soils and individual farms linked to soils within a single county.

- Third settlers were not just stand-alone economic men. They were also tied to local social, political, manpower and economic networks.[1] We will see in later chapters that an investor's life-course, especially during the first years of farm-making, also depended on a farmer's immediate neighbors. More information on the social aspects of settlement will be addressed in later chapters.[2]

Michigan's Lower Peninsula Counties

Michigan's Lower Peninsula has 68 counties stacked in eleven tiers from south to north. Their dates of organization, names, rectangular surveys, borders, sizes and land auctions changed over time. There were 26 organized counties at the time Michigan became a state. Before some of them were organized they were assigned to other existing counties for judicial and administrative purposes. Counties in all four of the state's most southern tiers were organized by 1839.

Twenty-eight counties bordered one of the Great Lakes. Only 26 of the other 40 counties had a box-like shape. Ten others had straight-line borders but were in irregular patterns.

It is not surprising that counties differed greatly in size from one another. The largest county had three times more acres than the smallest. If all other influences and factors were assumed to be constant, then one might expect that the largest county would have three times as many acres of the highest quality soils, farms and farm acres than did the smallest county. This was not so in Michigan.

The inter-county differences within this one state were also found in other states as well. This is one reason why more in-depth attention to variations within one state would represent what was happening more generally as the frontier moved west.

Soil maps for individual Michigan counties show a heterogeneous environment with soils that differ even within a few adjoining acres. And, of course, even the very best soils cannot overcome the constraints of climate, drainage and a short-growing season. How well a farmer managed his crops and soils further complicates any effort to attribute differences in farm-level productivity either to a particular county or to that county's soils only.

Access to markets is an additional influence on the east-to-west and south-to-north settlement history.

Despite the above questions about using counties as a statistical unit, counties are the reporting units for soils and for census information on

The six Great Lakes states of the Old Northwest Territory.

agriculture and population. We work with what is available and what is available for Michigan has parallels in other states as well.[3]

Counties were further subdivided into smaller governance units. The 1785 Northwest Ordinance defined the "congressional" township, but it was not until two years later that territorial governors were authorized to appoint civil officers in each county and township. The Act of 1825 further authorized the territorial governor and legislative assembly to divide the territory into townships and provide laws for the election of township officers. Elections turned local governments into both governance and political units.[4]

Local governments had a keen interest in the market for land because, among other considerations, taxes on land were the major source of revenue for all levels of government within Michigan.

County treasurers in Michigan were mandated to maintain tax assessment rolls with separate columns for "the school, library and school house taxes in one column, the highway taxes in another; and the township, county and state taxes in another column."[5]

Article XIV, Sec. 12 of Michigan's 1850 constitution mandated that property was to be assessed at its cash value and that these assessments were to be equalized every five years. Public officials could have a significant influence on the financial health of local communities.

In order to facilitate assessment and tax collections, it was in a state's interest to create as many new townships and counties as feasible. It was also important for the state (through the Auditor General) to have local governments auction lands that were delinquent on taxes. Not only were auction receipts shared, but they also put the land back on the tax rolls.[6]

Although it appears that all privatized land was taxed the same regardless of the soils on the land, this may not have been so in some counties.

Not all counties were equally endowed with the kinds of soils that prudent investors would want to cultivate.

During the closing of the American frontier old eastern social networks were replaced by new ones. Arriving settlers were not only tied to their land but also became members of new social, economic, political and marketing networks that were essential for both economic but social survival. Residents were required to pay taxes, elect one another to local self-governing bodies, and often to work for one another. There are no social network maps analogous to what the original land surveyors provided.

I have a considerable amount of social history materials for the one case-study county but lacking comparable information for other counties it is not possible to explore how the life trajectories of new settlers were influenced by their new homes' social networks.

A number of studies of voting and political life at the time suggest that new settlers in Michigan probably shared a common civic culture, one that Formisano labeled "Yankee Protestantism and pietism" among Michigan Whigs.[7] "Yankee Morality," according to Gray, gave priority to "church, school, and local government—as the bulwark of a communal order, without which barbarism, irreligion, ignorance, and anarchy—would reign on the frontier."[8] Sonya Salamon's study of four relatively contemporary prairie villages in Illinois concluded that "Ethnic identity, thus, is more predictive of behavior than is religious identification."[9] Kirkland, on the other hand, provided a less flattering account of the religiously-tinged culture among early settlers in one of Michigan's more southerly counties.[10]

New studies of local pioneer societies appear regularly but there is not yet the kind of evidence that lends itself to inter-settler community comparisons. For that reason I will issue my case-study social history elsewhere and keep the present study focused on dry numbers.[11]

County Soil Endowments in Michigan's Lower Peninsula

Steven Stoll noted that soil maps can change over time. In his *Larding the Lean Earth* (sub-titled *Soil and Society in Nineteenth-Century America*[12]) he reported used-up (eroded) soils in Pennsylvania and South Carolina. Other researchers made similar observations—for example, most pre–Civil War farmers "did little to maintain, let alone improve the quality of their soil."[13] Declines in crop productivity were reported in many parts of Ohio in the 1840s, and the same comments were made in 1848, 1850 and 1851 about exhausted lands in the southern counties of Michigan.[14] That is, soils were not forever.

Observations on exhausted soils are a necessary caveat to the applicability of current soil classifications to the soils in pre–Civil War Michigan. Soil inexhaustibility is a myth. This also means that the way a farmer managed his soils and crops also affected the yields from these soils.

Reading back in Michigan's settlement history suggests that southern-tier counties may have had less promising soils than what was generally thought at the time. This is because these counties were closest to eastern states and also because they were the first and longest to be farmed regardless of their soils. Soils that were cultivated in 1845 could have been degraded five years later. That suggests that crop yields from the same soils would vary over time (unrelated to weather and other influences).

Jethro Veatch was the first soil scientist to provide county-level soil information for Michigan. The ideal (farm) land, according to Veatch, would have "relatively high fertility of soil and durability expressed in sustained plant growth or yield," be relatively uniform over a considerable area, have "physical character favorable for good tilth," and be level or only gently undulating.[15] The rating scheme he used and the current chapter adopts "was determined upon the basis of the physical suitability for the prevailing types of farming, in conjunction with farmers' present and past experiences." Soils that he ranked as first class "for general agriculture" had to be suitable for the successful production of a number of crops.[16] In fact, his classification is based on an economic interpretation of pre–WW II agriculture.[17]

If settler-investors were prudent, then they would presumably have settled in counties with the most unclaimed higher-quality soils. Note the time reference. The supply of different classes of soils can change over time in the course of a county's settlement history.

Veatch developed his county-level descriptions based on twenty samples (each of approximately 1,152 acres) taken in each of the state's "full townships of 36 land sections."[18] He defined four different classes:

FIRST CLASS Land of highest value for general farming, on the basis of inherent productivity of soil. Virgin land highest in potential value.

SECOND CLASS Usable land of medium value for general farming. Virgin land has potential value and constitutes reserve agricultural land.

THIRD CLASS Land of doubtful value for general farming. Suitable locally for special crops, subsistence farms, and extensive grazing.

FOURTH CLASS Very low or no value for general farming. Small acreage suitable for high-acre-value crops under special conditions. Low value for extensive farming.[19]

These are general definitions and, as a result, Veatch's county-level percentages must be considered approximations. Moreover, he did not use a single statewide standard. Instead, the classifications varied by region—which probably means by tier as well.

The classification of land is on a local regional basis, so that the standards for making the ratings vary for different parts of the state, but it is hardly likely except in a few instances that the differences resulting from this procedure exceed the range from one class to another.[20]

This is an important qualification for which no compensating adjustments are possible.

The southern half of the Lower Peninsula has the highest percentage of first and second-class acres. Forty-seven percent of the southern half's 14,543,000 acres have Class 1 Soils.

Regionally adjusted estimates suggest the differences noted in Table 4.1 underestimate north-south differences in soil endowments (the physical geography of Michigan).

Table 4.1: Southern Tier Counties Had a Higher Proportion of Quality Soils

Lower Peninsular Region	*Class 1 Percent*	*Class 2 Percent*	*Classes 1 and 2 Percent*
Southern Half	47%	35%	82%
Northern Half	10%	24%	34%
Total Lower Peninsula	30.5%	30.5%	61%

Based on Veatch, Agricultural Land Classification and Land Types in Michigan, *62.*

Comparing Table 4.1 with Table 2.1 indicates that the Class 1 percentages for the entire Lower Peninsula (30.5 percent) are about the same as the statewide percentage of land that has "few or some limitations for cultivation" (31 percent).

Michigan statewide has 38 percent of its acres in higher-quality alifsol and mollisol soils, as also seen in Table 2.1. The percentages are similar but the classifications are based on different numbers.

If all the nearly 14 million alifsol and mollisol acres were in the Lower Peninsula, then 53 percent of this Peninsula's acres would be potentially productive and a magnet drawing farmer-settlers who based their locational decisions on the potential of soils to support the most marketable crops.[21] There would be a fairly close overlap of multiple maps and geographies: soils, markets for particular types of crops and maps of farmer-settlers.

But early land-buyers, of course, did not benefit from these soil science classifications. As noted earlier, some knowledgeable buyers used rules of thumb to assess the suitability of soils for farming. Based on these rules and others, early settlers in Michigan (according to Lewis) recognized six broad subregions—the Eastern Shore, the Western Shore, and four river drainage areas (St. Joseph River, Kalamazoo River, Grand River, and the Saginaw River).[22]

Consistent with Veatch's division of Lower Peninsula into southern and northern halves, still another classification found that the state's soils fall into two broad types: the gray brown Podzolic of the south and the Podzol of the north.[23] The line separating the two halves runs, as noted in the prior chapter, in a convex line from approximately Saginaw to Muskegon.[24]

This convex line is also the approximate division between *two vegetation zones*. The 37 counties south of a line from Bay City (just north of Saginaw) to Muskegon were populated by oaks and hickories, with some beech and maple.[25]

Veatch agreed that tree species in Michigan was a useful indicator of soil quality and agricultural land values.[26] This soil-vegetation correlation is important, for it suggests that lumbermen and farm-settlers were not in competition with one another for the same land. Lumbermen were narrowly interested in the forest vegetation that the soil supported, not the soil itself.[27] Once the trees were gone so were those who lumbered them.

Good agricultural soils (Veatch's Classes 1 and 2) could be found north of the Saginaw-Muskegon line, but soil and pre-settlement vegetation were not the only significant selection criteria that a farmer-settler might have considered. The same line through the center of the state also "marks the climatic limits of viable grained-based agriculture."[28] Below that line, farmers had a mean annual of at least 140 frost-free days, while above the line farmers could expect anywhere from 60 to 120 such days.[29] Calendars of frost-free days can and did change over time. It is unknown if potential settlers were aware of the lines that defined the length of a growing season or how different crops responded to the number of frost-free days.

Instead of a north-south dividing line for rainfall, the state has a triangular-shaped east-west gradient with more precipitation in the western half of the state.[30] An investor who focused only on soil could miss the climate constraints a new farmer would face.

In addition to classifying the physical, chemical and biological components of soil, drainage was important as well. It appears that up to half of the counties in the southern half of the Lower Peninsula were characterized as having "incomplete drainage."[31] It is little wonder that a survey party in Michigan swamps in 1821 refused to finish their work because of "the suffering from mosquito bites, both men and horses being weak from loss of blood and want of sleep."[32] Many earlier travelers commented on how unhealthy Michigan was, a state whose overflowed lands were a source of the ague (malaria).[33]

Still there were good farming soils in every Lower Peninsula County both above and below the Saginaw-Muskegon line. But not all counties and tiers of counties were equally endowed. Chances of selecting poor soils were higher in some counties and tiers than in others. A random selection of soils in soil-rich counties would be more profitable than random selections in soil-poor areas.

Chances of random success were relatively higher in twenty-eight counties that had three quarters or more of their land in Veatch's two top classes. Forty (59 percent) had half or more of their land in these two classes. At the other extreme, there were seven counties with half or more of their acres with Class 4 soils; fourteen counties had 40 percent or more of these acres. A farmer-settler could improve his (and farmers were overwhelmingly men) chances of success by deciding to buy land in soil-rich counties.

Choice of county was not, of course, sufficient to assure one had good soil to farm. Individual counties were heterogeneous with regard not only to soils but also with regard to other important features such as drainage and access to transportation and markets. Pressly and Scofield's analysis of county real estate values for 1850 to 1959 found that "even within an area as small as a county, the actual value of individual farms can be expected to range as much as 50 percent, and often more, above or below the county average."[34] Prospective farmer-settlers are unlikely to have that kind of information.

Given these variations, the use of any unit of analysis (tier of counties, individual counties or townships and sections within them) has inevitable problems. We will try to skirt this problem, especially in later chapters dealing specifically with Midland County. For the present, we will rely primarily on tiers of counties but will also note differences among counties within the same tier. This tedious but revealing coverage further indicates the challenges that new farmers had in deciding where to make their life investments. Later chapters will explore how harvests differed according to the class of a farm's soils.

Table 4.2, based on Veatch's (region-based) calculations, suggests that the proportion of poor-quality soils (Class 4) rises after tier 5, and that tiers 7 through 11 offer proportionally fewer high-quality acres than found in lower-tier counties. There are, however, sizeable inter-county differences within individual tiers, as also seen in this table that is based on Veatch's region-adjusted classifications.

Table 4.2: Not All Lower-Tier Counties Have More of the Best Farming Soils

Tier	*Number of Acres in Classes 1 and 2*	*Percent of Acres in Classes 1 and 2*	*Percent of Acres in Class 4*	*County with Highest Percent in Classes 1 and 2*	*County with Lowest Percent in Classes 1 and 2*
1	2,070,014	81	5	Lenawee (96%)	Cass (61%)
2	1,890,322	76	6	Washtenaw (85%)	Van Buren (64%)
3	2,238,769	79	7	Eaton (96%)	Allegan (63%)
4	2,855,876	86	4	Shiawassee (97%)	Ottawa (65%)
5	2,228,632	78	9	Sanilac (96%)	Muskegon (24%)
6	1,665,239	60	22	Huron (98%)	Newaygo (28%)
7	756,996	38	39	Osceola (55%)	Lake (12%)
8	640,658	29	42	Ogemaw (35%)	Roscommon (12%)
9	510,106	25	47	Grand Traverse (41%)	Crawford (7%)
10	632,637	40	32	Antrim (52%)	Montmorency (22%)
11	572,351	39	31	Charlevoix (46%)	Emmet (27%)

Source: Veatch, Agricultural Land Classification and Land Types if Michigan, *63–65.*

Given the small number of counties within any single tier, it is not feasible to conduct significant intra-tier statistical analyses. For some of the following tables, we will group the 68 counties into three categories: the four most southern tiers of counties, a transitional category of counties in tiers 5 and 6, and the northern counties in tiers 7 through 11. (Table 4.3) These are arbitrary groupings.

Tiers 1 and 2 close to Ohio and Indiana have a disproportionately large share of high-quality soils while tiers 7 through 11 have disproportionately more of the state's poorest quality soils. But counties in all tiers have both higher and lower quality soils. That was a challenge for an investor-settler. (Atack and Bateman reported analogous differences.)

Table 4.3: Another Perspective on Tiers and Their Soils

Tiers	*Total Acres*	*Percent of State's Acres in Classes 1 and 2*	*Percent of State's Acres in Class 4*
1–4	43%	56%	12%
5–6	22%	24%	17%
7–11	36%	19%	71%
TOTAL	101%	99%	100%

The Human Geography of Farmer-Settlers: 1850 to 1860

The analysis now shifts from soils to farms.

If farmer-settlers were rational economic decision-makers, they presumably only invested in productive soils and that Michigan's human geography would be the same as the state's physical, geography. The two geographies are not the same, a discrepancy at least partially attributable to the challenges of buying and selling in an information-poor market for land.

If the price of land with the best soils was the same throughout the Lower Peninsula, and if neither access to markets nor small changes in the growing season were important, then farm-settlers with perfect information would likely have made their locational decisions on the basis of soil quality only (with reservations already noted, for example drainage and access to markets). But the markets created to privatize land used criteria other than soils to price the land. The Graduation Act, military warrants, credit arrangements provided by state programs, the asking price set by speculators, and the absence of reliable information on lands, their soils and vegetation: all influenced the price of land and those who owned it. Furthermore, the availability of the best quality farmlands changed over time as new settlers bought and began to cultivate their land.

As the supply of acres with the best soils was converted to agricultural uses, new farmer-settlers presumably would be attracted to counties that still had large supplies of agriculturally promising soils. There would be leapfrogging rather than in-filling. Leapfrogging meant moving to higher-level, more northerly tiers and a shorter growing season, as well as less-developed physical and institutional infrastructures.

These more northerly counties were well forested with pine and other marketable species.

Farmers held less than half of the state's patented acres both in 1850 and 1860.[35] Although the proportion of patented acres in farms increased over the decade, the proportion of families that were farmers actually declined. Economies became more diversified.

According to census data, Michigan pioneers were more likely to be non-farmers than farmers. However, as noted earlier, the census definition of a farm excluded small operators, farm laborers, and sons living with their fathers and helping to farm their land.[36] Still, farming was not the only income-earning option for families.

Table 4.4 tracks the importance of farming in Michigan from 1850 to 1860. (I do not have county or tier-specific trend numbers.)

Statewide statistics can be misleading, as the relative significance of farm and non-farm patented acres varied by tier and county within a tier. We do not have summary statistics on the county-level acres that were patented but county-level information is available on the number of farms, farm acres, and the number of total acres. Again, these numbers are approximations, but the patterns these data reveal are unlikely to be affected by more precise measures. These patterns are reported by tier. Lewis displayed them by a series of maps of settlements (not farm-settlers) over time.[37]

Table 4.4: Trends in Farm Acres and Families, 1850–1860
Approximations Based on Different Sources

	1849–50	*1859–60*	*Decade Increase*	*Percent Increase Over Decade*
Patented Acres[1]	10,171,456	14,917,385	4,745,929	47%
Farm Acres[2]	4,383,890	7,030,834	2,646,944	60%
Percent Acres in Farms	43%	47%	56%[4]	
Families[3]	71,580	143,587	72,007	101%
Farms[2]	34,089	62,422	28,333	83%
Farms as a percent of all families	49%	44%	39%	

1. *For the years 1849 and 1859. Greffenius,* Development of Michigan Public Land Policy, *219 (statewide figures).*
2. *Joseph Kennedy,* Agriculture of the United States in 1860 *(Government Printing Office, 1864), 222.*
3. *Refers to Lower Peninsula only. Compiled from* Statistics of the State of Michigan, Compiled from the Census of 1860 *(John A, Kerr, 1861), 309.*
4. *This discrepancy seems to come from tabulation errors by the respective State census officials.*

Not all populated counties had farms. In 1850, 35 of the 37 counties reported in the Seventh Census had farms. By the time of the Eight Census in 1860, there were seven populated counties without farms. (Fifty-four Lower Peninsula counties reported residents, whereas 47 had farms.)

Some of these differences may be apparent only; the agricultural census, as already noted, excluded smaller (start-up) farms that did not meet the definitional standards that census-takers were instructed to use.[38]

All 28 counties in Tiers 1 through 4 had farms in 1850. By 1860, all six counties in Tier 5 had farms (up from four counties ten years earlier), and all seven counties in Tier 6 also were being farmed in 1860 (up from three in 1850). No farms were reported in 1850 for tiers 7 through 11 but six of the 27 counties in these two tiers attracted pioneer farmers by 1860.

The 21 counties without farms in both 1850 and 1860 are excluded from our subsequent analysis in this chapter. These 21 had approximately 2,273,760 acres of Class 1 and 2 soils, fourteen percent of the Lower Peninsula's total—but also 61 percent of the Lower Peninsula's Class 4 soils. (The 21 excluded counties held 28 percent of the total acres in the Lower Peninsula.) These more northerly tiers also had a shorter growing season.

Tiers 1 through 3 held 83 percent of all farms in 1850. These tiers added 45,870 new farms over the decade for an average of 15,290 farms per tier. Tier 4 counties increased their number of farms by twice the rate as the lower tiers. Starting with very few farms in 1850, tiers 5 and 6 had the highest growth rate, although they only added 3,107 farms, eleven percent of the new starts added during the decade. (Table 4.5) That is, many investor-settlers no longer found suitable soils in the soil-richer southern tiers but promising soils were available farther north.

Table 4.5: Lower-Tiers Had More Farms but a More Modest Rate of Growth, 1850–1860

Tier	*1850 Number of Farms*	*1850 Percent of All Farms*	*1860 Number of Farms*	*1860 Percent of All Farms*	*Increase in Number of Farms 1850 to 1860*	*Percent of All Farms Added 1850 to 1860*	*Rate of Increase in Number of Farms 1850 to 1860*
1	9,629	28%	16,398	26%	6,769	24%	70%
2	9,782	28%	14,477	23%	4,695	17%	48%
3	9,380	27%	14,995	24%	5,615	20%	60%
4	5,704	16%	13,081	21%	7,377	27%	129%
5	206	1%	2,679	4%	2,483	9%	1,205%
6	0	0%	640	1%	624	2%	3,900%
7 to 11	0	0%	255	0%	255	1%	
TOTAL	34,717	100%	62,525	99%	27,818	100%	80%

The tables above can give a misleading picture of inter- and intra-tier differences in new farm starts and the influences on them during the

1850s. There were declining supplies of land, with some tiers and counties having tighter supplies than others. Farmers who arrived before 1850 (and every year after) removed their acres from the supply available to new arrivals.

New arrivals, of course, could purchase an existing farm or portions of one. Many resident farmer-speculators no doubt made such sales. By 1850, three counties (Oakland, Washtenaw and Jackson) already had about 70 percent of their acres in farms (both improved and unimproved acres). Nine of the 34 counties that had farms in 1850 had half or more of their land reported as farms in that year.[39] That number nearly doubled (to 17) ten years later.

The number of heavily farmed counties (with 75 percent or more of their acres in farms) increased four-fold to eight.[40]

The most heavily farmed counties were in the lower tiers, the same tiers and counties in which the largest number of new farmers located during the decade. These earlier settlers had often already acquired the local supplies of the best soils. That is, *there was much more in-filling than leap-frogging* even though, as will be suggested, the in-filling was often on less promising soils.

Instead of soils being the magnet drawing new settlers, it is likely that the pattern of earlier migration decisions was also an indicator of profitable investment opportunities. In an information-poor market, such as the market for land that was created and managed by federal, state and local officials, many new settlers no doubt based their investment decisions on questionable and often misleading market information.

With a dwindling supply of more promising soils, it would seem that new farmer-settlers were in danger of making unwise locational choices. At least choosing to locate in tiers 4 or 5—and perhaps Tier 6 at the hypothetical Saginaw-to-Muskegon line dividing the Lower Peninsula by soil, vegetation and growing season—would provide a larger array of options. Of course, those selecting poorer quality soils in lower-tier counties could overcome some of the fertility handicaps through good soil and farm management, just as the advantages of higher-quality soils could be lost through poor management.

Farm and soil statistics (as in Table 4.6) can be deceiving, for not all the acres reported as farms were actually farmed—or to use the census term, *improved*. For example, although 70 percent of all acres in Tier 1 counties were in farms in 1860, only half these farm acres were improved. Counties in Tier 2 had the highest percentage of their total acres and total farm acres classified as improved in 1860.

The discrepancy between total farm acres and total improved acres reflected the early settlement and farm-making stage in Michigan. Farmers were in the near-continuous process of logging their land (or just removing the trees and their stumps) and preparing it for cultivation. The discrepancy also suggests that an unknown percentage of farmer-settlers bought more land than they intended to farm. They were farmer-speculators who sold off parts of their farms to newly arriving settlers.

Table 4.7 suggests that in both 1850 and 1860 the supply of land in lower-tier counties was not as tight as suggested by the percentage of all land in farms. On the basis of my review of Midland Michigan's deed books, it appears that the sources of land proliferated over time to include not only federal and state programs but also non-residents and farmer-speculators. Again, Table 4.7 suggests that farmer-speculators made in-filling possible. This pattern is also reflected in the large number of new farmers who settled in lower-tier counties during the 1850s. Because these new arrivals bought some unknown portion of their land from earlier settlers, it is not surprising that the average size farm declined over time.[41]

Table 4.6: Lower-Tier Counties Had Proportionally More of Their Land in Farms

	*50 Percent or More of the Counties' Acres in Farms**		*Percent of Tier Acres in Farms*	
Tier	**1850**	**1860**	**1850**	**1860**
1	2/7	6/7	46	68
2	2/3	5/6	55	71
3	3/7	3/7	41	58
4	0	3/8	20	40
5	0	0	1	12
6	0	0	0	4
7 thru 11	0	0	0	2

* *Numerator refers to number of counties with 50 percent or more in farms. Denominator refers to number of counties in the tier.*

Some historians referenced the challenge that new farmers had in making wise decisions in selecting land for their farms. Susan Gray reported that early settlers in Kalamazoo County "passed over" one township (Alamo) with over four-fifths of its lands that Gray classified as marginal ("fertile but requiring constant improvement for general farming").[42] Very early settlers in the third-tier Macomb County also were "apparently dubious about buying land" in a lake plain, although a more recent soil survey indicated that this area was well-suited to farming.[43] Other researchers found less astute settlers. Rose Moore, as noted earlier, reported that homesteaders between 1878 and 1890 were attempting to farm Grayling sand outwash plains unsuitable for agriculture in the seventh-tier county of Oscoda.[44]

Unwise decisions were also made by farmers in five lower-tier counties prior to 1850 and during the following decade. We need to make certain assumptions to support this statement—that is, if it is assumed that farmers who were enumerated in the 1850 agricultural census only bought Class 1 and 2 soils, then Tier 2 Counties already had 63 percent of their higher-quality soils in farms. (Table 4.8 presents the percent of Class 1 and 2 soils still available in 1850 and ten years later.)

Table 4.7: Farmer-Settlers Owned More Land Than They Farmed

	Improved Acres as a Percent of All Acres	*Improved Acres as a Percent of all Farm Acres*	*Improved Acres as a Percent of All Acres*	*Improved Acres as a Percent of all Farm Acres*
Tier	**1850**		**1860**	
1	21	46	36	52
2	25	46	41	57
3	18	45	30	51
4	8	37	18	44
5	.03	29	3	25
6	.03	30	.1	18
7–11	0	0	.3	16

Oakland County already in 1850 exhausted its supply of its best soils. At the end of the decade, Tier 2 counties only had six percent of Class 1 and 2 soils not in farms. And in addition to Tier-3 Oakland County, St. Joseph and Cass Counties in Tier 1, joined by Jackson and Washtenaw counties in Tier 2, had more acres in farms (improved and unimproved acres) than these counties had in their Class 1 and 2 soils.[45] If markets were information-rich, one might not expect some of these patterns.

Again, if new farmer-settlers based their locational decisions only on the quality of soils (land) available to purchase, then higher-tier counties presumable would have relatively more farms (and farm acres) than reported in the agricultural census of 1860. But instead of being attracted to more readily available good soils in tiers 3, 4 and higher, a large majority of new arrivals stayed closer to where earlier farmers had already settled.

The settlement pattern did move from south to north (as well as from east to west), but *existing farm operations seem to have exerted a stronger (gravity) pull than the attractiveness of a larger supply of good soils in higher tiers (the magnetic pull of quality soils).* Information on the market for land was richer on human than on physical geography.

Table 4.8: Using Up Class 1 and 2 Soils*

Tier	*Percent of Class 1 and 2 Soils Still Available*		*Percent of Available Class 1 and 2 Soils Available in 1850 Added to Farms by 1860*
	1850	**1860**	
1	44	16	63
2	27	6	79
3	48	26	46
4	76	53	30
5	99	85	14
6	99.8	93	7
7–11	100	99	1

* *All 68 Lower Peninsula counties.*

Other authors have suggested various non-soil influences on the pace and pattern of pioneer farm settlements. We have already referred to the importance of the general economy, events in other countries, federal and state land policies, and the distribution of wetlands. Few of these influences are place-specific, nor do they allow the use of even simple statistical techniques to estimate the quantitative contributions these influences had on particular areas within Michigan or elsewhere.

Among the Michigan-specific influences, Charles Davis noted the importance that the state's drainage system had for the distribution of "human habitations and the lines of communication—that is, the overlap of physical and human geographies. Of those primary human necessities which are limited in extent, water is one of the most important and its distribution profoundly influences human activities."[46] Benson had a similar observation on the importance of topography and water in noting that "[f] rom a central tableland watershed extending the length of the peninsula, streams and rivers flow topographically determined serpentine courses either east into lakes Erie and Huron or west into Lake Michigan."[47] The physical geography of Michigan waters, not just soils, influenced settlement patterns over time.

Early settlers found that with water came mosquitoes and malaria. They in turn gave parts of the state a negative image. But Michigan was not necessarily unique within the Old Northwest, for, as Hugh Prince noted, "[s]warms of insects are the most profuse and characteristic forms of life in all Midwestern wetlands."[48] Michigan, however, did have a large number of wetland acres, as seen in the swamplands that the national government granted to the state.

Where good well-drained soil was available, there would seem to have been little incentive for a settler to try farming in mosquito-laden wetlands. These areas were simply unhealthy, as indicated by visitors to various parts of the state. For example and as referenced earlier, John Gordon wrote in his journal on October 7, 1836, that the River Rouge in southeast Michigan was a place that "the New England emigrant might enjoy the ague & fever nine months in the year & and the bilious for the other three."[49] Farther north, the U.S. Army in 1823 moved its garrison from Saginaw to Detroit because the "pestilential swamps" in the area were a source of "an aggravated form of intermittent fever" that affected those housed in the garrison. At least nine young soldiers died along with members of their families.[50] It wasn't until much later that epidemiologists added their maps to the human and physical geographies then available in the mid–1800s.

Getting to one's land and marketing harvests from it also had an unmeasured effect on the timing and spatial patterning of farm settlements. Lewis mapped the road and railroad patterns in pre–1860 Michigan, and there is anecdotal information on how particular roads affected land purchases (but not necessarily settlement).[51] For example, John Gordon wrote in his journal in 1836 that all the land on a road somewhat west of the St. Joseph River had been taken (which again is different from being settled).[52] In her study of migration and settlement in pre–1850 Macomb County, Dooley found that "settlement progressed along established trails and along waterways which could provide a dependable supply of water..."[53] Trowbridge in 1837 also emphasized that a new 30-mile road that his company built between Allegan and Grandville soon attracted twenty new families to the area.[54]

New railroads and water transport significantly lowered the cost of shipping farm and other commodities. This allowed Michigan farmers to compete in more distant markets as well as in fairly nearby ones.[55] It should also have made the state a more attractive location to begin farming. Still, we are unable to estimate the size of the effects that new transportation infrastructure had on the locational decisions that potential land-buyers made. No doubt population growth sometimes preceded and led to the construction of roads; in other instances, the roads probably came first and facilitated settlement. Theories of unbalanced development are consistent with both time sequences.

Transportation is not just a background environment in which locational and investment decisions were made, but our current state of evidence and analysis does not make it possible to ascertain the relevant importance that transportation, undrained land, health conditions, and soil quality had on the spatial patterns of farm settlements either in Michigan or in other states.

Given these and other previously-noted data and analytical limitations, it should not be surprising that we are unable to statistically assess in precise quantitative terms the wisdom of the locational decisions that farmer-settlers made in different tiers, counties within tiers, and the soil quality found in these counties and tiers.

It is possible to link county-level information on soils to the economic returns from cultivating them. That is one indicator of collective economic rationality and the wastage associated with how the American Frontier was closed. The next chapter uses the present one's county-level evidence in conjunction with evidence taken from the 1860 agricultural census. But it will be necessary to move below statistics aggregated at the county level and move to the level of individual farms. That will be done in later chapters.

5

Rates of Return on Investments in Farming

Overview

This chapter begins with a summary of several studies that estimated rates of return on investments made by mid-nineteenth century farmers. A separate annex explores some of the major biases found in evidence used by historians in their studies of this century's farming and the closing of the American frontier. Our discussion will cover costs and prices of farms and farm-making, the time frames used to estimate rates of return, and differences among several types of investors. Counties, the units of analysis used in this chapter, differ in their access to major urban markets. We will see that this access influenced the per-acre value of land independent of soils. A later chapter will revisit the effects that type of soil had on the wisdom of the decision-makers in the single case-study county.

Both inter and intra-state analyses that are limited to soils unfortunately overlook the effects that weather and the growing season had on farming in states and regions within them.

Weather, rates of return, costs and prices are not terms that are deeply explored in general narrative histories. Nor do narrative historians always clearly distinguish geographies, markets, economics and the several social science disciplines.

The present number-heavy multi-disciplinary chapter explores some of the many decisions that farmer-investors had to make in starting their new lives on the frontier. A good way to begin this chapter is with the summary section.

Earlier studies had interests that go beyond what is covered here. For example, Atack and Bateman (with co-author Parker) "evaluate the attainments of the yeoman agricultural *system* at the peak of its prominence on the eve of the Civil War."[1] Their Chapter 14 is titled "The Profitability of Northern Agriculture: Economic Survival and Resource Allocation."[2] It provides information on inter-state differences in rates of return earned by farmers in the antebellum North. New settlers in the mid–1800s were unlikely to have been aware of what these much-later researchers documented.

Again, the present chapter explores some possible reasons why farming (especially in different parts of Michigan) was not necessarily the best way for most antebellum families to build wealth and initiate sustainable flows of adequate income. Of course, some promising alternatives to farming were only available to individuals with access to capital.

There is little narrative history in this chapter although there is hopefully a clear story line. Readers will find that line in the chapter's summary, always a useful starting point in any study.

Earlier Studies on Rates of Return on Investments in Farming

In 1845, fifteen years before the 1860 census that Atack and has colleagues used, the Secretary of Treasury reported that "the profit of agriculture [nationwide] varies from 1 to 8 percent."[3] By 1860 these rates averaged 6 to 10 percent on "current production" and an additional 3 to 7 percent in capital gains. The average Illinois farmer earned an estimated 10.8 percent rate of return without capital gains, a sharp contrast with the negative 0.5 percent return by the average Michigan farmer. When capital gains are included, Illinois farmers enjoyed a 19.1 percent rate of return, well above Michigan's 5.8 percent.[4]

Michigan farmers, according to these estimates, survived by selling some of their land to new buyers who in turn would survive by continuing the buy-sell-buy cycle. These farmers were "earning less than the opportunity cost of the labor and capital that they employed."[5]

Atack's sample of nine Michigan counties (with one township per county) included the two counties in Tier 11 that had farms in 1860, and one of the seven Tier 6 counties with farms.[6] These three counties account for one-third of the two researchers' Michigan sample but none of the seven counties in Tier 3. The two counties in Tier 11 were home to 85 farmers who had an average of about 117 total acres per farm.

It is likely that Atack and Bateman's state-wide results are biased by their sampling plan. The large majority of the state's farmers were settled in the more soil-rich southern tiers of counties. A sample of counties or townships is not the same as a sample of all farms and farmers.

Although the sample used by these researchers did not allow for inter-tier comparisons, the list of their counties indicates that 92 percent of the farms located in Tiers 6 and 11 were settled some time during the 1850s. These farmers were decision-makers early in their farm-making, as suggested by their having an average of only fifteen improved acres per farm.

The agricultural economists' analyses are based on total acres, not those actually being cultivated or used as pasture. These researchers note that although Michigan farmers with 40 acres or less had an average loss of 21.3 percent, if a farmer had 120 more acres (160 in all), he could expect an average return of 12.5 percent.[7] These acreage totals, however, refer to a farm's total land, not to acres actually being cultivated. There is a difference between these two numerical universes as well as north-south differences.

Overall, the researchers concluded that the "highest profit rates were to be found in a band of about 200 miles wide through northern New York State, southern Michigan and northern Indiana, and the northern half of Illinois ..." Profit rates to the north of this belt were negative.[8] These aggregated rates are potentially biased in several ways including what we will see is an ecological fallacy, not just the spatial (county) units that were sampled.

Given the nature of their sample (counties or townships within them), it is not possible to assess the impact of farm size on farmers' well-being independently of tier in Michigan. And these researchers' conclusions on the importance of farm size do not agree with Donald Parkerson's study of New York farmers. Atack and his co-researchers estimated that 43 percent of farmers who had less than 40 acres were unable to feed their families or livestock with a recommended diet, whereas only 19 percent of the farmers with 80 or more acres suffered a similar deficit.[9] Parkerson used a different yardstick on food deficits in his study of farms in mid-century New York. Even with meager yields, "a farm family of six could feed itself by planting just twelve acres of corn or its equivalent."[10] If this yardstick was applicable to Michigan (and if farmers in these northern counties could cultivate corn), then the average farmer in the two counties in Tier 11 lived just above the minimal survival level. Moreover, cultivating crops, as will be seen, was not a farm family's only source of income, an important consideration during early farm-making years.

Atack and his colleagues are clear about the many assumptions they make in their analysis of 1860 census data—for example, assumptions about the cost of labor, including the family's own sweat equity. On the other hand, they could have been more critical of the information collected by the census enumerators. Farmers themselves reported on the number of their improved acres, the bushels of wheat and corn they harvested, the value of their livestock, the value of their farms, and other items included in the analyses of those who designed the 1860 census. Atack's team was working with self-reported estimates, typically rounded off in even numbers. As far as I could discover, no one has closely examined the validity of these estimates. (Validity issues are covered both in the present chapter's annex as well as in later chapters. Historians are, of course, aware of the limitations of the evidence they use.)

If researchers wish to distinguish between rates of return with and without capital gains, then estimates are also needed of the prices farmers paid for their land and prices they charged when they resold it, as well as any dollar outlays and sweat equity they expended on the land. Any multi-year estimates of earnings from current farming activities also need to recognize variations in the market prices of commodities and, therefore, farmer's income (rates of return on investments) during a particular year.

Analytical refinements need to be addressed as well. For example, Paul Gates faulted early studies of speculators' profits for not considering compound interest, the costs of ownership other than the original purchase price of the land, and a time dimension that recognizes that speculators liquidated their investments at an uneven rate.[11]

Researchers have addressed these critiques but doing so required the collection of non-census data. For example, Allan and Margaret Bogue's study of land speculators' profits on the frontier was based on cost, sale, and tax figures obtained from federal land-entry books (tract books), county records, and business records.[12] Robert Swierenga reviewed the income flow and capital-theory analysis of the Bogues and others in his own analysis of land parcels patented and first resold in central Iowa. His analysis incorporated length of ownership, government entry fees, realtors' commissions and taxes in his calculations.[13]

Atack and Bateman were fully aware of the data and methodological issues raised by these authors. But lacking their own data, Atack and Bateman relied on estimates made by others in reporting inter-state differences in the average cost of buying 40, 80 and 160-acre farms, as well as the cost of livestock owned and the mean value of machinery. Using the results from these other studies, the authors estimated that a Michigan farmer with a 40-acre farm paid $18.85 per acre; this dropped to $16.03 for an 80-acre farm and $17.33 for double this size.[14] The assumption "seems" to be that a large majority of these farmers bought their land from speculators and other farmers, not from the federal or state governments. This may be a correct assumption for many but hardly for all tiers and counties. Relying on aggregate statistics opens the research to the earlier-referenced ecological fallacy in which a few farmers can distort the totals reported by all farmers.

It is not clear whether the cost of different-sized farms included the cost of clearing acres for cultivation. Farms differed in the number of their improved acres, and there is no evidence that per-acre costs differed for farms with 40 or 160 acres. Costs might, however, have differed on land with hardwood versus softwood (pine) trees. Removing trees was a labor-intensive time-consuming challenge in heavily forested Michigan. Farmers had other significant costs as well—for example, building the family's house, buying equipment and livestock, and supporting a family until harvests generated sufficient income for the family's maintenance.

There are both general estimates of farm-making costs as well as estimates specific to Michigan,[15] but not to inter-tier and inter-county cost differences that would allow us to estimate the rates of return on farming different soils in different parts of the state.

There are at least three related reasons for mentioning these estimates. First, farm-making was a process, and the decisions a farmer made depended on how far along the farmer was in this development trajectory. That is, farmers differed in the contexts in which their decisions had to be made. Second, the more time and resources a farmer devoted to clearing his land for cultivation, the less time there was for cultivating the improved acres. And, third, these time and financial investments made over time affected the rate of return on them, the time horizon for making such a calculation, and the base on which they were made—that is, on total farm acres or more narrowly on improved acres only. All these number-heavy considerations are relevant both to human geography and to an understanding of the closing of the American frontier.

The existing literature expresses farm-making costs in terms of both dollars and days of labor required to clear one acre. These estimates nationally and for Michigan in particular seem to have different definitions of what it means to clear an acre of trees. Some authors limit their estimates to cutting cordwood; others to cutting and removing the fallen trees and brush; others to removing stumps as well, and still others to using the cut timber to fence the cleared land.[16]

Farmers clearing their land of pine trees were able to realize income from their cuttings. Some (not all) hardwood forests did not provide as many similar benefits.[17] That is, farmers in Michigan's pine forests were harvesting and marketing a crop they neither planted nor cultivated. This, of course, was not a sustainable source of income. Moreover, pine stumps had a longer life than hardwoods, so that stump-pulling to prepare cut-over land could consume some of the revenue from selling the cut pine trees. More importantly, as we will see in later chapters, relatively few farmers selected land that had pine trees. This vegetation was associated with poorer quality agricultural soils.

Estimates of the time to clear (improve) an acre and the number of acres that a farmer could clear in a year differ quite widely, although Williams concluded that the time and costs of clearing did not decrease during the century. Based on his review of nineteen estimates of "time requirements" made between 1800 and 1890, Williams found a wide range of between 13 and 36 man-days per acre. This range did not include the time and costs required to remove stumps. It would take approximately 32 man-days to clear an acre completely, although an 1851 issue of the *Michigan Farmer* estimated that manpower and dollar requirements were slightly lower if the work was initiated during the winter months.[18] This kind of market information was not available to aspiring new settlers.

Based on his research on New York farmers, Parkerson estimated that a "good man" under the best of conditions could clear an acre of "cordwood" in the off-season.[19] Danhoff has a much higher figure—from 10 to 15 acres cleared during a pioneer's first year on his land. When man-days are converted to dollar wages current at the time, then the cost per-acre of clearance was estimated to be between $3 and $15 in the late 1830s. Other estimates were $6.25 per acre in 1838 for chopping, clearing and fencing in Macomb County, and $10 per Michigan acre in 1849.[20] Again, these estimates differ in their definitions of clearing. And the evidentiary bases for the estimates are rather thin. But what is important for present purposes is that Michigan farmers throughout the state made significant investments of time and money in their farm-making—that is to human and capital investments that followed the initial decision on where to settle. There is no information that to-be settlers had any of this information to factor into their migration and investment decisions.

For many farmers, there were no doubt limited opportunity costs for their sweat equity, as there were few outside sources of income. The absence of these opportunities could add to the complexities of estimating the value of an acre of improved land at any one time and the rate of return on that land. Estimated rates of return on a statewide basis conceal significant intra-state variations. In theory, one might want to base returns on improved acres only, not on different size farms.[21]

There is evidence that tenants and farm-owners differed in their decisions on how to use the acres available to them. These decisions in turn affected their investments, returns on them and the associated labor, and the income from farming the land. Farther west, prairie renters may also have given more emphasis to livestock production rather than to crops, and they invested less in equipment.[22] These differences are reflected in the analyses that Atack and Bateman made of tenant versus owner-farmers. For example, the average midwestern farm-owner on an 80-acre farm had five times more money tied up in his farm than did a tenant working the same number of acres ($1,716 vs. $325).[23]

The capital outlays of an average midwestern tenant who farmed 160 acres were only one-seventh of the average owner-farmer's outlay working the same number of acres.[24] Despite these differences, the average farmer-tenant in Michigan only earned $7 less during 1859–60 than a farmer working his own land at the time.[25] The tenant's income was $78; the owner's $85. This was only about half of what an Illinois farm-owner realized.

Atack's team made a number of assumptions in calculating their estimates, but the resulting incomes were well below the $363 annual earnings of all American employees in 1860.[26] If these figures are approximately correct, then farmer-settlers and farm tenants in Michigan might have been better off pursuing non-agricultural employment. At a minimum, it would have been a wiser decision for both owners and tenants to have started farming elsewhere than in Michigan. (My own maternal grandparents did not take this advice.) These estimates provide answers to Kuhn's two questions.

Anecdotal information suggests that many Michigan farmer-settlers added to their income by working "in the woods" or for other farmers.[27] In later years, farmers were part-time (really "temporary") farmers and lumbermen. Working in the woods or in lumber mills was during the fall and winter. Workers could farm their land during the planting-to-harvest months, and professional loggers were also available for labor-intensive work during the peak harvesting season. The survival strategies of new farmers (especially in higher-tier counties) and lumbermen required this dual employment track. Similarly, as noted in Parkerson's research on New York State, farmers there cut and marketed cord wood on their land as well as on properties owned by others. This was true for Michigan's Midland County as well.

From the farmer's perspective, the rate-of-return calculation might have been based on his overall income-earning possibilities as well as those for the other members of his family—not just on how many acres he farmed. We do not know what farmers were most attempting to maximize—their farm income or total family income. Presumably both were important and both influenced the likelihood that farmers would continue on their land or move on. Human geographies of farming were constantly changing.

There are significant data problems in estimating the rates of return on both farm acres and on an individual farmer's own labor.[28] The present concern is with the wisdom farmers made in selecting their land and managing it. If their choices were truly wise, then Michigan's physical and human geographies would have the same approximate maps. They were not close to being the same.

Estimated Yields of Corn and Wheat

Existing data allow for three approaches for assessing the wisdom of the multiple decisions that Michigan farmers made in selecting soils and where to begin farming. Wisdom also applies to how well a farmer managed his soils and crops. Presumably good management would produce higher yields on Class 1 and 2 soils than on poorer quality land.

The first approach examines corn and wheat productivity figures by counties and tiers that differ in their supply of different quality soils.

The second approach links county and tier-level soil and yield data with the value of farmland. Here it seems reasonable to expect that counties and tiers with both high yield and larger supplies of Class 1 and 2 soils would also have higher values assigned to their farms and farm acres.

The third approach links farms to larger markets for farm products independent of the soils that were cultivated. We will see that the size of local markets for farm products might help explain why soils were not the only or even major influence on the value of individual farms and by extension rates of return on the investments farmers made in the mid–1800s.

Still we might assume that farmers would only select the highest quality soils to cultivate. If we further assume that an acre of these best soils would yield more bushels of wheat and corn than could be harvested from poorer soils (Classes 3 and 4), then we would expect fairly clear inter-county and inter-tier differences in per-acre yields of wheat and corn that in turn would be reflected in higher returns on investments. Of course, the real world and its markets were more complicated. Crops differed in their optimal growing environments (e.g., rain, temperatures, and growing season), and farmers differed in how well they managed their soils and crops. Moreover, we have also seen that farmers, even in the most heavily farmed counties, left a good portion of their land unimproved. Finally, we do not know which soils were sown with corn and which with wheat or other crops (e.g., potatoes) that will be discussed in the chapters limited to the case study of Midland County.

Despite these unknowns, we do have anecdotal and state census estimates of per-acre yields for corn and wheat. The anecdotal information also comments on why individual farms differed in per-acre yields. For example, good management practices paid off, but there were thought to be relatively few progressive farmers at the time. That is, a farmer's wise choice of soils could have led to a wasted investment if unwise soil and crop-management practices were adopted.[29] Expressed somewhat differently, a farmer's rate of return on his investment depended both on the soils he cultivated and on the how he managed his resources.

Contemporary observers commented that Michigan farmers, as well as those elsewhere, were doing little to protect and enhance their soils. The physical environment (geography) was not a constant. The U.S. Patent Office reported that farmers in southeastern Michigan gave little attention to saving or applying manure. On the other hand, farmers in the state's southern tiers of counties were making extensive use of gypsum in the 1840s.[30] According to an article published in the *Journal of Agriculture* in 1856, a farmer in Ypsilanti had already discovered that a rotation of clover, corn and wheat produced good crops—that "wheat soils of America stand less in need of manure than of good cultivation."[31]

Alternating between wheat and corn—missing the clover—was a road to lower productivity. An 1848 observer writing in the *Cultivator* commented that this two-crop rotation practice in southern Michigan "is such that land which has not been more than twelve years cleared from its primitive forest has, if not run out, become at least thoroughly run down."[32] Lower yields also resulted from poor drainage and inappropriate plowing. Recent studies have found "significantly lower yields on eroded soils."[33]

With the state of soil and agricultural science and practice at the time, it is little wonder that by the 1840s there were reported declines in soil productivity in Ohio, Indiana, and Wisconsin.[34] These reports run counter to Atack, Bateman and Parker's claim that "productivity, measured by yield per acre, changed relatively little for most crops during the nineteenth century," although they too recognized that as soil nutrients were depleted, yields dropped from the initial yields from newly cleared land.[35]Again, just has the human geography could change over time so could physical geography do the same.

This anecdotal evidence points to further complications in assessing productivity per acre. Soil was not a fixed asset able to produce the same bushels of wheat and corn year after year. Since Michigan's lower tiers had the most acres of continuously-cultivated acres, and given the farming practices adopted on depleted the soil, we would expect that some of each of Veatch's four classes of soil would have slipped a level by 1860—that is, some of Class 1 soils would be less fertile than Class 2, and some Class 2 soils would be only as fertile as soils in Class 3 or, even, 4. This downward drift, however, would only apply to soils classified in the 1830s, not in the 1930s and 1940s, the date of Veatch's research.[36] The physical geography of soils was not a constant. The effects that the degradation of soils had on human this geography were probably not apparent until well after the initial settlement of Michigan's soils.

Left out of these mental measurement gymnastics are temperature, the growing season, and moisture. Crops that did well in some environments did less well in others. Wheat did better in drier and cooler climates that were relatively free of wheat rust and wheat blast. Corn did better in moderate climates.[37] Corn was also better adapted than wheat to "naturally very poorly drained soils."[38] There were analogous differences in the nutritional needs of livestock. Horses "can survive and be healthy on a pasture where cows fail to thrive and reproduce."[39] And, of course, the farmer and his family had their own nutritional needs and the need for a crop mix that spread peak labor demands in accordance with available labor. Farmers were challenged by a number of significant decisions that could affect the family's health and welfare. We focus here only on how these decisions might have affected corn and wheat yields.

According to Lewis, Michigan's Lower Peninsula was at the northern edge of the corn-growing zone. His map of corn production in 1860 parallels the state's farm settlement at the time. Wheat production follows the same pattern, although Lewis reports that wheat-growing gravitated towards counties with large areas of (oak) openings and prairie lands.[40]

When overlapped with one another, these maps by Lewis suggest that Michigan farmers practiced mixed farming and that the total harvests from their crops were unsurprisingly relatively higher in counties and tiers with the largest number of farms and improved farm acres—as well as the largest number of acres of Class 1 and 2 soils.[41]

Were farmers in the illustrative sample county of Midland (see the following chapters) any wiser than the county's original Amerindian cultivators? There is no evidence that Midland's Amerindians made wise investments in the lands they farmed. This did not mean, however, that the yields obtained by these early cultivators were low by then-current standards. The "Saubiewan Indians" in 1852, for example, cultivated corn, potatoes and bean "Upon the Corner of Ses: 1, 2, 11 and 12" in Township15 N R 1 W. None of these four sections had good soils (primary or secondary) but, still, the crops "grow large, and do well here" according to the federal surveyor's questionable field notes. The surveyor also reported "Indian" fields but not crops on them in two other sections in the same township. Neither section had good soils. Other fields were observed in T 13N R 2

W and T 14N R 2E that included one section (27) with good soil as the primary classification and another section (21) with good soil as a secondary classification. Amerindians were no wiser investors than those who later occupied native lands.

Given the hypothetical importance of Class 1 and 2 soils farmed in the state, it seems reasonable to expect that Michigan corn and wheat yields per acre would compare favorably with yields in neighboring states. In fact, as seen in Chapter 2, the Commissioner of Patents supported this assumption for wheat but reported just the opposite for corn. For the period 1843–1856, Michigan farms had a median output of 21 bushels of wheat per acre and a range of 12 to 30. These were the highest yields in the Old Northwest, whereas the state was at the low end for corn yields, with a median of 30 bushels per acre and a range of 15 to 40.[42]

At mid-century, American wheat yields were in the range of 10 to 13 bushels per acre. Another estimate put wheat yields in the range of 15 to 16 bushels per acre whereas German, English and French farmers had nearly double that range at about the same time (24 to 26 bushels per acre).[43] At least two and probably more European countries were agriculturally more profitable to work than what was current in America at the time. (But information is not readily available on the cost of land and labor to allow for estimates of rates of return.)

If we accept these estimates at their face value, then Michigan wheat farmers made a wise decision in moving to the state, but farmers who emphasized corn would have done better elsewhere or by sowing wheat rather than corn.[44] And just as there appear to have been inter-state differences in the productivity of their soils, so we might assume similar inter-tier and intra-tier differences within the state. That might have been so, but the evidence to support this assumption is biased and incomplete.

Two major sources of evidence are now available but were not so in the 1800s. First, we have scattered anecdotal reports. In June 1864 (and applicable to the 1863 growing season), the state's Secretary of the Board of Agriculture sent a long list of questions (including questions about productivity) "to the farmers of Michigan." There was an effort to improve markets by providing reliable information. Respondents from seven counties provided productivity estimates for corn; two additional counties provided estimates of wheat yields per acre.[45]

The second evidentiary source is from the state census of 1864. It also has farm-level information for the 1863 growing season's number of acres sowed with wheat and the same for corn, as well as the bushels of each crop "raised in the preceding year."

"Hard numbers" do not necessarily make this a reliable source.

Township supervisors were authorized to conduct the census, but a post-mortem by the Michigan's Secretary of State concluded that "the law has in many cases been misapprehended; hence has arisen inaccuracies, or in some cases *an entire failure* to report upon important points suggested."[46] Supervisors were to collect this information "at the time of taking a list of the taxable property of their township, ward or district." Due to a "want of experience and aptitude ... caused many returns to be inadequate and defective."

Historical geographers and agricultural economists, along with other researchers, are often left with questionable evidence. And potential investors making their locational decisions were also left in an information desert. Land was bought and sold in an opaque market. Again, it is no wonder that soil and settlement maps were different from one another.

County and township officers had other time and political burdens during this period, as they played key roles in enrolling and recruiting volunteers to serve in Michigan regiments during the Civil War.[47] Both the federal and state censuses had other weaknesses—for example, they relied on self-reported information, including acres planted and bushels harvested. Publications based on these censuses also included typographical errors and/or miscalculations.

In short, the 1864 state census data are as suspect as the anecdotal information reported by the Secretary of the State Board of Agriculture.

Table 5.1 reports corn and wheat productivity figures (bushels per acre) for nine counties responding to the Board of Agriculture's questionnaire. Both the Board's and census figures refer to the 1863 crop year.[48]

There are significant differences for corn; much less so for wheat. Obviously, the Board of Agriculture's respondents were unable to collect county-wide information, but both sets of yields fall somewhere within the statewide ranges estimated by the Commissioner of Patents for 1843–1856 (12 to 30 bushels of wheat, 15 to 40 for corn). The Commissioner's ranges are too broad to derive statewide or intra-state averages.

If a new settler already knew these productivity levels before making a locational decision, and if the yields were fairly constant over time (or at least retained their inter-county differences), then a wise settler with plans to cultivate corn would have selected Hillsdale over Monroe. The aspiring wheat farmer would make the same decision. Unfortunately there is no really reliable information on the sales prices of these different crops and the incomes they yielded for those cultivating in different parts of Michigan (despite the estimates provided in the 1860 agricultural census).

These two sets of productivity figures do not reveal major inter-tier differences, with the possible exception of the two counties in Tier 4. Genesee and Ottawa had the least promising wheat prospects.

If we expand our coverage to include all counties with farms in 1863, not just those with information reported by the Board of Agriculture, then tier effects are seen for corn. Again, our measures provided in the State's 1864 census are crude and questionable. Still ten out of thirteen counties in Tiers 1 and 2 had corn yields of 25 or more bushels per acre, while only two of the fifteen counties in Tiers 3 and 4 were as productive. None of the eight counties growing corn in Tiers 5 and 6 met this productivity level.

Wheat yields followed a similar pattern—with all thirteen counties in Tiers 1 and 2 reporting over 11 bushels per acre, while only three of the fifteen counties in Tiers 3 and 4 reached the same standard.

These are admittedly crude indicators that probably display the influence of growing season and climate, not just the importance of soil and farmer-management skills.

If the self-reported numbers in the state census are approximately correct, there is almost as much intra and inter-tier differences. For example, counties in Tier 2 had the highest corn yields (29.1 bushels per acre) whereas Tier 6 counties had 10.8 fewer bushels (18.3 per acre). But within Tier 2, both Kalamazoo's and Washtenaw's 32 bushels per acre were 8 more than what Wayne County's corn growers harvested. The inter-county intra-tier differences for wheat yields display similar spreads—Van Buren County in Tier 1 had 6 more bushels of wheat per acre than Ottawa and Lapeer counties in Tier 4, but there is the same 6-bushel gap within Tier 1 between Van Buren and St. Joseph counties.

In antebellum America, much of agriculture was narrowly local. Investor-farmer-settlers were unaware of these differences.

There were many American lands of opportunity along with many opportunities to waste one's investments. Studies of the closing of the American frontier can easily overlook what was actually happening on specific grounds. That, is there are multiple histories of the closing of the American frontier and of American agriculture.

An aspiring farmer who was aware of these differences would presumably have demonstrated his wisdom by avoiding Emmet and Mason counties in Tiers 7 and 11 in favor of Oakland and Berrien in Tiers 3 and 1.[49] In fact, this settlement pattern was followed in general. Still (if these productivity figures are generally correct), a large number of farmers either settled in low-productivity counties—or counties differed significantly in the management skills of their resident farmers.

Table 5.1: Anecdotal and Census Sources Differ in Their Wheat and Corn Yields for 1863

		Corn (Bushels per Acre)		Wheat (Bushels per Acre)	
Tier	*County*	*Board of Agriculture*[1]	*State Census*[2]	*Board of Agriculture*[1]	*State Census*[2]
1	Berrien	45	31	12 to 15	17
1	Cass	40[a]	26	12 to 15[c]	13
1	Hillsdale	60 to 80	25	20[d]	14
1	Monroe	18	25	10 to 13	12
2	Calhoun	35	28	15	15
2	Kalamazoo	45[b]	32	15[e]	14
3	Macomb	No Information	Not Applicable	15 to 25[f]	11
4	Genesee	40 to 60	23	15	7
4	Ottawa	No Information	Not Applicable	12 to 50	11

1. *Third Annual Report of the Secretary of the State Board of Agriculture of the State of Michigan for the Year 1864 (Kerr, 1864), 10, 12, 16, 20, 22, 28–30, 42, 48, 52, 57, 61.*
2. *Census and Statistics of the State of Michigan, 1864 [Kerr, 1865].*
   a. *Down from 60 from earlier years*
   b. *When well-tilled, up to 80.*
   c. *Down from 25 in an earlier year.*
   d. *Down from 40 in an earlier year.*
   e. *When well-tilled*
   f. *Up to 35*

There is some suggestion that poor soil and crop management might have affected wheat more than corn yields. Wheat yields dropped in five tiers from 1853 to 1863, increasing in only one tier. Corn yields, on the other hand, increased in all tiers except one during the same decade. There is still much to be learned about the history of farming in the state of Michigan as well as in other states as well.

Dollar Values of Farm Acres

As indicated earlier, this chapter references quantitative evidence relevant to agricultural economics. Twenty-first century investors would search for such market-relevant understanding before making their decisions. But the market for land during the closing of the American frontier was information-poor. It is no wonder that many wasted investments were made during the closing of the American Frontier.

Farmers no doubt differed in how well they managed their operations. A new settler who bought an existing farm might very well have been able to produce higher crop yields per acre than the farmer who sold him his farm. But our county-level census data do not accommodate an assessment of farmer management skills. (And again, we are subject to statistical ecological fallacies,[50] among other difficulties.) But if we make the admittedly unrealistic assumption that all farmers were equally good (or poor) managers, then we might argue that soils and climate were the most significant determinants of productivity and, furthermore, that differences in productivity would be reflected in the (self-reported) values of farms. These farm-level values could in turn be converted to per acre values for both total and improved acres separately. Different assumptions could be made with similar end results. The calculations could, in theory, be linked to soils and the physical geography of Michigan.

That is, regardless of soil, growing season and climate, *farm management might have had the most influence on farm values*. Under different sets of assumptions, we would expect fairly clear inter-tier value patterns. And, in fact, there is a tier gradient but one different from what was reported for corn and wheat yields per acre.

Table 5.2 distinguishes between the per-acre dollar values of farm acres in general from the same values for improved farm acres in 1850 and 1860. The dollar entries refer to the averages among a tier's counties (an average of averages). The tier pattern in this table differs from the yield pattern described earlier. Instead of dollar values trailing off after the second tier, as suggested by some of the crop productivity figures, the transition for values based on total acres in 1860 is after Tier 4 and not until after Tier 6 for improved acres in the same year. (Information for this and other follow-on tables was drawn from federal agricultural censuses and other earlier-referenced state sources.)

What mattered for land values seems to be a farmer's work and financial investments in clearing land and other farm-making tasks. The resulting improved acres generated a stream of income from crops presumably grown on more as well as on less productive soils.

The statistical profiles reveal some unexpected variations. For example, corn and wheat productivity levels declined after Tier 2 whereas the value of an acre of improved land on which this wheat was cultivated did not show the same pattern in 1860! An improved acre has approximately the same value in Tiers 1 through 6.[51]

We need to make an immediate exception to this physical and financial generalization, for, again, there are sizeable intra-tier differences in these values. Most strikingly, in 1860, Wayne County (with Detroit, the state's largest city) farmers valued their land at $72 per improved acre, $33 more than similar acres in fellow Tier-2 counties Calhoun and Jackson. The gap between high and low-valued counties in other tiers are $20

(Tier 1), $11 (Tier 3), $9 (Tier 4), $28 (Tier 5), $55 (Tier 6) and $28 (Tiers 7 through 11). Clearly more than productivity influenced self-reported farm values. *Market access also was important,* as counties in Tiers 1, 2 and 3 that were close to Detroit had relatively high values. And markets refer here to population size—that is, the consumers of farm harvests.

Table 5.2: Cash Values of Improved and Total Acres, 1850 and 1860

	Dollar Value Per Improved Acre				Dollar Value Per Total Acre			
Tier	*1850*	*1860*	*Increase*	*Percentage Increase*	*1850*	*1860*	*Increase*	*Percentage Increase*
1	$15.6	$47.9	$32.3	207%	$12	$24.4	$12.3	102%
2	$16.2	$49.5	$33.5	207%	$12	$27.3	$15.3	128%
3	$13.4	$44.6	$31.1	232%	$10.4	$21.4	$11	106%
4	$11.25	$46.1	$35	311%	$8.9	$20	$11.1	125%
5	$3.75	$40	$34.5	920%	$8	$10.2	$3.25	41%
6	$4.5	$45	$32	711%	$7.5	$8.7	$2.5	33%
7 to 11	NA	$34.5	NA	NA	NA	$0.7	NA	NA

If market size had the primary influence on land values, then there should be a high correlation between county population totals and county land values regardless of tier level or an east-west location. And, in fact, *in 1860 the correlation between population and average value per total farm acre was a very high .89—higher than the .43 between population size and the value of improved acres.*

To the degree that farmers based their locational decisions on building wealth, then *market access would likely have played a more significant role than soil quality.* But this also suggests that the link between soil quality and per-acre crop yields is a rather weak indicator of how and what drove changes in the human geography on the closing American frontier. That is, we see that human geography (the spatial distributions of populations) at Time 1 influenced trends in this geography at Time 2 somewhat independently of the underlying physical geography. Earlier-arrived farmers took the better soils and drove up the price of their lands available for sale to newly arrived investors. This was a land market analysis somewhat independent of soil quality.

That market size was probably a more powerful influence than the supply of higher quality soil is also supported by the negative correlation of –.46 between 1860 county population totals and the hypothetical number of Class 1 and 2 soils still available for new farms in 1860. Five counties, according to the assumptions made in this calculation, had all of their best lands in farms; another four had fewer than 25,000 of these acres

(Class 1 and 2). The larger population counties of Oakland, Washtenaw and Wayne were among these nine.

Some lower-tier counties had ample supplies of Class 1 and 2 soils, so it might be argued that the value of land is also a consequence of higher crop yields than would be expected from such soils. However, the correlation between population and yields of corn and wheat are only half or less than the correlation between population and land values. (The first correlation was for 1863; the second was for 1860.) There are, of course, questions about the quality of the data on which these correlations are based. Still, these simple two-variable correlations indicate the general order of magnitude among these different population, market and farming features.[52]

New settlers who decided to begin farming in counties with higher land values could, by definition, be expected to pay more for this land if bought from speculators or resident-farmers. Regardless of where new farmers located, and regardless of the yields they could expect from whatever management practices they adopted, investors in every tier could expect some capital gains over the decade. The estimated per acre price index increased by only two points from 25 to 27 in 1860 (eight percent over the decade),[53] whereas in Tiers 1 through 4 there was at least a 100 percent rise in the per-acre value (total acres). An improved acre rose at double that rate.

Economic (market) forces evidently had a significant influence on changing settlement patterns (human geography).

Value-Added Farming

To this point we have focused on the wisdom of the locational decisions that farmers made, not on how they managed their soils and crops. Wisdom was assessed based on the soils that a farmer was cultivating. Yet if building wealth was a key factor in the decision to select land and farm it, then these on-going farming decisions are important. Important, yes, but beyond the present research's terms of relevance. Still, a slight detour beyond locational decisions will reveal the obvious—that not all farms and farmers were the same. The context for decision-making differed by a farm's size and access to markets, not just by the physical environment represented by type of soil and climate. To explore this tangent to our research, we focus on farmers or farms, not per acre yields.

Given our county-level data, it is not possible to trace with certainty the steps a successful farmer took to add value to his farm. But it appears that clearing more acres and cultivating them were obviously central to farming success. After a certain number of improved acres were available, the farmer added value by diversifying into animal husbandry. This is most clearly reflected in the number of milch cows and sheep on a farm. Dairy farming (milk more so than butter and cheese) depended on access to larger markets. A farmer who used manure from his cows to fertilize his land could increase crop productivity. This was important for providing feed for livestock.

Panel data for individual farms (where information is collected on the same farms over a period of time) were not available for the present study, so the information we have is only suggestive of the changes in the types of decisions some farmers made over time and how these decisions influenced Michigan's human geography. We rely on cross-sectional one-time-only information. This information, however, reveals a correlation of .80 or above between a county's average cash value and three other county-level averages: the number of milch cows per farm, corn yields per acre, and the total number of improved acres.

The dairy and livestock strategy that added value to a farm also supports the contention that farmers, through some of their own actions other than the locational decisions they made, could add to the selling price of their farm. This was not just a feature of speculation but, instead, the result of farmers' decisions that added value to their farms.

Michigan's antebellum farmers were not only farmers but also settlers. They exerted Herculean if not Sisyphean energy in clearing and farming their land.[54] Farming was a tough life, one that paid off for thousands of pioneers and their families (including my own maternal ancestors, pioneer farmers in Michigan's Midland County). But farming was also a risky business. The general economy affected the demand for crops that in turn affected commodity prices, the welfare of families and human settlement patterns. Weather, transportation costs and facilities, pests and disease—all resulted in poor years as well as good ones. Some farmers defaulted on their mortgage payments and were forced into bankruptcy. Others could not pay their property taxes and, as a result, their lands were offered at tax auction sales. Other information suggests that a good number of frontier farmers were not successful. They abandoned their farms.

This conclusion is based on the 1860 census enumerator sheets for Midland County. Column 1 of the census form instructed enumerators to number the county's "dwelling houses" in "the order of visitation." Midland had 183 dwelling units (including a hotel and other lodging arrangements). Nineteen (ten percent) of these were unoccupied. On the basis of the occupation of the heads of households in the dwelling units just before and just after these unoccupied units (and also drawing on information from the 1860 agricultural census for the county), it is quite likely that up to 16 of the unoccupied units were abandoned farms. (Nine percent of all dwelling units in the county.) Farming in the forest was not a wise decision for these families.[55] And for the many reasons already mentioned the maps on farmer-settlers and the different soils available to potential cultivators changed over time.

Summary

This and the previous chapter report both general and specific findings. The former will be covered first, as they were not emphasized. Both are placed in a larger context of how an imperfect market for land made it difficult to make rational economic decisions on where to invest in farming. That concern was also placed in a context of the overlap between two geographies, one represented by classes of soils (physical geography), the other by where farmers bought and cultivated these soils (human geography). This chapter and others explore the spatial overlap between these two geographies as well as how the market for land was influenced by the access this land had to consumers of farm harvests.

Counties in Michigan differ in their two geographies thereby inviting research on why the relationships between these two geographies on the nineteenth century frontier changed over time. Human geographies responded not just to the physical world but also to changing market systems as well as the drag and pull of earlier settlement patterns and the forces behind them. Water systems, drainage, growing season and differences in how individual crops responded to different soils were components of the complex often labeled as the "physical environment" or physical geography. This and the previous chapter deconstructed these general geographical categories and linked them to some of the influences on how America's frontier was closed during the nineteenth century.

The convex Saginaw-to-Muskegon line divides the Lower Peninsula's 68 counties north and south of this line into different predominant soil profiles, pre-settlement vegetation, and growing seasons. This line also generally separates the major interests of land-buyers. North of the line the interest was primarily by lumbermen in search of pine forests; south of the line the interest included both farmer-settlers and non-resident speculators. As this two-Michigans distinction suggests, the market for land in the state was much larger than the market for farmland only. This distinction also clouds the meanings that can be attributed to trends in new acres patented by the General Land Office and the State of Michigan. Demand for new acres did not accurately reflect an interest in starting new farms or settlements.

As of 1860, large areas of the physical environment in both halves of the Lower Peninsula remained untransformed. Although very large proportions of some lower-tier counties were in farms, the actual number of improved acres was much less that the total number of all farm acres.

A single focus on the quality of soil can overlook the importance that other environmental influences had on locational choices and success in farming. The growing season seems of particular importance in Michigan with, again, a north-south divide within the Lower Peninsula. However, a broader perspective on the selection of land to be farmed warns us against adopting a simple geographical determinism.

The institutional and legal environment described in earlier chapters set the rules for acquiring land and taxes on it. Without these laws and the organizations that implemented them, there would not have been the timed-settlement that Michigan experienced. Moreover, differences in crop yields within a tier and the apparent success of some farmers in more northern counties suggest that good farming skills can, to a degree, compensate for environmental constraints. With modifications, we could accept Daron Acemogulu's view that "it cannot be that the climate, ecology, or disease environments of the tropical areas have condemned these countries to poverty today."[56]

On the other hand, there is evidence that "[c]limate, terrain, and other physical factors of space affect behavior far more than they do cultures."[57] There is no evidence that farmer-settlers differed significantly in their cultures,[58] but surely there were differences in farm-making tasks and at least initial cropping practices adopted by settlers above and below the Saginaw-to-Muskegon dividing line.

Shifting from the general implications to some of the specific findings in this and the just-preceding chapter, we note that although good farming soils are found in every tier, the lower tiers have relatively more of them. The supply of these acres was reduced as new farms were established, but despite the declining supply in these tiers relative to what was available in higher-tier counties, the lower tiers continued to draw large numbers of new farm settlers. Filling-in rather than leapfrogging to higher-level tiers was the predominant settlement pattern, one that was produced by an aggregation of individual investment decisions.

A good majority of new farmers stayed close to where earlier farmers had already settled often buying the original owner's excess land that was held for speculative gains. Yes, the settlement pattern did move from south to north (as well as from east to west), but existing farm operations and farmers willing to sell some of their holdings seem to have exerted a stronger (gravity) pull than the attractiveness of a larger supply of good soils in higher tiers (the magnetic pull of quality soils). These general trends hold true at the tier level, but there are often quite wide differences among counties within the same tier with regard to the endowment of higher quality soils and farm-settlement trends over time.

Each new cohort of farmers had to repeat the farm-making process of earlier arrivals. This meant more time and money was devoted to removing the forest cover and, also, to farming with fewer improved acres. Fewer acres were not sufficient to provide the farm family with the basic necessities it needed. But farmers were able to garner a positive rate of return by selling some (or all) of their farms to new settlers who presumably would face the same challenges. Speculative profits were possible in every tier of counties.

We can only speculate on speculative opportunities, for more information would be needed to determine likely rates of return with or without speculation. Even information collected by the 1860 agricultural census is questionable, as key terms and concepts were ill-defined and the information collected by the enumerators was self-reported without independent assessments of their accuracy. Anecdotal information is not a substitute for good census evidence. This is seen in comparisons between this information and the numbers that appear in the censuses separately conducted by the federal government and the State of Michigan.

Some reports indicate that Michigan wheat farmers had higher yields than farmers did in the four other states of the Old Northwest. This relationship between soils and crop yields is an overlooked component of physical geography. Corn farmers did worse. Within Michigan, yields per acre for each crop were highest in Tier 1 and 2 counties. Tier 3 and 4 counties had relatively lower yields, while farmers in Tiers 5 through 11 did quite poorly. These two crop patterns (for corn and wheat) suggest that climate and growing season had a greater impact on yields than did soil quality only. However, there were sizeable intra-tier inter-county differences in corn and wheat yields.

High yields of corn and wheat are found within every tier of counties. Still within-tier differences suggest that many farmers made unwise decisions both with regard to where they settled and with regard to how they managed their farms. Good management practices no doubt contributed to a farmer's success within any county or tier on different classes of soil. And what might have been good farming practices back east might not be especially relevant to farming in different Michigan counties.

Because the relative supply of higher quality soils and per-acre yields were more generous in lower-tier counties, we expected that the value of farmland would follow a similar pattern. This was not the case. Instead of values trailed off after the second tier, as suggested by some of the crop productivity figures. The downward transition for values based on total acres in 1860 was after Tier 4 and not until after Tier 6 for improved acres in the same year. This anomaly is partially an artifact of a farmer's access to markets for his farm products—that is, the economic geography of markets and marketing.

The value of farmland was much higher in the more heavily populated counties. Population size is a surrogate indicator of the size and strength of the market for a farmer's outputs. Farmers seem to have adjusted to these larger markets by switching from traditional grain crops to higher value-added dairy farming.[59]

The vagaries of weather, crop diseases, and market conditions were risk factors affecting the wealth, welfare and survival of farms. A large proportion of the state's antebellum farmers managed their farms and finances well enough to survive and prosper, but there is also evidence from bankruptcy sales and vacant houses to suggest that many farmers had to abandon the time and financial investments they put into buying land and transforming it into a working farm. That their neighbors did not suffer the same fate suggests that farmers differed in the wisdom of the management decisions they continually made.

Most but not all of the "findings" reported in this chapter are based on statistics aggregated at the county level. We will see that because of the earlier-referenced ecological fallacy, it is appropriate to shift the analysis from aggregate to individual farms, the focus on the following chapters that place one multi-soils county in the middle of Michigan's Lower Peninsula in a larger economic, market, political and social setting.

Annex: An Assessment of Questionable Evidence

> "The aggregates we bandy about so casually today are subject to a margin of error of between 10 and 20 percent, and when it comes to economies of the past, that figure is nearer 30 percent."
>
> —Fernand Braudel, *The Perspective of the World, Civilization & Capitalism 15th-18th Century, Volume 3* (Harper & Row, 1982), 300.

> "Certainly our comparisons of the original [1860 census] data with the published summaries would provide sufficient evidence to impeach any work based upon these published figures."
>
> —Atack and Bateman, *To Their Own Soil*, 115.

Instead of perfect quantitative evidence, we seem to be swimming in a swamp of unreliable data. Atack and Bateman discovered transcription, tabulation and printer errors in published census summaries.[60] By retabulating data taken from the original census manuscripts, these authors and their colleagues were able to correct "numerous errors and omissions." Other scholars working with published patent and other data on land discovered and attempted to correct analogous inaccuracies—such as those in Donaldson's baseline compilation of federal records that he prepared in 1880 for the Public Land Commission.[61]

My own compilations of patent information taken from annual reports of the Commissioner of the General Land Office give different annual totals than those reported by Jones and other writers. Some of these typically small discrepancies result from changes in the reporting year (from the calendar year to the fiscal year, a shift begun at the end of June 1850). Others come from updated (corrected) data reported in occasional multi-year compilations. And still others from poor eyesight and mistakes by researchers themselves.

These observations do not justify the criticisms that narrative historians might make against cliometricians—of garbage in and garbage out. Cliometricians in turn charge traditional historians of writing Ouija board event-focused stories based on anecdotes taken from archives and secondary sources that suffer even greater problems than quantitative information's shortcomings.

Perhaps we need to accept the 10 to 30 percent margin of error that Braudel reports for studies on the "economies of the past." At the same time, we need to have a better understanding of the sources of these margins, for they extend well beyond the transcription, tabulation and printer errors discovered by Atack and Bateman. For convenience sakes, three sources of error will be outlined: sampling, measurement, and interviewer biases.[62]

Sampling Errors: A universe (such as all farms in a particular township or state) is a sample in which 100 percent of the relevant targeted units (farms) are selected. We have drawn heavily on the very valuable work of Atack, Bateman and Parker for their 100 percent samples of farms in their sampled counties and townships. By matching the 1860 agricultural census lists with the population census from the same year, these authors (and others) are able to distinguish farmers without farms (tenants) from resident farm owners. Unfortunately, detailed farm-level data are only available for the units enumerated in the agricultural censuses, so the definitions that the census used for a farm affected the data available for secondary analysis and the published reports on this census.

To be included in the agricultural census of 1860, census enumerators were instructed to exclude farms that did not produce "one hundred dollars in value." "Produce" refers to a list of crops (but not necessarily livestock).[63] Pressly and Scofield report that the $100 minimum value could be from a combination of products for both home use and sale.[64] An enumerator would presumably have to collect information from farmers before deciding whether to include or exclude the respondent from the agricultural census.

Farmers in their initial farm-building stages were still farmers but not yet with sufficient improved land and crops to warrant the designation of "farmer." If they defined themselves as a farmer in the population census, then they could be considered a farmer without a farm—that is, a tenant. But the size of their farms, the number of different kinds of livestock, and harvested yields for various crops would not be recorded. That is, an enumerator's complete 100 percent coverage of all resident farmers would not yield an agricultural census that included the universe of all officially designated farmers.

There were other coverage problems as well. For example, the farm was the unit that is included in the agricultural census. This meant that farmers' sons were typically classified as either farmers without farms (if they reported in the population census that they owned real estate) or as farm laborers.[65] Other researchers found that the census enumerators missed a number of residents in the highly mobile population of the time.[66] Even some of the more prominent residents of Midland County, Michigan were not enumerated in the 1860 census.

Measurement Errors: The 1860 census did not provide definitions that enumerators were to use for some key terms in the census. For example, the special instructions that enumerators were given stated that the "value of farms" meant "the actual value of the whole number of acres returned to you as improved and unimproved." Other sources not included in these instructions stated that the monetary value of a farm means "estimated current market value of farm lands, fences, permanent improvements, and buildings." (The value of farm houses was not asked as a specific question until the 1930 census.) Apparently excluded from the value of the farm were the monetary value of farming implements, the value of livestock, and the crops produced on the farm.[67] This confusion on what is included or not means that concepts such as "per-farm" or "per-acre values" lack precision—that is, the numbers given for these concepts may or may not include the same underlying elements. And there is no way of determining if there was any consensus among enumerators in the definitions they used.

This lack of precision suggests that readers need to be tolerant of the validity of the measures used in this chapter. There also are questions about the reliability of farm-level information recorded by enumerators. This is suggested by the unexplained anomalies between the 1860 federal census and the 1864 state census, as well as between the 1850 federal census and the state census of 1854. These anomalies refer to the published reports for these four censuses. Some of the anomalies (e.g., huge increases in a county's population) seem to be printing errors.

Both the published census and original enumeration sheets on which they were based include various rounding errors. Atack and Bateman, among others, found that "ages are heaped in five and, particularly, ten-year intervals."[68] Analogous rounding errors are found in the agricultural census for Midland County, Michigan—most significantly for farm cash values (rounded off to $100 intervals), improved acres (rounded to five-acre levels), value of livestock, bushels of corn and wheat, etc. There is much more differentiation in the values that the county tax assessors assigned to 73 farms. Unlike the census, these rolls were important to county officials responsible for assigning values and collecting taxes: treasurers were authorized to receive from two to four percent of the dollar amounts they collected.[69] Michigan had its own version of Roman tax farming.

Interviewer Bias: The enumerators were to assist farmers "to estimate fairly and accurately the amount of his crops, when he keeps no exact account; and in all instances it is desired to make the nearest approximate returns which the case will admit of."[70] Census information was self-reported, as it is today. Either the farmer or the census enumerator was to know the market cash value of the farm and to know how many bushels of different crops were harvested. We do not know how many farmers knew these numbers and how many of the figures were suggested by the enumerator. There was only one enumerator in Midland county, a lawyer fairly new to the community. We do not know what training, if any, he received prior to entering the field, and there were no follow-on studies to assess the accuracy of the information provided.

Skilled narrative historians working with diaries, government records and other historical documents would certainly examine the quality and reliability of the information included in these sources. Manuscript census forms warrant the same critical examination. Absent a critical review of sampling, measurement and interviewer biases, we necessarily assume in the present study that census information does not fall outside acceptable margins of error. This is an important and perhaps questionable assumption.

Land and Soil Surveys: Both the present and earlier chapters referenced problems relating to the cadastral surveys used to identify acres that were later classified by soil scientists well after much of Michigan was settled by farmers. I assume that the land surveyors eventually produced acceptable maps. But, as we will see, the assessments that the surveyors made of soils were of questionable value as will be explored in the following chapters. Again, settlers were making locational decisions in an information-poor market. No wonder so many poor decisions were made. But if farmers abandoned their poor soils then it is likely that over time there was a closer overlap between Michigan's physical and human geographies.

Analytical Limitations: Lawyers, historians, social scientists and all of us in our everyday lives make inferences based on what we consider adequate evidence. Even if the evidence used in the present study is 100 percent accurate, we still would be limited in the kinds of inferences we could make based on this evidence.

Two constraints are especially significant. First, most of the census information comes from 1860 only. We do not have time-trends that might allow us to make certain kinds of assumed cause-effect linkages. However, it is clear that some data are not likely to be dependent variables whose variation we wish to explain. They include soil and pre-settlement vegetation types. And we can read into our data certain timelines—for example, the date a farm was patented and the state where a farmer was born. Soil can, under some circumstances, be a dependent variable—for example, when it becomes the object of decisions made by land-buyers. (Do farmers select the best soil? Do lumbermen pick the best pineland?)

The second constraint is the frequently-referenced ecological fallacy—that we cannot make inferences about individual farms based on aggregated farm data for an entire county or state. There is a difference between individual correlations and ecological ones. Atack and Bateman are able to avoid this fallacy when they analyze data based on information provided for individual farms.[71]

Since these authors and others working with individual farming units report the strength of certain relationships (using different statistical formulae) based on a number of reasonable assumptions, it would have been helpful to test alternatives to their assumptions. Such sensitivity analyses are standard in other technical reports. I believe that Atack and Bateman were correct in not turning their manuscript into a treatise for a specialized audience (perhaps an error made in the present chapter). At the same time, some of the more powerful statistical procedures that econometricians and social scientists employ can give a false sense of precision to data with a sizeable margin of error attributable to sampling, measurement and interviewer biases. My own approach is to rely primarily on simple cross-tabulations and two-variable correlations. This approach at least has an advantage over the use of such vague terms as some, few, many and most.

Geographic Level 4: One Multi-Soils County

6

Moving from Macro to Micro-Level History

Background and Context

Earlier chapters used aggregate statistics on soils, the settlers on these soils, and the economic effects of farming the soils at the state level in the Old Northwest Territory and at both the tier and county level within the State of Michigan's Lower Peninsula.

This chapter begins a transition to a combined quantitative and narrative history of farmer-settlers in one multi-soils case-study county in Michigan. This is a shift from aggregate (or ecological) data to information about individual-level decisions that were made by the original patentees and holders of deeds in Midland County prior to 1860.

Individual owner-cultivators were the county's first generation of wealth-builders who presumably were driven by rational financial self-interest in their selections of land and farming of the land. By relating their selections of soil (land) that they acquired through patents and deeds together with information taken from the agricultural and population censuses of 1860, it is possible to hazard some general assessments of the wisdom of the investments made by these first-generation individual farmers who were far from the stronger markets for farm products in the southern tier of Michigan counties.

The settlers who closed the American and Midland's frontier migrated during America's "great transformation."[1] The "rapidly expanding economy ... was causing massive dislocations, frequent depressions, and widespread unemployment."[2] Based on their analysis of samples of the original enumerators' sheets from federal population censuses, Patricia Hall and Steven Ruggles found that the "highest [population] mobility occurred in the first half of the nineteenth century ... [and] the high levels of nineteenth-century migration resulted from long-distance westward migration to farms."[3] Midland is part of that settlement history.

Migration and settlement rates and patterns in turn affected both the physical environment and the larger legal and institutional context that influenced the decisions that individual farmer-settlers and other investors made. Much of the most desirable lands, as earlier documented, was patented, cleared of vegetation, and cultivated with commercial crops that could be sold in the expanding national and international market. Congress also made changes in land policies, as seen in earlier chapters. The combined results of these individual but interrelated trends was a constantly changing matrix of time, space, physical environment, institutions, laws, the economy, markets and society.[4]

As complex as this often-disjointed multi-component matrix was, the decisions that individual buyers of land made permeated if not drove the movements of the larger matrix. Both self-interest and time were part of the matrix and its history. Individual decisions, however, were based on incomplete and often erroneous information about the soils that investors could most profitably cultivate. It was a flawed market that could and did result in wasted family and national investments.

Our current state of knowledge does not allow us to assess the precise impact that each component of the matrix independently had on the total complex at particular moments or over periods of time.[5] But this has not prevented historians from accepting the analytical challenge of weaving these influences within a larger interpretive framework. Some have adopted a teleological approach, as suggested by the title (if not the text itself) of Robert Wiebe's *The Search for Order 1877–1920*.[6] Others, especially historians researching individual communities, border on tautologies by formulating broad themes (for example, the decline of the patriarchal family, the increasing power of the market, and the influence of political parties) and then shoehorning their evidence into these themes with only minimal attention to contrary (contradictory) materials and hypotheses.[7] The thematic approach of some historians appears to be primarily a way to organize chapters. Themes in traditional narrative histories are treated as both claimed causes and their self-evident teleological effects (Whig History or presentism).

These various national, regional and local studies are much more ambitious than the present research. But while the focus here is on the decisions made by investors individually and collectively, especially resident farmers, these decisions shaped the rates and patterns of settlement, how these rates and patterns changed the physical environment, and, of course, the implications these individual choices had on national, state and local tax revenues, how the revenues were used, and both the national politics relating to the privatization of America's land resources and the local politics relating to economic and community development. Again, all these interpenetrating influences were propelled in part by the self-interests (or selfish interests) of the investors who acquired land with the anticipation that their land would be a source of livelihood and wealth. That is a history built on the selfish economic interests of individual farmers.

Pioneer farmers, of course, were not the only investors. In fact, they were only a small minority of landowners in many counties including Midland County. Speculators held most of the land in some counties. And pioneer farmers were themselves speculators, as were resident non-farmers who owned land in the counties where they lived.

Not all farmers were at the same stage of their development. New arrivals had less time to clear their land of its forest cover.

Farming at the end of the nineteenth century was different in many respects from what was common in antebellum Michigan. As a result, a longer-term time perspective on income from farming and speculative gains could significantly affect the rates of return from investments made before 1860. But surely most of the antebellum farmers and other investors had passed from the scene by the end of the century.

Before we can begin an analysis of the case-study county, we need again to recognize that the available evidence is not error-free. In addition to the limitations noted earlier, the population census for Midland missed a few residents.[8] The agricultural census did not enumerate smaller farms, and data reported for individual farms are estimates at best. Soil and vegetation maps classify 640-acre units (a section of one square mile) and thereby fail to identify variations that might be found on an individual farm.[9] Many patents obtained through military warrants do not list the names of the patentees.[10] And biographical information comes from vanity publications common at the time.[11]

The information analyzed in the following chapters is both incomplete and sometimes biased. On the other hand, a focus on a single county allows the researcher to record and analyze data on the universe (a 100 percent sample) of land, patents, deeds, soils, vegetation and residents.[12]

7

The County's Physical Geography

According to the U.S. Department of Agriculture's most recent soil survey of Midland, the county has "about 332,800 acres, or 520 square miles."[1] In theory, a perfectly squared 16-township county would have 576 square miles or 368,640 acres.[2] However, four of Midland's townships were only four miles wide rather than six. This is because, as Yates explained, "Michigan was surveyed from east to west [and] by the time the survey reached the meridian in Midland County there were only four miles left instead of the six miles in the standard township."[3]

Midland's coordinates of 43.875° in the north and 43.375° in the south place the county on the northern border of "Yankeeland," the "latitudinal zonation" of latitude 42° to 43° north that was heavily populated by migrants from New York State.[4] This was more than a cultural divide. It had agricultural implications as well, for Midland was on the northern fringe of the corn belt and south of an average of 60° F summer temperature.[5] The growing season (the number of days between the last frost in the spring and the first in the fall) varies by year. In nine out of ten years recorded for Midland from 1930 through 1974 the county had 128 days whose "daily minimum temperature during growing season" was higher than 32° F. The last spring freezing date was as late as May 26 and the earliest fall freezing date was as early as September 22 or before. Early settlers did not have this kind of information. Two years in ten had less than 25.6 inches of precipitation.[6] The western-most townships had an average of about two inches of precipitation more than the eastern portion of the county—with 30 to 32 inches in the west and fewer than 30 in the east from 1961 to 1990.[7]

Midland's marginal agricultural potential is also revealed in Veatch's soil classification system. While nearly half (46 percent) of the county's soils fall into his top two region-adjusted classes,[8] 42 of the Lower

Peninsula's 68 counties had a higher proportion of these farm-friendly soils. Only 19 had a higher proportion of the lowest class soils. As seen in Chapter 4, lower-tier counties were generally better endowed with good soils, and their growing season was longer as well. Again, the market for land in Michigan did not benefit from this kind of information.

Midland's variety of soils and physical geography more generally are found throughout Michigan's Lower Peninsula, although in different relative proportions. So what we find on man-land (soil) relations in Midland can hopefully be a mirror of what we would find both statewide and Territory-wide.

But, of course, latitude, longitude, square miles, soils and climate do not capture all of the important geographical features of Midland, especially how the county fits into the larger water and drainage system that in turn had implications for both agriculture and lumbering.

The entire Saginaw Valley drainage area had approximately 864 miles of water on which logs could be floated.[9] In addition to the Tittabawassee, at least part of Midland's Pine and Chippewa Rivers[10] could also handle logs.

The County's 16 Townships and 528 Sections[11]

According to a 1979 series of Soil Conservation Service's maps, Midland had seventeen creeks feeding the county's three major rivers and several smaller ones.[12] Seventeen percent of the county's 528 sections were on a creek; about thirty-nine percent were on a creek or a river. (The map descriptions are not always clear on the distinction between river and creek. Today there are also many drains.)

Charles Davis observed that Michigan's drainage system gave a pattern to the surface of a landscape that "affects the distribution of human habitations and the lines of communication," and the distribution of water "profoundly influences human activities."[13] For example, the Village of Midland was situated at the junction of the Tittabawassee and Chippewa rivers—known at the time as the Forks. (It was also a juncture for earlier Amerindian trails.)

This river system with the Tittabawassee as its spine provided waterborne transportation for people, supplies and logs. But the combination of waterways and a fairly level topography had its drawbacks, at least for farmers, for, as Davis noted, a flattish ground moraine without a gradient sufficient to carry off water rapidly results in incomplete drainage patterns—that is, swamps and wetlands.[14] Soils alone do not define a county's physical geography.

Midland, according to Davis, was in a "mature dendridic area."[15] A

State of Michigan report in 1893 described Midland's surface as "slightly rolling, except the extreme southern portion, which is quite level.... There are no swamps of any size."[16] These reports are at odds with J.O. Veatch's map showing Midland as having a "Flat surface area greatly in excess of slopes, which are low in gradient or, if steep, are short."[17] More specifically, a research team from the State's Department of Environmental Quality reported that Midland's "[p]oorly drained portions supported large swamps."[18] These diverse if not incompatible descriptions taken from official documents remind readers of the importance of referencing multiple sources relating not just to physical geography but to human geography as well. Researchers, not just investors, should not rely on a single source of market and other information only.

A focus on the general term "swamps" can be misleading, as there are different kinds of wetlands. The original land surveys of the county found a large number of wetlands, even though there might not have been extensive swamps.

Wetlands had to be drained before they could be cultivated on a sustainable basis. Moreover, wetlands were breeding grounds for mosquitoes and malaria.

According to its locational, topographical, geological, weather and physical features, Midland was at the margins of an optimal farming environment. It was certainly not equal to what farmer-settlers might find in lower-tier counties and in other parts of the Old Northwest. And the mix of soil types, as well as the distribution of wetlands, meant that wise decisions were needed to take advantage of what agricultural opportunities the county provided. If wise choices were made, the harvests from the soil could be more easily exported to outside markets by the use of the county's navigable rivers, a point we will return to later.

Federal Surveys and Resurveys of the County

The Federal land surveys described in earlier chapters were not an end in themselves but a means to achieve three other objectives.

- First, surveys were the base on which the boundaries of a piece of land could be legally delineated. These boundaries in turn gave some legal security to the landowner, and this in turn helped reduce the risk of buying, using and selling land. No land surveys, no market for land.
- Second, township and section boundaries had to be in place before the land could be "proclaimed" and then offered at auction and follow-on private sales.

- Third, the surveyors were required to keep notes on the soils, vegetation and wetlands they encountered in the course of laying out township and section boundaries. These market-relevant notes were available to potential investors as a way to improve their knowledge of the land, to identify places for personal inspection, and to maximize the wisdom of the choices that investors might make.

This and the following chapters introduce the most widely available market information on lands that were being privatized by antebellum speculators and farmer-settlers. We do not know how many back-east farmers and speculators actually inspected soils before investing in them. Investors and their agents had access to the field notes prepared by the surveyors who mapped townships and sections within them. We will see that these notes were of questionable and often misleading value. Investment decisions were being made in information-poor markets, a major theme in the present study.

There are at least two criteria on which to base the usefulness of the private sector land surveys commissioned by the General Land Office. One is the accuracy of the technical measurements (the boundary lines). Inaccuracies could be attributed to technical factors but also to outright fraud. The other criterion is more difficult to assess, as it refers to how complete and accurate the surveyors' observations were, as recorded in their field notes that describe the county's physical geography.

Potential patentees and their representatives (land lookers, agents, and timber cruisers) were able to read these notes, an important resource for identifying better soils and trees so that wise investment decisions could be facilitated.

Federal surveyors began their work in Michigan in 1815 with drawing two lines, a base line along an east-west axis and a prime meridian, a south-to-north line that happened to run through Midland (through my maternal ancestors' farm). The county had two ranges of townships on each side of the meridian. From a current technological perspective, the surveyors relied on rather simple aids—magnetic compasses and chains.[19] Again, there were 80 chains to a mile, 100 links to a chain. A chain was 66 feet long; a link was 7.92 inches. Ando Linklater has written an engaging history on this rather archaic measurement system.[20]

Bruce Catton's brief visual image of the results of a surveyor's final product will help readers to understand the usefulness of the rectangular survey. Surveyors:

> laid out the country into townships six miles square, with each township thus containing thirty-six square miles [in theory, for, as seen earlier, Midland had

> a truncated system]. Measuring six miles along the base line to east or west of the Principal Meridian, the surveyor erected a monument and then ran another north-south meridian from it. From the principal meridian, in turn, at six-mile intervals, east-west lines were run, so that the whole state was laid out in a gigantic grid; and the long north-south strips running the length of the territory were known as ranges—No. 1 east, No. 5 west, and so on. The grid defined the townships, and each township in turn was measured off into thirty-six sections by parallel lines a mile apart: a section, accordingly, was one mile square and contained 640 acres, numbered from 1 to 36, the top row reading from east to west, the next row coming west to east, and so on.[21]

To the surveyor, a theoretically perfect acre equaled ten square chains.

There were two types of surveys for each township: one covered the township's external boundaries, while the other drew the section lines within the township. Indian reservations were included in the surveys and were considered part of the townships in which they were located.

Midland's initial surveys were conducted in 1831 and 1832. Ten townships were proclaimed for sale by public announcement during 1832 and 1833. The other six followed in 1834.

Sales were executed at auctions, after which "the remaining unsold lands were classified as 'offered' and were open to private entry" at the then-designated price per acre "or they could be entered with any of the various forms of scrip or military bounty land warrants." With one exception, there were no caps on how many acres of federal land an individual could buy at the auction or by private entry.[22]

All except one of Midland's sixteen townships were open to private entry by October 1834. The map of soils that we have today was, of course, not available to early settlers who created the county's human geography.

All the surveys in the state were done by contractors who were designated as Deputy Surveyors and were paid on a per mile basis "for lines actually run." These deputy surveyors were responsible for hiring and supervising their assistants, supplying the survey team, and preparing the plats and field notes.[23]

Surveyors in Midland and its adjoining counties encountered major problems. According to Yates, the first surveyor sent to Midland "was killed by the Indians in 1831."[24] That was an extremely cold winter with deep snow that forced two surveyors to abandon their work until spring only to encounter "new hardships and difficulties" when the swamps thawed so that the surveyors "were constantly wading in ice water." One survey team on a re-supply mission to Saginaw "traveled part of the way through the woods in a canoe because the water covering the ground was so deep that the pack horses could not wade through it." This team left their work incomplete "for they believed it was useless to continue." One surveyor wrote that "[m]any of the northern townships laid out by me cannot in my opinion pay the expense of surveying." All the surveyors working in this multi-county area "agreed that the country was undesirable for settlement."[25]

Given the difficult working environments statewide and the technologies employed by the surveyors, it is perhaps not surprising that there were some technical errors. One section of the state's base line drawn in 1816 suffered "gross inaccuracy" and had to be re-run in 1824.[26] There were errors in county lines as well, including Midland's boundaries.[27]

Fraud, rather than technical errors, seems to have been more common, and certainly the misinformation in such surveys could adversely affect decisions that potential investors might have made. Surveys in 400 townships north and west of Saginaw Bay were found to be fraudulent and had to be resurveyed.[28] "In some cases the field notes of the township subdivisions were actually faked; in many instances the surveyors did not even run the lines or ran where the going was easiest. Their notes were, of course, worthless."[29]

At least five Midland townships had to be re-surveyed in 1852 after patents had already been issued. (The external lines for T 14N R 2E were resurveyed earlier in 1840.) But it is not always clear whether technical deficiencies were more important than outright fraud. This is seen in Deputy Supervisor Austin Burt's "Remarks" on his re-survey of T 13N R 1W (Porter Township):

> the old survey was found to be *mostly* fraudulent, the bearing trees to many of the corners not agreeing with the field notes, as to timber course or distance. Many of the lines were not run, and those that were, some of them—especially the east and west lines—only those closing to the North Boundary were but thinly marked on one Side, and do not intersect at the corners for which they were run.... the old work was so blind that it could not be clearly identified, and lines that were considered Random without being connected and did not intersect at the Corners for which they ran.[30]

There is no information on any problems the fraudulent Midland surveys might have had on investors but there was an effect on the State's sales of swampland. The Commissioner of the State Land Office wrote in his annual report dated December 1, 1855, that he "was notified in February last ... of the re-survey of considerable tracts of land, embraced in the lists of swamp land." As a result, the swampland in these areas were "suspended on our books" pending the results of the re-surveys.[31]

Just as boundary lines could be faked, so could the notes taken on the vegetation, soil and wetlands along these lines. These fake observations on the physical geography would have misled potential investors. Surveyors' notes made in the process of running lines also could be incomplete or incorrect for other reasons. The time of year that the surveys were conducted could explain possible biases in the field notes made available to interested parties. These notes were to help potential investors to identify land for possible purchase. (The original notes themselves are in the archives of the Bureau of Land Management in Springfield, Virginia—as well as copies housed in the Michigan State Archives.[32])

As noted earlier, surveyors were instructed to "note the occurrence of wetlands, comment on the agricultural potential of soils, and note the quantity and quality of timber resources as they were encountered along each section line." Wherever trees were noted, their species and diameters were to be specified.[33]

Edwin Tiffin, the Surveyor General, as noted earlier gave these detailed instructions in 1815:

> all rivers, creeks, springs and smaller streams of water, with their width, and the course they run in crossing the lines of survey, and whether navigable, rapid or mountainous; the kinds of timber and undergrowth with which the land may be covered, all swamps, ponds ...the quality of the soil and the true situation of all mines, saltlicks, salt springs and mill seats, which may come to your knowledge are particularly to be regarded and noticed in your note books.[34]

Soils were to be designated as first, second or third rate for agricultural purposes, also as noted earlier. In addition to these observations made during the running of lines, surveyors were to give a general (summary) description of the entire township.

Table 7.1 presents some illustrative written comments the surveyors made on individual townships in Midland County. With only a few exceptions, these notes are fairly negative on the townships' agricultural potential. Soils are commonly classified as second and third rate, and large areas of some townships are too wet to permit farming. This picture of swamps is consistent with the explanations the surveyors gave for not finishing their work on time.

Since their notes were used by the state to designate land to be granted to it under the Swamp Land Acts of 1848, 1850 and 1860, it is relevant to note that it was only in the 20th century that classifications were developed giving greater specificity to wetlands—for example, distinctions among marshes, swamps, and bogs, each with different types of vegetation. This attention to vegetation is useful in identifying the locations and extent of wetlands in a township. However, even these more precise delineations (for example, marshes) have been found to be vague and imprecise.[35]

The terms used by Midland's surveyors were similarly vague, although they gave sufficient locational information to allow potential patentees to make their own personal inspection. That was possible because the points at which a wetland were entered and then exited were specified by chain and link (47:50 "enter swamp & marsh"; 39.97 "leave burnt land"). However, these specifications only referred to the line being run, not to the distance the wetland covered on either side of the line. That these could be sizeable distances were reflected in the re-survey of T 13N R 2W: "... it is interspersed with swamp and much wet land." Designations of class of soil and type of wetland were based on imprecise criteria. And, again, imprecision could have given misleading information on which to base decisions on which lands to visit and possibly.

There is one imperfect indicator of the accuracy of the surveyors' observations, but two important assumptions must be made for this assessment of reliability, if not validity. First, it is assumed that the original surveys of townships that were later re-surveyed were deficient on technical grounds. The lines were drawn but not as precise as expected. Fraud was of minor significance. Second, the time of the year and the years themselves of the original and follow-on re-surveys did not significantly affect the number and extent of wetlands. For example, a re-survey would agree with the original surveyor's note that "This mile is nearly all swamp" (as was the case for the east line of Section 36 in T 16 N R 1 W).

Table 7.1: Selected Comments on Townships by Surveyors

	Township	*Soil*	*Trees*	*Wetlands*
13N.1E	Mount Haley	Poor; sand		Very wet
13N.1W	Porter	Second, and poor second. Second and Third Rate; rich bottom land	White Pine	Rather wet and swampy. Tamarack swamp
13N.2E	Ingersoll	Third rate; South-east good. Land miserable; level and rich	Hemlock	Principally swampy; considerable swamp
13N.2W	Jasper	Third and second rate; good second rate; poor second rate; good second rate. Rich bottom soils; good soils	Pine 50" in diameter	Swamps and much wet swampy; very swampy
14N.1E	Homer	Poor; generally poor along the river; good along the banks; the remainder is generally poor		Swamp and marsh

	Township	*Soil*	*Trees*	*Wetlands*
14N.1W	Lee	Poor second	White pine 30" in diameter	Swamp and marsh
14N.2E	Midland			Sometimes overflows
14N.2W	Greendale	Mostly third rate; first rate	First rate	Mostly swampy; low and wet; naturally wet
15N.1E	Lincoln	Generally poor except river bottom; small percentage of second rate, rest third rate. "It is a poor township."		
15N.1W	Jerome	Very poor except for bottom of Tittabawassee and Salt Rivers. Bottom lands and northwest corner better.	Large white pine; pine windfall	Many swamps in south and east. "This mile is all swamp."
15N.2E	Larkin	One third is second rate; remainder is poor	Pine	
15N.2 W	Geneva			
16N.1E	Hope			
16N.1W	Edenville	Land miserable; Northwest side of Tittabawassee "first rate." "This is a very poor township." First rate; rich bottom course; second and third rate. Good farming lands along rivers and streams. Land miserable indeed.	Pine 40" in diameter; pine second rate.	This mile is nearly all swamp; willow swamp
16N.2E	Mills	Poor township		Too wet for cultivation
16N.2W	Warren			Alder marsh

A hand tally of the number of wetlands reported in the original surveys and in the re-surveys in five townships indicates that the above assumptions are probably incorrect. There appears to have been widespread fraud that provided seriously misleading information on which to make investment decisions. The re-surveys had nearly three times more mentions of wetlands than did the originals. In Jasper Township (T 13N R 2W) the re-survey found more than fifteen as many wetlands as reported by the original surveyor.

If surveys were to perform their intended purposes, they had to have technically correct lines that would remove any questions about the legal boundaries of privately-owned land. The original surveys in at least ten of Midland's sixteen townships met this technical standard. Surveys in five of the remaining six townships were fraudulent and had to be redone in 1852. For a period of twenty to twenty-one years, patents in these five townships were open to challenge, although I have not found any such cases. (But I did not look for them.)

An ancillary purpose of the surveys was to provide information on soils, timber and wetlands that would assist potential investors in making wise decisions. Again, for twenty to twenty-one years, fraudulent information was provided for at least five townships. Moreover, the classifications used for soils and wetlands were imprecise and open both to fraud and subjective assessments. Still, the information provided in the surveyors' (and re-surveyors') field notes should have helped potential investors in their decision-making processes on which lands, if any, they might purchase. Investors who ignored these notes opened themselves to unwise decisions.

The Challenge of Inspecting Before Investing in Midland

Given the questionable and limited information available to potential investors, it would have been prudent to personally inspect land and its access to markets before buying and settling. That would have been a physical challenge for even the most prudent investors. This is seen in the county's access to the outside world.

Again, Midland's window to the outside world was Saginaw, and the route to that window was the Tittabawassee River and its tributaries.[36] Surface roads seem to have played much less of a role than water transport in linking Midland to Saginaw and then larger markets. As earlier noted, the state's focus was on connecting Saginaw to Flint and Detroit, not to Midland. "When Michigan became a state [in 1837] there appears to have been between Saginaw and Detroit a barely passable wagon road." The national government extended its own road work five miles north of Flint by 1835 but the state was responsible for completing the road to Saginaw in 1841.[37]

Michigan's frontier was presumably closed by settlers moving over difficult east to west routes. Even getting to Michigan was a challenge, let alone traveling to inland Midland in the middle of the new state.

A 32-mile plank road connecting East Saginaw to Flint was begun in 1848, a project that supposedly "resulted in a rapid increase in immigration and settlement."[38] There was steady progress in physically linking Saginaw, Midland's window to outsize markets via an evolving transportation network in the lower tiers of Michigan counties. However, the road link between Midland and this network, via Saginaw, was considered primitive at the time.[39]

Road conditions farther south were also difficult, as Edwin Cross reported in his Civil War pension file. His coach overturned during an April 1862 storm on a road from Flint to Detroit. Daniel Sanford's pension file reports an accident on a plank road between Flint and Holley. "There were many planks out at the time." Not much seems to have changed since the 1830s when Kirkland reported that the "roads near Detroit were inexpressibly bad. Many were the chances against our topping load's preserving its equilibrium."[40] Similarly, John Gordon's diary written from near Kalamazoo in October of that year stated that "The road west is so bad at this season that it is desperation to attempt it in the stage, or rather wagon. The passengers walk most of the distance and are repeatedly upset ..." In the spring of 1844 in the same area, "the prairie mud was up to the top of the fences."[41]

The poor state of Midland's roads and lack of them in the 1850s should not come as a surprise. There was no plank road connecting Midland and Saginaw and, as a consequence, the roads were impassable for part of the year. This is seen in Thomas Sprague's explanation for keeping his new Civil War recruits from making the short trip from Midland to Saginaw. Sprague wrote the Mustering and Discharging Officer in Detroit on April 9, 1864:

> the men referred to were raised in the forest in the counties north of this when in the fall of the year the roads, such as they are, are almost impassible, being literally without bottoms. There were no publick conveyances by stage or otherwise. ... As soon as the frost had rendered the roads passable, the citizens of the county turned out with their teams and transported the men to Saginaw without expense to the Government thereby saving the Government at least one hundred dollars.[42]

Midland's river system provided the county with its accessibility advantage. One early source claimed that the Tittabawassee River was "boatable for 40 to 50 miles above the river's junction with the Chippewa and Pine Rivers."[43]

According to Yates, a man named Dan Osborne ran a 7-ton pole boat three times a week between Midland and Saginaw. Osborne's boat was followed in 1858 by a 25-ton side-wheeler steamboat. It was replaced in 1860 by another boat that could float during low water levels. The upriver trip from Saginaw to Midland took 12 hours.[44] Potential investors could also travel by horse and foot, timely, exhausting ways to inspect land before investing in it.

River boats made it possible to ship goods and farm harvests in and out of Midland at a lower cost than by horse-drawn wagons, and by substituting boats for wagons, there was less need for horses and manual laborers.[45] If potential investors were aware of the transportation infrastructure, they might have seen that farming in Midland offered some cost savings although there is no evidence that investors incorporated this travel technology and cost in their investment decisions.

Paul Gates estimated the benefits of river over road transportation. A 2-horse team could haul a ton only 25 miles a day. Atack's research team assumed that, if the mean distance to a market was 50 miles, then "moving 1,000 tons would have employed at least ten teams full time for a year."[46] The Midland-to-Saginaw road probably would also have required heavier horses, more feed for them, and more teamsters.[47] But only one Midland man in the 1860 census identified himself as a teamster. The county in 1860 had neither the human nor animal power required for an expanding and prosperous road-based physical transportation system. Even if the county overflowed in rich soils, there were limited opportunities to market the harvests from the farms that new investors were cultivating.

Transportation technology did have financial advantages. Atack and his colleagues found that farmers who were served by cheap water or railroad transportation had higher "surpluses" than farmers in townships that depended on wagon haulage.[48] The advantages were even much greater for lumbering.[49]

Potential investors would also have been advised to know that Midland's river transportation was not problem-free. The navigation season on the Great Lakes was from about the middle of March to the end of November, so that alternative transportation means were required for at least three or more months a year. Commercial riverboat transport also competed with the booming companies that filled the rivers with logs from bank to bank. It was not until 1861 that these companies were required to leave a navigation channel open at all times.

Midland benefited from its physical system of rivers and the access they provided to outside markets through Great Lakes shipping. This industry had been expanding for years, especially since the Erie Canal opened in 1825.[50] Lewis reported that "only two steamers plied regularly between Detroit and Saginaw in the mid–1830s but by the early 1850s five were in regular service on the Saginaw River itself. At mid-century, annual arrivals at Saginaw averaged around twenty-five, and as many as ten or fifteen ships connected Saginaw with Buffalo and other lake ports."[51]

These transportation developments indicate that the physical environments in which settlement and land-purchasing decisions were made changed over time. But improved transportation would have little importance if Midland's soils were unsuitable for farming and if the county was devoid of commercial-quality timber within a short distance of a river that could float cut logs to saw mills. That is, excellent transportation facilities cannot substitute for good agricultural soils and extensive pineries.

Chapter 8 will describe the county's soil resources, the market-tradable component of Midland's physical geography. One of my *Michigan Historical Review* articles covers the county's lumbering history.

Summary

This chapter covered some of the physical features of the land about which investment decisions were made along with the then-available information about these and other features. We saw that

1. Midland was at the margin of an optimal environment for farming. The growing season was relatively short; the county had a high proportion of poor soils; and there was a good amount of wetlands. Decision-makers had to be careful in the choices of land they bought to farm.
2. Contract surveyors laid township borders and section lines, and they also entered into their notebooks information on the soils, vegetation and wetlands encountered along the lines surveyed. Both the plats and notebooks were made available to potential patentees to help them make wise decisions on which lands to inspect personally or to buy unseen. Fraudulent surveys and notes were prepared for at least four of Midland's sixteen townships.
3. It was expensive and difficult for potential investors to personally inspect land before making their investments.
4. The physical barriers to onsite assessments of investable lands were also barriers to marketing the harvests from these lands.

Despite all these market-related imperfections, there were many settlers who moved to Midland and began farming the county's questionable soils. Chapter 8 will draw on soil classifications made by soil scientists in order to assess the likelihood that a farmer-settler could benefit from investing in this one county that was endowed with both promising and poor soils.

8

The Market and Privatization of Land in a Case-Study Frontier County

Turner was partially correct in arguing that cheap land drew investors to the frontier but in marginal areas such as Michigan's mid-state county of Midland, most investors were speculators and lumbermen rather than farmer-settlers. All investors operated in imperfect land markets designed and implemented by federal and state governments as well as private sector speculators. These markets led to a wasteful use of scarce national resources at the time the frontier was being closed.

We saw earlier that there were many justifications for farmers to invest in Michigan's southern tiers of counties that were endowed with potentially productive soils and were close to markets for the harvests of farms. But despite Midland's smaller relative supply of the most promising soils as well as its distance from markets, farmers (including my maternal grandparents two or three decades after the Civil War) invested in this county. The demand for Midland's lands, however, was more likely related to the county's endowment of pine trees rather than its ample supply of farmer-friendly soils. Duncan Wayne, my maternal grandfather, harvested the trees on his land for income that allowed him to farm the cleared land along the county's Pine River.

The following chapter provides information on this county's soils and farmers who were cultivating different classes of soils. The micro-level evidence taken from individual farms can then be linked back to the earlier macro-level statistics regarding both inter-state and intra-state variations in rates of return associated with different endowments of soils. These linkages provide answers to Kuhn's questions about "better off."

The present chapter takes a broad market-wide perspective on the privatization of the county's land with background information on a database that could link investors to different classes of soils (and vegetation, as covered in an article separate from the present study). That database also allows for linking privatization trends to legislative changes in how land was to be priced. It also makes it possible for the following chapter to assess the wisdom of individual farmer-investors by linking crop yields to the soils that were cultivated. That linkage confirms the inter-state and inter-county macro statistics patterns reported in earlier chapters.

The archival research procedures covered in this chapter will hopefully be helpful to other researchers interested in how to assess some of the consequences associated with the imperfect markets for land on the American frontier.

Land Patent and Deed Records

As noted earlier, a land patent transfers land ownership from a sovereign (the U.S. Government) to a buyer or grantee. Patents are the best form of a warranty "deed," and are the first record in a chain of titles to a piece of the public domain.[1] Once GLO approved a patent, it was entered into a tract book for a surveyed county, whether the county was organized or not. The tract book includes the name of the patentee (if known), the number of acres in the patent, their location within a section, the cash paid if procured under a Cash Act, the legislative authority for issuing the patent, and the dates of both the application and award of the patent.

We earlier covered two general types of patents that were used to acquire most of Midland's acres. The first were patents issued to specific individuals under the 1820 Act (at a minimum of $1.25 an acre), the Graduation Act (with different prices per acre depending on how long the land was on the market unsold), and military warrants. The 1820 Act and the Graduation Act were considered "cash sales." Not all of the patents issued under military warrants gave the name of the patentee. In fact, 117 (23 percent) of the county's 518 warrant transactions (as explained below) recorded in tract books do not identify the patentee. Earlier chapters also described military scrips.

The second general type of patent was a pass-through from the federal government to the State of Michigan. It had its own patenting procedures for section 16 lands (set-asides to generate revenue in support of public schools), swampland, salines, and several other earmarked purposes. But in Midland, most of these acres were passed through to the St. Mary's Canal Company and the railroads. These private firms in turn marketed the lands granted to them under the construction provisions approved for these enterprises.

I recorded information for individual patents as listed in the original tract books archived in the Bureau of Land Management's Eastern States Office in Springfield, Virginia.[2] Online sites with patent information are limited to cash sales, not military warrants nor the large grants to the state for its own disposal or as a pass-through to the canal and railroad companies.[3] One must rely on the Bureau of Land Management's tract books and the surveyors' notebooks for information on soils or vegetation.

The first of the three following photocopies shows the official record of a patent issued on September 9, 1834, to Gardner Williams for 3.84 acres in one "range" within one of Midland's sixteen townships. (No information is available on why only 3.84 acres when the minimum number was much higher.)

A second photocopy shows his patent along with others issued for the same township, range and section.

I entered this information into an Excel spreadsheet along with information on soils and vegetation as described in this and later chapters.

Individual patents can also be accessed online in the format provided by the third photocopy.

Another necessary technical note: Patents are the physical paper trail of individual decisions. Some patents covered two or more sections. For example, Joseph Copeland's August 1854 patent for 560 Midland acres covered three different sections within Ingersoll Township.

Only one of the 518 section investments using military warrants was by an 1860 resident of Midland. Warrants were a cost-saving tool used primarily by lumbermen and larger speculators. Benson found in her tally of 147 townships that timberland buyers "obtained twice as much land by warrant as through cash sales."[4]

Individual applicants accounted for only half of all acres applied for in 1850. All the initially patented physical geography had a uniform per-acre price independent of the assumed future potential dollar returns from these investments. Speculators could, of course, use other criteria in their own pricing practices. We will see later that higher quality soils yielded higher harvests that justified a higher per-acre cost of the soils in post-patent markets—that is, land sold by different kinds of speculators, existing farmer-settlers and others.

A patent might also include two or more sub-sections within a single section. Copeland's patent for 560 acres included four different parcels within Ingersoll's section 28 (suggesting that he was deliberate in his selections).

The soil classification refers to entire sections. Patentee decisions refer to an individual section. That is, *the patent is not the unit of analysis. The section with its soils and vegetation is the unit.* That, of course, overlooks intra-section differences in soils, a potentially significant caveat in the present analysis.

The examples below indicate how these rules were applied to record decisions based on both the time of a patent application and the sections included in the patent.

- The multiple sub-sections within the *same* section of a patent are treated as a single decision. For example, Copeland's patent for 520 acres included W1/2NE, W1/2SE, and SE/SW within section 13-N 2-E.21. These three are treated as a single time-specific decision, not three separate ones. However, having three different sub-sections while not patenting the others suggests that Copeland was not making blind selections.
- A patentee with two different patents referring to the same section is treated as two separate decisions. For example, David Cramton (also spelled Crampton) had two patents that included single references to the same section 13-N 2-E.25. These are treated as two separate time-specific decisions.
- Each section covered in a patent is considered a separate decision. For example, Copeland's patent for 520 acres included one sub-section in 13-N 2-E.19, four sub-sections in 13-N 2-E28 and three sub-sections in 13-N 2-E.21. These eight sub-sections are treated as three time-specific decisions, one for each of the three sections specified in the patent.

Yes, these are rather complicated decision rules.

These rules were made early in the present study. Another set of rules based only on sub-sections would have ballooned the database with attendant data-management and interpretation challenges. This, of course, is not a valid analytical excuse but one based on practical considerations. Another set of rules might affect the data arrays to be presented in this and the following chapters.

Again, *the individual section, not the patent, is the unit of analysis.* To simplify the terminology appropriate to this distinction, I will interchangeably refer to "sections" and to "decisions," although the use of "patent," "patentee" and "deed holder" will also be appropriate in some instances.[5]

Despite repeated checking and re-checking patentee names and related information, I suspect that there is a small number of errors. Error rates are minimal for patents issued to individuals (as confirmed by checking information obtained from tract books with information provided by the Bureau of Land Management's online GLO search facility). I suspect that any errors would represent only a few hundred of Midland's approximately 320,000 acres.[6]

The following chapters will also report on after-patent sales (the transfer of title to the physical land). All these transactions as well as the original patents were (at least in theory) to be entered into Midland's own deed books. However, information on sellers (grantors) and buyers (grantees) is incomplete. In part, this is because the first patent applications for land in Midland County were made in 1832 (but the first four actually awarded were on September 10, 1834), five years before Michigan entered the Union and 23 years before Midland was organized as a county and started keeping its own deed books. As previously noted, some of these early patents and deeds were recorded in Saginaw's deed books, and it is possible that some were recorded in Oakland County as well.[7]

Aggregate Statistics on Patents and Deeds in a Frontier County

By June 1, 1860, Midland's 512 sections subject to federal patenting attracted 1,745 patent entries. In addition, the State of Michigan received all sixteen township section 16s that were set-aside in the Northwest Ordinance for the support of public education. (No federal patents were issued for land in these sections.) Table 8.1 summarizes the number of section entries and acres issued under different federal laws.[8] Information on soils will be introduced in Chapter 9.

Also by June 1, 1860, 78 percent of the county's approximately 332,000 acres were no longer under the authority of the General Land Office.

Sixty-nine percent of all the 1,745 section entries were made by individual investors (including partnerships), but these owners claimed slightly less than half (48 percent) of the patented land.

This discrepancy (69 percent and 48 percent) is largely a result of the large number of acres covered under the multi-section patents granted by GLO to the state for subsequent transfer to the railroads planned for the county.[9] That is, these grants created a large private sector-operated market for land within this and other counties. There is little information to suggest that these private markets were any more transparent than the public sector ones.

As seen in the first photocopy, on September 15, 1832, Gardner Williams was awarded the first patent in the county. It was for 3.84 acres (not the normal minimum of 40 acres) in what today is Midland Township (T 14 N R 2E.20). It was not until August 9, 1851, that the first resident enumerated in the 1860 census applied for a patent. Stephen Benson applied for two patents in the former Chippewa Indian reservation (T 14N R 2E: 34 and 35).

Over time, 317 names appeared on the 1,190 section applications made by individuals. They included 29 partnerships in which two or more individuals are listed on the same patent.[10] These are minimum numbers because, as noted earlier, 117 of the 518 patentee decisions using military warrants did not give the name of the patentee.[11] The owners of these patents presumably held the hard paper copy of the patent as proof of ownership. These numbers again refer to the holders of patents.

Only 43 (14 percent) of these 317 or so patentees were listed in the county's population census of 1860. They account for five percent of the 1,190 section entries and six percent of all 115,649 acres covered by patents issued to individuals. They claimed less than three percent of all land that GLO transferred by June 1, 1860, to individuals and the state for its own disposal or for pass-through to the canal and railroad grantees.

That is, *non-residents (speculators, lumbermen, the state, and private corporations) were the primary investors in Midland's antebellum land market*—at least for the patent side of the market. The county's land was owned by outsiders few of whom ever lived in the county or had a stake in the lives of residents. Investors in land are not the same as investor-settlers, many of whom acquired their lands from speculators.

The closing of the American frontier is different from the shrinking supply and physical geography of public lands available for investment and settlement. Non-resident investors presumably anticipated that they could sell their property to private settlers and lumbermen at prices sufficient to justify the speculators' own investments.

A relatively small number of patentees held large amounts of land. Each of these three investors held title to over 5,000 acres for a combined three-owner total of 16,318 acres. Another four investors held from 3,000 to 4,999 acres each. Twenty-eight individuals by themselves or in partnership with others patented at least 1,000 acres each. These twenty-eight (about nine percent of the minimum of all 317 patentees) held 51,928 (45 percent) of the 115,649 acres patented by individuals under the cash and military warrants acts. Many of these investors were lumbermen interested in the county's vegetation, not its soils.

The market for land was different from what historians cover in their studies of the closing of the American frontier. Their focus is on settlement, not the privatization of land or the imperfect market for that land.

This patentee information indicates that land in Midland was privatized presumably by wealthier investors from outside the county and mostly from outside the state of Michigan itself. Land was a national market commodity subject to market forces shoe-horned into channels largely dictated from Washington, D.C. National concerns and national markets drove the eventual economic and settlement history of the state of Michigan including this one illustrative county.[12] Turner saw cheap land as the force pulling settlers west. Speculators (and lumbermen), not settlers, were the first to respond to those market signals.

Midland was only one of a number of counties in which these large investors held patents. GLO records indicate that Charles Carroll and his partners, as well as Charles Merrill, Joseph Copeland, Franklin Moore and others, held patents elsewhere in Michigan.

Merrill and Eber Ward (whose cousin David Ward became one of Midland's major lumbermen after 1860[13]) relied almost entirely (93 percent) on the lower-priced military warrants to procure their patents to sections in Midland.[14] Merrill began as early as 1836 to acquire Michigan pinelands, well before he closed his operations in Maine in about 1850.[15]

Midland's situation was not unique. As noted earlier, Benson reported that 320 large lumbermen acquired 304,811 acres throughout the state.[16]

Not all of the large investors in Midland lands were lumbermen. On the basis of deed records, it appears that the previously mentioned Joseph Copeland, the county's second largest landowner (with 5,238 acres patented before June 1, 1860) was primarily a speculator who, it appears, relied on other people's money. He was later forced into bankruptcy.

Just as non-residents had multi-county land holdings, at least some Midland residents themselves had similar holdings in other counties. William Copeland (perhaps a relative of Joseph Copeland, the speculator) reported in his Civil War pension file that during the war he wanted to return to Midland to sell land he owned in various parts of the state so that he could buy a home for his wife and child.

As this pattern of investments in land suggests, Midland's patent and settlement history must be placed in the larger context of public land law developments, what was happening elsewhere in Michigan and the Old Northwest, how the market for land was organized, and national economic conditions more generally. Midland was only a very small part of a larger national market and system that itself experienced irregular financial fillips and crises.

Early patent activity statewide was depressed by the Black Hawk War and a cholera epidemic in 1833 and 1834.[17] And as seen in earlier chapters, Michigan lands were privatized at a slower rate than experienced by three of the state's neighbors in the Old Northwest. Moreover, large supplies of Michigan land were put on the market well ahead of demand for them. This gave potential investors a wide range of choices (that is, more acres in more counties to choose from). This privatization path could have lowered the demand for land in more marginal areas of the state, including Midland County. GLO proclaimed 3,415,673 Michigan acres open for public purchase during 1831 and 1832, the time Midland and its 320,000 acres first became available for privatization.[18]

"Demand" and "sale" refer here to patents entered by investors either through cash sales or military warrants. Grants to the state for its own distribution or as pass-throughs to the private canal and railroad companies were not strictly market-driven, although both these companies and the state selected soils, vegetation and land they judged to be most attractive to potential investors. Of course, as seen in the minor importance of residents in the county's land market, it appears that a large proportion of the 317 or so individuals whose names are recorded on patents also anticipated logging the land or selling it to others. Relatively few acres were being farmed.

Individual patent-holders had to pay cash or military scrip for their patents or warrants.

The history of land privatization is different from the history of those who settled on the land.

Table 8.1: Patentee Decisions and Patented Acres Under Different Laws

	Section Decisions		*Acres Patented*	
	Number	*Percent*	*Number*[c]	*Percent*
Section Decisions by Individuals				
Cash Sales[a]	672	39%	72,293	29%
Military Warrants	518	30	42,355	17
SUB-TOTAL	1,190	69%	115,648	46%
Section Decisions by the State for its Own Distribution				
Section 16	NA	NA	10,240[b]	4%
Swampland	211	12	35,620	14
Salines	10	1	2,243	1
SUB-TOTAL	221	13%	48,103	19%
Section Decisions by the State for Pass-Through to:				
Canal Company	115	7%	17,536	7%
Railroads	219	13	67,600	27
SUB-TOTAL	334 19%	85,136	34%	
TOTAL	1,745	101%	248,888	99%

a. Includes sales under both the 1820 and Graduation Acts.
b. Based on the assumption that each section contained 640 acres.
c. Numbers are rounded up.

Except for the saline and section 16 grants to the state, individual patentees accounted for all patent applications through 1849. The 163 section decisions made before 1850 under the 1820 Act accounted for 30 percent of all section decisions under this act through May 1860. These 163 investment decisions accounted for 36 percent of all the Midland acres covered by this Act. (See Tables 8.2 and 8.3.)

Patent applications for sections under the Graduation Act with its reduced per-acre costs were first submitted in 1853, and by 1855 they exceeded sales under the 1820 Act. Their lower cost provisions that were central to Turner's closing the frontier thesis were not (at least in theory) to benefit large speculators although a maximum of 320 acres per patentee was initially in effect.[19]

That is, the federal government in Washington continued to change market rules including both the supply and the price of land as was well as state and large private entities entitled to well-defined acres of soils and vegetation. This was a national market that played out locally with several different de-nationalization paths.

In his many studies, Gates reminds us that the land market was really a nationally-directed one but in order to understand what was happening in Midland County one had to understand what was happening both in Lansing, the state's capitol, and in Washington.

Cash sales were soon dwarfed by acres patented under various military warrant arrangements. These warrants accounted for half (51 percent) of the acres patented by individual investors in 1851. The percentage rose to a high of 92 percent the following year before falling to 75 percent in 1853.

Table 8.2: Number of Patents by Year and Program

	Section Decisions by Individuals			**Section Decisions Via State Pass-Throughs**		**Section Decisions for Land to be Administered by the State**		
Year "Applied" for Patent	*Act of 1820*	*Graduation Act*	*Military Warrants*	*Private Canal*	*Private Rail Road*	*State Swamps*	*State Salines*	TOTAL
1832	4							4
1833	5							5
1834	2							2
1835	2							2
1836	95						2	97
1837	49						8	57

	Section Decisions by Individuals			Section Decisions Via State Pass-Throughs		Section Decisions for Land to be Administered by the State		
Year "Applied" for Patent	*Act of 1820*	*Graduation Act*	*Military Warrants*	*Private Canal*	*Private Rail Road*	*State Swamps*	*State Salines*	Total
1838	0						0	0
1839	0						0	0
1840	0						0	0
1841	3						0	3
1842	1						0	1
1843	0						0	0
1844	0						0	0
1845	1						0	1
1846	0						0	0
1847	0						0	0
1848	1						0	1
1849	0						0	0
1850	9		4			4	0	17
1851	43		19			0	0	62
1852	14		101	2		0	0	117
1853	40	2	135	61		193	0	431
1854	173	24	117	0		12	0	326
1855	68	70	67	52		1	0	258
1856	19	18	58	0	1	0	0	96
1857	1	2	2	0	1	0	0	6
1858	0	0	0	0	0	0	0	0
1859	6	13	15	0	217	0	0	251
1860	0	7	0	0	0	0	0	7
No Information						1		1
Total	**536**	**136**	**518**	**115**	**219**	**211**	**10**	**1,745**

Table 8.3: Acres Transferred from Federal Ownership by Year and Program

	Section Decisions by Individuals			Section Decisions via State Pass-Throughs[4]		Section Decisions for Land to be Administered[4] by the State			
Year "Applied" for Patent	*Act of 1820*	*Graduation Act*	*Military Warrants*	*Private Canal*	*Private Rail Road*	*State Swamp*[1]	*State Salines*[2]	*State Section 16*[3]	*Yearly Total*
1832	280							10,240	10,520
1833	398								398
1834	365								365
1835	312								312
1836	11,241						588		11,828
1837	7,112						1,655		8,767
1838	0								0
1839	0								0
1840	0								0
1841	80								80
1842	80								80
1843	0								0
1844	0								0
1845	70								70
1846	0								0
1847	0								0
1848	38								38
1849	0								0
1850	711		360			1,209			2,280
1851	2,734		2,884			0			5,619
1852	649		7,764	120		0			8,533
1853	2,865	320	9,425	8,560		32,452			53,621
1854	20,086	3,622	9,120	0		1,680			34,508
1855	6,943	9,107	6,614	8,856		240			31,760
1856	1,219	2,196	4,988		400				8,803
1857	33	274	160		120				587
1858	0	0	0		0				0
1859	180	1,482	1,040		67,081				69,783
1860	0	897	0		0				897
TOTAL	**55,395**	**17,899**	**42,355**	**17,536**	**67,601**	**35,620**	**2,242**	**10,240**	**248,888**

1. *The year was not designated for one 40-acre patent.*
2. *Acreage information could not be determined for two additional patents.*
3. *It is assumed that each of the 16 sections had 640 acres.*
4. *Numbers are rounded up.*

It seems reasonable to assume that the changing flat or uniform pricing of public lands helps explain why early (pre-scientific) farming patterns, the human geography, did not replicate the county's underlying physical geography. Information-poor markets mattered.

The relative importance of individual patents varied according to the number of acres granted to the state. Swamplands claimed by the state accounted for most (60 percent) of all the acres sought for patents in 1853. The canal company accounted for 28 percent of the acres sought in 1855, and the railroads accounted for 96 percent of the sought-after acres in 1859.[20] That is, land transfers were independent of market demands and actual transfers of ownership to individuals, partnerships and corporations other than the canal and railroad companies. These non-governmental entities were to market Michigan's and Midland's land.

The large number of acres claimed by the state and private corporations (54 percent of all acres with patent applications made through June 1, 1860) reduced the supply of land that could be acquired by means of cash acts and military warrants. Most of Midland's farmers, as we will see, procured their land from the secondary market, not directly from the national or state governments.

The number of more market-driven patent "applications" fairly well tracked Michigan "sales" and "acreage" figures identified by Jones, Cole and Oberle.[21] Midland's three highest Cash Act application dates were 1836 (11,241 acres), 1854 (23,708 acres) and 1855 (16,050 acres). Both Jones and Cole also report 1836 as a high point of patent awards (associated with "Michigan Fever"). Midland's high marks for 1854 and 1855 match Jones' statewide figures. Two of the county's three high years for acres under military warrants also match those given by Jones and Oberle.[22] (These authors' figures refer to awards; mine refer to applications.)

That is, the market for Midland's lands fairly well tracked the market more generally in Michigan and its adjoining states. But, again, market "sales" are different from settlement decisions—the populating of the American frontier.

The market was well ahead of settlers in at least the state of Michigan. These early investors were paying land taxes to local governments and the state. They, the investors, had a financial interest in recouping their investments by either selling land at marked-up prices or by themselves exploiting their private physical geography. That was what lumbermen did (and then abandoned their cleared lands so that land taxes could be avoided).

Midland's market for soils varied over time presumably in partial response to national economic conditions. Gates, Jones, Cole and others have written that land sales were highly responsive to the course of the larger national economy. The Panic of 1837, for example, helps explain why applications dropped off in that year and did not recover until the 1850s. Cash sales also plummeted after the Panic of 1857. Tables 8.2 and 8.3 show that this same financial crisis affected both cash sales and the use of military warrants in Midland.[23] The market for lands was one of many interrelated financial and other markets. Local land markets and follow-on settlement patterns were responsive to changing national markets.

Financial crises depressed new applications for patents nationwide while at the same time these crises (e.g., those of 1837 and 1857) led to wholesale foreclosures. "Many of the banks that failed in this period came to destruction because they had lent sums too generously on absurd appraisals of land which, when commodity prices fell, could not be sold after foreclosure for a fraction of the sum they had lent on it. During these periods of depression, court dockets in the newer parts of the country were clogged with foreclosure cases."[24]

Midland's deed books provide partial support for this same trend in foreclosures. It is "partial" because the foreclosures refer only to tax sales recorded after the county began to chronicle land transactions in 1855.[25] (There were some bankruptcy cases as well.[26]) Moreover, deeds were only recorded for land actually sold at auction. Unsold land was removed from the county's tax rolls and transferred to the state. Their status in Midland's deed books is unclear.

Tax auctions allowed lumbermen and speculators with access to finance to acquire land at below patent-level prices. The buyer was only required to pay the unpaid taxes and interest on them. Midland County itself (rather than Saginaw to which Midland was administratively attached) held its first tax auction in 1855, a year in which only three properties were awarded to successful bidders. This jumped to 64 in 1856, 61 in 1857, and a large increase to 105 the first year after the financial panic of 1857.

Again, we have seen several different ways land was first privatized and later trucked and traded. There were multiple types of markets for the nation's physical and economic resources.

Summary

Gates and others are correct in arguing that in order to understand the closing of the American frontier one must first understand how the lands on the frontier were first privatized and later sold in follow-on markets. The present chapter explored how imperfectly designed and implemented markets for land influenced investment decisions that led some settlers to invest in one illustrative frontier county.

Patents were the legal documents transferring ownership (title) of federal land to private individuals or the State of Michigan. A patent specifies the location of the land covered by the patent. Location is expressed as a section or a fraction of one. Other information on a patent include the name of the patentee (except for some obtained by military warrants), the number of acres, what was paid for them, and the dates of both the application and award of the patent. Patents were entered in tract books specific to each surveyed county whether the county was organized or not at the time. These tract books are the sources of patent information used in this and in the following chapters. Land patents and deeds are legal documents that say nothing about the physical world of soils and vegetation.

There were two general types of patents, one to individuals and the other a grant to the state for its own disposal or as a pass-through to designated canal and railroad companies. This chapter referred to patentee decisions relating to individual sections, not to the patents themselves. A single patent could record multiple investment decisions involving two or more sections.

Midland's tract books as of June 1, 1860, recorded 1,745 section entries (market investment decisions) of which 68 percent were by individuals, nineteen percent as pass-throughs and thirteen percent by the state itself. Acreage figures provide a different percentage distribution with 47 percent of all acres patented to individuals and 34 percent as pass-throughs to railroad and canal companies.[27]

Since not all military warrants provided the names of the patentees, there were likely to have been more than the 317 names listed as patentees. Eighty-six percent of the patentees did not reside in the county, and a relatively small number of these patentees owned a large proportion of all the acres that were patented in the county. The 28 who had patents to over 1,000 acres each (all non-residents that included some partnerships) claimed 45 percent of all acres patented to individual investors.

Midland was part of a much larger imperfect market for land, as many of the outside investors patented lands elsewhere in Michigan.

Except for the township section 16s and saline acres granted to the state, cash sales accounted for all patents until the advent of military warrants in 1850. Slightly over half of all acres patented to individuals in 1851 used these warrants.

Midland's first swampland grants to the state were made in 1851, but 1853 was the major year for these transfers. Pass-throughs to the St. Mary's Canal Company stretched from 1852 to 1855, while the pass-through railroad grants were almost entirely awarded in 1859.

Trends in the number of patented acres followed the health of the larger economy. Tax-auctioned land followed the same national financial trends.

Readers are reminded that land sales were initially to generate national revenues to retire the debt that several states transferred (traded) to the central government in return for relinquishing these states' claims to land west of the Appalachians. The federal government created and managed a national market that was assigned multiple objectives over time that included large land transfers to individual states for their own management and revenue-raising. State and local governments depended on land-based taxes, so the market for land was a central concern for all levels of government.

It appears that the supply of land well exceeded the demand for it. Investors could be choosy. But we also have seen that not all land had equal potential value, although differently valued land was not priced differently as was seen in the earlier reference to how the Habsburg Monarchy's classified arable land into nine discrete categories according to supposed fertility. American land markets were defined prior to the birth of soil science and modern economics. It was not only an imperfectly priced market but also one suffering from incomplete and often entirely erroneous information.

We turn next not to land in general but to identifiable soils on the land—that is, the physical geography of this county.

Readers are reminded of the multiple interests of this research that places physical and human geographies in the larger context of the closing of the American frontier. That larger context includes government policies and private sector entities related to the imperfect market not just for land but also what the land could yield in tradable crops and lumber.

9

Those Who Farmed or Left Their Soils

Earlier chapters laid the evidentiary basis for answering Kuhn's questions on the wisdom of farmers who decided to settle in Michigan. Would these farmers have been better off investing in some states or counties rather than in others? This chapter provides answers to these questions by comparing crop yields from different quality soils that were trucked and traded in very imperfect man-made markets.

Statistics aggregated at the county and state levels are subject to an ecological fallacy that allows a few tail-end cases to distort averages. Responding to this possible fallacy requires information on individual farms, their soils and the harvests from them. Farmers cultivating few acres of productive soils could have higher total crop yields than farmers who cultivated larger numbers of poor-quality soils. Testing this obvious assumption is done by focusing on individual farms for which information is available on both soils and crop yields. What we find for this one county, it is suggested, is very likely to represent farm-specific soil-and-crop yield relationships at the county and state levels. And as seen in earlier chapters, market failures help explain why so many farmer-settlers invested in unpromising soils, part of the history on how the American frontier was wastefully closed.

This chapter provides an example of how bottom-up histories can be linked to top-down ones. Doing this requires:

1. Identifying individual farms differing in total acres, not just improved ones.
2. Linking individual farms to the soils on them.
3. Information on the dollar value of yields from farming these soils.
4. Information on the likelihood that farmers cultivating different quality soils would survive the decade from 1860 to 1870.

The soil classifications used in this chapter are relatively recent creations. What little was known about these soils in the mid-nineteenth century will be introduced as well. We do not know how many acres were planted in different crops. Only harvest yield information is available, and those yields are estimates provided by farmers themselves. That is, we work with the incomplete and sometimes only estimated numbers.

Identifying Individual Farmers and Their Farms

I took the names of farmers listed in the 1860 agricultural census and then searched where they were farming based on information reported in patent and deed records.[1] While the grantee-grantor indexes (also known as forward and reverse indexes) at the beginning of these records were helpful, the poor quality of a number of microfilms may have contributed to my overlooking some deed-holders (either as sellers or buyers). The early deed books also included some apparent double-entrees. All in all, the deed information is likely to be incomplete.[2] Moreover the legal descriptions of resold lands occasionally departed from the terms and approach used in rectangular surveys and instead used the language of metes and bounds. For example, on September 17, 1851, Stephen Benson's sale of land to Sophrona Jane Townsend was described as "commencing at a stake near the river on south side of the small creek emptying into Tittabawassee river below Stephen Benson's house and running thence ... on line of Indian reservation." The half-acre that James Major and his wife sold to the School District of Ingersoll was described as "commencing in the center of the State Road..."

Patent and deed information is not available for all the 72 farmers listed in the 1860 agricultural census. Because some farmers both bought and sold land, their sales need to be subtracted from their buys to discover the net acres they owned as of June 1, 1860. This process yielded usable information for only 31 farmers, 43 percent of the 72 farmers reported in the 1860 population and agricultural censuses. Even this information is incomplete because although I was able to locate all the patents for all the farmers who had them, the same was not so for deeds.

Some of the missing farms could have been cultivated on a tenancy basis, and farmers with patents also rented additional acres. For example, Daniel Springstead, operator of the county's largest farm with 1,200 acres reported in the agricultural census, only had a single patent for 80 acres and his deeds were for city lots only. Midland's 1860 tax rolls reported he had 477 taxable acres. That is, there are discrepancies among several data sets.

Unnamed holders of military warrants are a second possible explanation for some of the discrepancies. Third, I had to discard other farms because the farmer held land in two or more sections with different soils in them. It was not possible to identify which sections were being farmed and provided the information that was recorded in the agricultural census.[3] My analysis obviously has several caveats.

Information on crops and land values is based on what a farmer reported in the agricultural census, even though the census generally reported more acres than what the net numbers were.

These 31 farms had 3,462 total acres, 43 percent of all farm acres in Midland. Because farms with two or more sections with different soils were excluded, it is not surprising that these 31 had relatively more small farms (23 percent with 40 or fewer acres vs. seven percent of the other 41 farms) but fewer unimproved acres (consistent with their smaller overall size).

There were cropping differences as well—with 61 percent of the 31 farms cultivating Indian corn (vs. 34 percent of the other 41 farms) and 58 percent cultivating wheat (vs. 40 percent of all other farms in the county. These differences are also reflected in farm values: 42 percent of the 31 farms had their land valued at $15 or more per acre while only 24 percent of the other 41 farms had similar value. The two groups of farmers did not, however, differ in their rates of residential persistence over the decade.[4]

Although the small number of 31 farms to be analyzed below seem to have been more prosperous than the 41 for whom sufficient information is not available, there are differences among these 31. For example, harvests of Indian corn by these 31 ranged from 40 to 300 bushels while wheat harvests ranged from zero to 150 bushels. There is also an array of farm sizes, ranging from 40 to 1,200 acres. No information is available on how many acres were planted in different crops and thereby the per-acre yields from different quality soils.

Only eight percent of one farm's acres were improved, while ten farms had half or more of their acres similarly classified. Most if not all farmers continued to invest time and money in developing their operations over time.

Behind the terms "farms" and "farming" are differences in farm size, number of cleared (improved) acres, and crops cultivated. That is, the farming "sector" is too broad a classification for historians interested in how the cultivation of differently priced land influenced sustainable long-term settlement patterns.

Farmers no doubt differed in their farming experiences and knowledge. The 1884 *Portrait and Biographical Album of Midland County, Mich.* includes short sketches of forty-three residents who arrived in the county before 1860. Seventy-nine percent of these 43 were farmers in 1884, but only 30 percent of them reported having had farming experience prior to arriving in the county. Some of these new residents had earlier land-market experience, as sixteen percent had invested in land before taking up residence in Midland. But farming was relatively new major occupation for most of these men. They may have had little experience with soils or with farming.[5]

As noted earlier, rather than the pull of cheap land, Stephen Thernstrom argued that migration was a safety value for the surplus labor force in Eastern urban centers. "Surplus" apparently referred to non-farmers, those who switched their occupations when they closed the frontier.

There is no compelling reason to indicate that Midland's early pioneer farmers were any different from farmers in Michigan's southern tiers of counties or in other states. W. J. Baxter of Michigan's Hillsdale County estimated that in 1864 "That fully fifty per cent of all the improved lands in the State are cultivated each year without profit, and even at a positive loss, is probably true."[6] Atack and his team reported that Michigan farmers in 1859 only realized a .057 rate of return per dollar invested. Yeoman farmers in the state had rates of return as low as a negative 12.8 percent. Moreover, "only 43 percent of farms under 40 acres farmers could feed neither their families nor their livestock the recommended diet, whereas only 19 percent of those holding more than 80 acres fell short of this standard."[7] Farming was not a wise investment for many settlers. Others did fairly well, at least over time.

The Soils These Pioneer Farmers Were Cultivating

Soil science is a relatively new discipline. Investor-farmers in the nineteenth century, as noted earlier, had to rely on rules of thumb and very questionable public accounts at the time. Federal surveyors in 1831 and 1832 made the first systematic observations of Midland County's soils. As seen earlier in Table 7.1, assessments were not particularly favorable. Negative comments outnumbered positive ones by about three to one. (This ratio leaves out townships that had both negative and positive comments on their soils.) The surveyors were not soil scientists; they too relied on crude rules of thumb common at the time. Still, these field notes identified sections that investors might be advised to avoid or to give closer attention.

Less helpful were the 1860 census enumerators' observations on Midland Township: "The soil of this township is of a dark sandy loose & gravel mixture." Ingersoll and Jerome townships had favorable assessments: "This township contains excellent soil for agricultural purposes."[8] The enumerators failed to observe that these townships also had poor soils and drainage problems. Township is too general a unit of classification.

If we were to accept at face value some early comments on Midland soils, then it would appear that the entire county was a veritable treasure of good farming acres. The *Michigan State Gazetteer and Business Directory for 1863/64* claimed that the county's "soil is unsurpassed for farming purposes, being a rich black loam, which produces wheat, corn, potatoes, etc., in the greatest profusion."[9] That was not true, and woe to the historian or investor who relied on public relations statements.

Michigan's Secretary of State in 1893, as noted earlier, claimed that Midland was a county where "There are no swamps of any size.... The soil of the southern portion of the county is mostly clay; that of the northern part is a clay loam, while the western and eastern portions have a sandy loam.... The 'stump lands' of this county have a good soil, and wherever cultivated have produced good crops."[10] The state welcomed the money invested in land perhaps because taxes on land were the major source of government revenues.

A Modern Soil Survey

The 1975 soil survey conducted in Midland used the National Cooperative Soil Survey Standards and Procedures to classify soils, design and name map units, and to identify local special soil features.[11]

The survey team prepared two types and scales of maps, one for "detailed planning" and the other a "general soil map for broad land use planning." The 73 detailed maps of individual sections are at a scale of 1:15,840. The digitized form of this map can identify a soil type down to a three-acre parcel. The color-coded general soil map is at a scale of 1:190,080. It glosses over the within-section heterogeneity of soil types revealed in the more detailed maps.

Midland has twenty-eight soil types. The detailed section maps display the areas separately identified based on these types. Most (but not all) of these twenty-eight are combined to form seven soil complexes that are considered "map unit descriptions." Each of these seven has an assigned number and color code that serve to identify where the soils are found in the general soil map.

The survey team characterized the twenty-eight soil types in two ways, first by the "potential" of the soil for farming, and, second, by the soils' capability. "Capability" refers to the degree of limitation on the use of the soils for agricultural purposes. Limitations are either "few," "modest," or "severe."

Midland only had five of the possible eight capability classes, as it lacked any soils "that have few limitations that restrict their use," and there are also no soils of the two lowest capability categories.

The assessment of "potential" is only given for the seven map units used in the general soil map. Acreage numbers are given for these seven, but accurate county-wide acres are not available for the eight capability classes. The report did estimate that there are 70,395 acres of best soils (those with moderate limitations). All of these require that "major management" attention be given to "wetness."[12]

Table 9.1 lists the acres, farming potential, and capability classes of each of the seven soil complexes used in the color-coded general soil map. Table 9.2 collapses these seven complexes into three "farming potential" levels: good, fair and poor.

Nearly one third (30 percent) of the county's acres have soils with a good potential for farming (leaving aside the need for drainage). One half of Midland's acres have soils with only a poor potential for farming. They too have wetness and other management challenges.

These quality rankings are supported by two sets of productivity statistics. First, the soil survey team collected data on "yields per acre" for seven different crops cultivated on each of twenty-one different soil types. (Crops were not cultivated on the other types.) These yield numbers were based on data assembled "from farm records and from field or plot experiments on the same kinds of soil" elsewhere. Moreover, the experimental plots were managed "under defined practices" and not necessarily from Midland County itself with its particular climate and water conditions. And the average yields per acre expected of principal crops were "under a high level of management."[13] Of course, antebellum farmers lacked the modern technology required today for a "high level of management."

The second set of supportive evidence comes from the soil rental rates offered farmers under the Conservation Reserve Program administered by the USDA's Farm Service Agency under the Federal Agricultural Improvement and Reform Act of 1996 (as amended).[14] This program allows for an "Environmental Benefits Index" to be assigned to particular acres. In addition, an "Erosion Index" is assigned to "cropped wetland" to yield an "Erodibility Index" that is converted to rental rates "based on the relative productivity of soils within each county, and the average of the past three years of local dryland cash rent or the cash rent equivalent."[15] These estimates refer to the years immediately preceding 1979.

Rental rates in Midland ranged from a high of $102 per acre down to a low of $39 per acre.[16] The rate scale follows the seven-category (and the combined three-category) ranking introduced earlier.[17]

Table 9.1: Soil Quality Classes

Map Units	*Percent of County's Total Acres*	*Acres*	*Farming Potential*	*Capability Class*
Lenawee-Bowers-Wixom	13%	43,264	Good	Moderate Limitations
Parkhill-Londo	14%	46,592	Good	Moderate Limitations
Intersoll-Pella	3%	9,984	Good	Moderate Limitations
Total "Good" Potential	**30%**	**99,840**		
Belleville-Wixom	12%	39,936	Fair	Severe Limitations
Wixom-Belleville-Pipestone	12%	39,936	Fair	Severe Limitations
Total "Fair Potential	**24%**	**79,872**		
Kingsville-Pipestone-Covert	45%	149,760	Poor	Very Severe Limitations
Cohoctah-Sloan	1%	3,328	Poor	Impractical to Remove Limitations
Total "Poor Potential	**46%**	**153,088**		
TOTAL	**100%**	**332,800**		

Table 9.2: Three Levels of Farming Potential

Farming Potential	*Acres*	*Percent*
Good	99,840	30%
Fair	79,872	24%
Poor	153,088	46%
TOTAL	332,800	100%

These yield and rental rates support the seven-fold classification listed in Table 9.1.

Post-1979 fieldwork found that the "soil delineation and map unit components" used in the *Soil Survey* "were accurate."[18] This follow-up work provided a test of "reliability." The "validity" of the categorization ranking was provided by the yield and rental rate calculations.

Instead of drawing on the power of the 73 detailed maps and the heterogeneity they provide, I used the General Soil Map to manually classify each of Midland's 528 sections with regard to their primary and, as relevant, secondary soils based on the 7-category color codes used in this map. The resulting classification yields a gross categorization. Only the predominant soil types are recorded. This approach still recognizes within-township and within-section variations of soils absent in other studies.[19]

Yes, the author recognizes that the above descriptive paragraphs provide more technical information than many readers will likely need. Future researchers, however, will hopefully benefit from these details.

The Soils of Midland's 528 Sections

As we will see again in later chapters, a farmer-settler's first step in building wealth from farming required the wise selection of the most promising or "good land" and certainly to avoid "poor land." Table 9.3 reconfigures the information in the prior two tables to estimate the county-wide stock of acres of each of three broad categories. The focus is on the most and least promising, not the entire range of combinations made possible by classifying the primary and secondary soils of each section.

The soil classifications are limited to primary and secondary types, not to the number of acres of each class. A farmer, of course, had to be concerned with drainage, not just with soil quality.

Farmer-settlers would have the greatest chance of making a wise investment decision by limiting their land purchases to sections that only had good land (both the primary and secondary classifications were "good"). There were 100 such sections, one-fifth (19 percent) of the county's sections. And it would have been unwise to start farming in one of the 162 (31 percent) sections that only had poor soils.

If each of the 100 sections with good land only had 640 acres each, then potential farmers could select from a stock of 64,000 of the most promising agricultural acres in the county.[20] Few of these acres were farmed as of June 1860. The agricultural census of that year reported that the county's 72 farmers reported their farms having 7,992 acres of which only 22 percent (1,796 acres) were "improved."[21] Start-up farmers who did not meet the census definitions of a farm were not included in these numbers.

In addition to these 100 good-good sections, there were another 60 whose primary (but not secondary) soil was good, and another 61 had good soil as a secondary type only. If we assume that the primary classification accounted for two-thirds of a county's acres (leaving one third for the secondary classification), and if we assume each section had 640 acres of land of all types of soil, then Midland had a stock of around 104,611 acres (approximately 30 percent of the county's total) with good soils. This is only slightly more than 99,890 acres classified as having "good" farming potential in Table 9.2. We are not too far off.[22]

A Shrinking Supply of the Most Promising Soils

By the end of 1852 farmers and others patented 4,042 acres in sections with any good soils (four percent of the 99,840 acres in this classification). By June 1, 1860, an additional 60,912 of these acres were patented for a total of 64,954 acres, 65 percent of the acres in sections with this classification. But all kinds of land were being patented. The same increases in patented acres are found for poor soils.

The map of the most promising physical soils of course was not the same map of lands that were privatized. And privatization was different from being settled by farmers. We are dealing here with multiple physical and human settlement maps.

These acreage numbers suggest that in every year, including 1860, aspiring farmer-settlers had at least some supply of Midland's best agricultural soils awaiting financial investments. This was true even more than a century later. According to the county's soil survey of 1979, "About 30,000 acres of potentially good cropland and 80,000 acres of fair to good cropland is currently idle grassland, wild pasture, or low grade woodland."[23] However, as noted earlier, there was no direct way to assess the productivity of different soils.

Also as noted earlier, it is possible that some investors, including farmers, based their selections on non-soil criteria—for example, access to more settled areas as reflected in how close the section was to neighboring Saginaw or, after 1855, to Midland Village or to rivers that provided access to outside markets and services.

This rural county's evolving human settlement history was shaped by more than the qualities of different soils. Here the focus is on the investment decisions made by farmer-settlers, not non-farmers. Their decisions, as explored in earlier chapters, were made in multiple information-poor markets for land. How those markets influenced the closing of farming frontiers is the focus of the present study. Soil-science-based classifications of land that was trucked and traded are central to the present analysis.

Table 9.3: The Declining Supply of Federal Land with Favorable Soils

			Number of Sections[a]	*Number of Acres*[a,b]	*Acres Patented Pre 1853 (%)*	*Acres Patented as of June 1, 1860 (%)*
Soil	*Primary*	*Secondary*				
	Good	**Good**	97	62,080	1,432 (2%)	43,145 (69%)
	Good	**Not Good**	156	99,840	4,042 (4%)	64,954 (65%)
	Poor	**Poor**	158	101,120	11,692 (1%)	71,654 (71%)
	Poor	**Not Poor**	246	157,440	20,881 (13%)	114,162 (73%)

a. Excludes all sections 16.
b. Each section is assumed to have 640 acres.
c. The numbers on these lines are included in the totals in the lines immediately below them. For example, the 97 "good-good" soil sections are included in the 156 sections in the next lower line.

The 31 farmers included in the present analysis were working different soils. Sixty-one percent were in sections with the primary soil classified as "good"; 35 percent were in sections without any good soil at all.[24]

A farm family could not easily survive on a very small holding. According to the 1860 agricultural census, thirteen percent of the county's farms had 40 or fewer total acres; 44 percent had 80 or fewer acres. Only eight percent had 40 or more "improved" acres; 58 percent had 20 or fewer such acres available for cultivation or pasture.

It seems reasonable to assume that a difficult life could be made worse by working not only less friendly farming soils, as many Michigan farmers did, but fewer acres of them.

Again, Midland was not unique. Kirkland's report on the difficult living environments of early Michigan settlers found "the interior of many a wretched dwelling, with almost nothing in it but a bed, a chest, and a table; children ragged to the last degree, and potatoes the only fare."

Farmers had their good years (for example, 1860 was good for wheat) but poor ones as well.[25] But subsistence farming was not a realistic choice under conditions of food deficits. Even the more prosperous farmers suffered during poor seasons.

Many if not most farmers had to have non-farm sources of income. As already noted, pension files of Midlanders who served in the Civil War reported that "working in the woods" was a common source of non-farm income (whether paid in cash or in kind).

William Higgins (in his pension file) described himself as a "woodsman," whereas the population census classified him as a farm laborer. Even that was misleading, as he and his farm were enumerated in the 1860 agricultural census.

Neighbors interviewed in the course of William Patterson's pension application probably best described the survival and growth methods followed by some early settlers: "he has worked for us and we have also worked together at different times . .. [we] worked at farm work, logging, hoeing and other work such as is generally done on farms." The census classified William as a day laborer living with his farmer father, mother and five other siblings. His pension file also suggests that he and one brother were "half-Indian," suggesting that some farmers and settlers benefited or were harmed by knowledge inherited from non-whites who occupied Midland in earlier years.

The pension files and the published literature also suggest that frontier men held multiple jobs and employee-employer relationships. Farm owners might work their own land and both logged and farmed for others during the same year.[26] It would take time for a new farmer to realize returns on his investment.

The census was conducted or dated on June 1, which was not during the logging season. Even if the occupation listed in June was the one identified as central to a resident, this resident might have earned more income that year from one or more other pursuits.

Moving beyond job titles as recorded in the federal and state censuses, we are missing the self-designations that settlers and others assigned themselves. For example, was farming a "job," an "investment," a "way of life," or even a steppingstone in one's time on earth? Perhaps those in a still relatively non-hierarchical society had multiple ways to designate their lives and to present themselves to others (that is, to socially-define themselves).

Pioneer farmers could also increase their welfare by clearing their land of trees, some of which may have had market value. That is, horizontal growth through adding improved acres was a major option, as vertical growth through improved seeds, fertilizers, and other technologies lay in the future.[27]

Whatever farming strategies were available, one would expect that farmers would be able to plant more crops with higher yields from them on good soils rather than on poor ones.

Crops and Soils

Farmers seem to have adjusted to their soils and environment by the crops they cultivated. For example, 84 percent of the farms with "primary good" soils cultivated Indian corn whereas only 27 percent of the farms without any good soil had the same crop. This pattern was repeated for wheat: 79 percent of the farms with primary good soils cultivated wheat whereas only 33 percent of the farmers without any such soils planted this crop. The Irish potato was the only crop grown on all farms.[28]

These percentage differences are based on small numbers, but the cultivation pattern is consistent for the county's two major crops. Some of this pattern, however, could be an artifact of inter-township differences not only in soils but also in the weather and ready access to nearby markets. Ingersoll Township in the far southeast of the county was close to Saginaw and the Tittabawassee River that provided a link to markets and services outside of Midland County.

All thirteen Ingersoll farms cultivated Indian corn and eleven cultivated wheat, whereas only one-third of the other eighteen farms cultivated corn and just 39 percent cultivated wheat. Ingersoll farmers also benefited from harvesting a crop they did not plant: maple syrup. All of the township's thirteen farms harvested maple syrup for processing into sugar and molasses, whereas 44 percent of the farmers in other townships had this same resource to add to the farm family's income and welfare.

Farming in this one county was not a mono-culture operation. In addition to cultivating different crops, farmers also had foul and livestock.

According to Easterlin, Alter and Condran, "farm value may not be a bad indicator of farm income differences, except that it may understate the relative position of farms in the newest settlement class."[29] It also seems reasonable to expect that good soils allowed the cultivation of more valuable crops that in turn added to the value of the farms that harvested the crops. And, in fact, the present data support the supposition that good soils directly or indirectly contributed to higher farm values as measured by the value of improved-acres (based on information from the agricultural census). Forty-seven percent of farms with primary-good soils were valued at $50 or more per improved acre. Only half that rate (27 percent) had the same value for farms with no such soil. The difference is even greater for poor soil.

These differences are suggestive. Different measures (dollar amounts), cut-off levels (over $50 and over $15 per acre), and type of land (improved or total acres) yield similar patterns but with dissimilar degrees of contrast.

The link between soils, land values, income (from yield estimates) is also seen in the dollar value of market garden sales. Thirty-two percent of the farms with primary good soils had sales of $50 or more whereas only nine percent of the farms with no such soils had a similar level of income. (The dollar figures refer to the agricultural year preceding June 1, 1860.[30])

Contrary to the inter-township cropping patterns that highlighted the favorable position of Ingersoll Township, this township's farmers did not have as high a value per acre as farms in other townships. That seems to be partially attributable to location relative to the Tittabawassee River. It added value to a farmer's investment: 80 percent of the ten farms in sections on this river were valued at $50 or more per improved acre whereas only 24 percent of the other twenty-one farms had as high a value. If these river farmers were able to sell their farms at these per-acre prices, then they could reap capital gains. But farmers working good soils were likely to realize higher levels of sustainable income.

In addition to farming, farmers as well as their non-farming neighbors were speculators. We saw earlier that the 1850-to-1860 increases in land values were found in all tiers of counties in Michigan's Lower Peninsula, although tiers differed in their relative proportions of good farming soils. The secondary market for land witnessed increasing prices-per-acre whereas government land available for patenting had relatively modest uniform prices that were well below those in the follow-on market. That discrepancy probably encouraged some investors to patent land whether or not they planned to settle on their holdings. They, the investors, were gambling.

Atack and his team reported that "Every farmer was a speculator in the sense that a relatively large fraction of total farm profits resulted from capital gains on land. Many, if not all farmers, when given the opportunity, bought and hoarded more land than they could cultivate intensively, hoping eventually to sell at a profit."[31]

Speculative profits were especially important among Michigan farmers for as noted earlier, Atack's team estimated that the state's farmers' negative rate of return on their farm investments in 1860 turned positive from the capital gains of selling one's land. A wise farmer would not have wanted to make life worse for his family by selling land for less than what it cost to buy in the first place.

If Midland farmers were like those elsewhere in the state, then they too would have had the speculative fever that Caroline Kirkland recounted in her memoir on southern Michigan pioneer life during the 1830s: "The possession of a large number of acres is esteemed a great good, though it makes but little difference in the owner's mode of living." She goes on to identify the negative consequences of speculation, as "the habit of selling out so frequently makes that *home*-feeling, which is so large an ingredient in happiness elsewhere, almost a nonentity in Michigan."[32] Her conclusion adds to our understanding of what really happened during the closing of the American frontier.

One English observer noted that "The people of the West became dealers in land, rather than its cultivators."[33] Based on what was has become a common perception of the farmer-speculator, some second-generation

Western historians asked whether "mid-continent pioneering [was] really home seeking after all?"[34]

Speculation was not, however, a winning game for all investors. This is seen in Midland's deed books' entrees on tax sales. Over one-fifth (26,506 acres) and probably more of all Midland lands patented through cash sales or military warrants (115,649 acres) were forfeited by their owners. A large proportion of all patents resulted in capital losses, not gains. For a small investor, a speculative fever could be a terminal one.

The long annex to this chapter has other information on residents who were land speculators.

Persistence

Good soils allowed farmers to cultivate marketable crops, and sustainable good crop yields made it possible for farm families to survive in Midland. That relationship speaks directly to the concern with how the physical geography of the frontier influenced the frontier's human geography. Farmers who cultivated poor soils were likely to have been more dependent on non-farm income such as "working in the woods" or working for other farmers. Some of the constraints imposed by poor soils were not always barriers to eventual farm success. At least in the short term, the technology available to compensate for poor soils was limited. Farmers working poor soils would find it difficult to survive as farmers over the decade.[35]

Other factors also influenced occupational change and geographical mobility. The 1860s witnessed four years of Civil War, the opening and settling of new states, improved approaches to farming, and a larger, more diversified economy and occupational opportunities. Americans were on the move; there was a mobile labor force and the American frontier continued to move. Farmers on poor soils may have had an extra or compelling reason to exit farming, but there were also pulls and pushes that affected the entire adult labor force, farmers and non-farmers alike. Midland was no exception.

Midland's 1860 population census included 266 men who listed an occupation. At least seven men perished during the Civil War, and another four non-servicemen died two of whom were survived by their widows.

Fifty-seven percent of the known 257 remaining men (and their widows) left the county by 1870. The highest rates of out-migration were among laborers (68 percent) and craftsmen (67 percent), followed by a combined group of professionals, businessmen and managers (65 percent).

Farmers were the least likely to leave Midland: only 43 percent of the 72 farmers in the 1860 agricultural census moved out of the county by 1870.[36] But eight of the 41 persistors shifted occupations over the decade, leaving the occupational persistence rate of 42 percent for this category of farmers.[37]

Investments in farming were not lifetime commitments. Changes in the larger economy allowed farmers who wasted their investments in an information-poor market for land to find other income-earning opportunities many of which were agriculturally and land-related.

No doubt many farmers who left the county were still in farming but in places thought to have more opportunity for success that what these early settlers experienced in Midland. On the other hand, Midland attracted 154 new farms over the decade.[38]

Farmers with both large and small farms were likely to leave. Again, the previously mentioned Daniel Springstead, the largest farmer with 1,200 acres, left the county. Out-migrants also came from farms with different cash values.

The quality of a farm's soils was one among a number of influences on decisions to leave or not. Seventy-three percent of the eleven farmers who had no good soil left their Midland farms by 1870. However, 42 percent of the farmers cultivating soils with a primary soil classification of good also were not in the 1870 agricultural census.

Closing the American frontier was not the same as planting a stable population of immigrants, farmers and non-farmers alike.

Summary

The first of the two parts of this summary covers local-level farm or agricultural economics. The second and perhaps more important is what farm-level economics can tell us about the role that imperfect land markets played in the closing of the American frontier.

Based on inter-state differences in the number of good farming soils, we suggested in Chapter 2 that a wise pioneer farmer-investor would not have made Michigan his first choice as a place to settle. But, of course, Michigan counties differed in their supply of good farming acres and a climate favorable to farming. The wisest pioneer-investors who settled in the state would have started farming in a lower-tier county, not in a marginal mid-state one.

Wisdom in both the inter and intra-state comparisons assumed that farmers would benefit more from cultivating good rather than poor soils. It was not until the present chapter with detailed soil information that this assumption could be empirically tested in the single mid-state county of Midland.

Two of our three tests supported our initial assumption. First, farmers who had good soils were more likely than their neighbors working poorer soils to cultivate two important crops (wheat and Indian corn) and to have higher earnings from their market gardens. Farming was more profitable on good rather than on other soils. Second, this profitability resulted in sustainability as suggested by the higher persistence rates of farmers cultivating the county's best soils.

On the other hand, soil quality seemed to have had no effect on speculative gains or losses. This finding is consistent with what we reported for the 68 counties in Michigan's Lower Peninsula. Land values were inflating in tiers of counties with proportionally fewer good quality acres as well as in counties with the highest proportion of the best soils. And land values were rising in zones with short as well as long growing seasons.

Farmer-settlers were both cultivators and speculators. When their extra holdings were sold to others and when the farmer's existence depended only on what his family could realize from cultivating their remaining soils, then many cultivators realized the facts of economic life: many chose to move on. That was much more likely for farmers who unwisely invested in land with unpromising soils.

The market for (cheap) land in Midland, Michigan and the Old Northwest departed from the economists' assumptions about perfect markets based on perfect information. To the degree this was so, there was much wasted investment and family suffering—as well as gain.

These Midland findings are based on a relatively few speculators, fewer farmers, limitations in our soil classifications, several important assumptions, and other information gaps. Improved data and larger numbers of farmers and residents might have produced even more striking differences attributable to the physical geography of soils. As it is, the consistency of the results supports the assumption underlying the inter-state and inter-county differences in the wisdom of farmer-settlers. Soils mattered, and wisdom (or luck) paid.

The second of the two parts of this summary links the Michigan and Midland histories to the larger history of the closing of the American frontier.

As complicated as the market for land was in Midland, this current chapter reported a fairly active market for land, not just unpatented land but land already held and later re-sold in a county that was well-endowed with exploitable pine forests.

We have also seen that there was much wasted investment, an inefficient use of scarce national and family resources. Waste and inefficiencies were built into a market that lacked transparency and was also rife with blatant dishonesty that began with those who mapped the land and later those who marketed it. And an information-poor market helps explain why the county's physical and human geographies differed from one another. That discrepancy is one indicator of the wasteful use of scarce national and personal resources.

Perhaps there was no reasonable alternative settlement policy at the time. Nevertheless, from a national economic perspective, scarce resources were wasted and many investors and families suffered. At the same time, the frontier and land that Turner's frontier thesis classified as cheap continued moving west.

Annex: Land Speculation in Midland County

Information on Midland residents' participation in the county's land market was taken from both patent and deed records. Patent information is limited to the initial privatization of federal lands. Information on the subsequent sales of this land comes from deeds recorded by the county's register of deeds. The gains and losses of non-residents must await later research except for sales at tax auctions.[39] I recorded all of these.

Other data limitations will be noted later with regard to tax auctions and capital gains or losses. Suffice it to note that I do not claim 100 percent coverage of all deeds or of all relevant information in these deeds whether owned by farmers of others. However, we are able to analyze a high (but unknown) proportion of all the deed transactions effected by the 1860 county residents. Moreover, the analysis of tax sales is based on 100 percent of these transactions.

Participation in Midland's land market was widespread among the county's 1860 residents. There were at least 114 different "resident landowners" at one time or another prior to June 1, 1860. Twenty-one of these residents held both a deed and a patent, whereas 25 held patents only and 68 were limited to deeds only. (That is, there were 46 patent-holders and 89 who held a non-patent deed.)

At least one member (or resident) in 98 of the 164 occupied dwelling units (60 percent) had at one time or another either a patent or a deed prior to June 1, 1860. Over half—57 percent—of the heads of household had been owners. Forty-six residents paid $4,510 for 65 patent applications comprising 6,852 acres. Eighty-nine residents paid more than $26,391 for 198 deed transactions comprising 7,898 acres and 52 transactions for lots in Midland Village. (Insufficient dollar information was available for 22 of these transactions.)

Resident participants in the after-patent land market displayed no more wisdom in their investment choices of soils than did resident patent holders. Less than half (46 percent) of the deed holders of rural (non-village lots) acres bought land in sections whose primary soils were "good." And only four percent of the deeds were in sections with any pine at all, but because there were more deeds, there were numerically more good-soil selections (67) than for federal patents (36).[40] It seems likely that these unwise investments were attributable to information-poor markets. The investments were unwise not just because of the absence of what later become soil science but also because of other market failures that contributed to what economic historians have referenced as a "speculative mania or fever" and asset bubbles.[41]

Not all farmers owned land recorded in the tract and deed books prior to June 1, 1860, but 76 percent of them did. The other 24 percent may have been overlooked in the deed books or were tenants.[42] Resident non-farmers were also market players. Fifty-six percent of the businessmen, professionals and managers had land, followed by half of the craftsmen and, even, thirteen percent of those classified as laborers. "Land fever" seems to have been widespread and endemic.

Over half (53 percent) of the 114 patentee and deed holders were sellers as well as buyers. These sixty sellers had 102 sales from 76 deeds and 23 patents.[43] (No information was available on three sellers.) I have complete buy and sell information for only 51 of these transactions. In addition to incomplete information, I have also excluded sales of village lots, apparent land swaps (with the seller only charging a single dollar) and the multiple transactions by John Larkin, a major player in the local land market, especially as the developer and seller of lots in Midland Village.[44]

The 51 transactions were for only 2,716 of the 4,219 acres included in the owners' original deeds and patents, but the sales of these acres yielded approximately 116 percent of the original purchase price for all 4,219 acres. That is, the sellers paid an average of around $2.09 for an acre of land that they later sold for an average of $3.35 an acre—and they still owned 36 percent of their original acquisition to sell or use at a later time.

These aggregate numbers cover only half of all buy-and-sell transactions. Moreover, there were both successful and unsuccessful speculators. Forty-one percent of the transactions were at a loss or only for what was original paid per acre. One quarter of the transactions yielded capital gains of two dollars or more per acre. That is, relatively few transactions accounted for a good share of the overall speculative gains. (I did not incorporate either inflation rates or time spans in this analysis.)

As referenced earlier, it seems that speculative gains were likely for all kinds of soil and growing conditions in the Lower Peninsula. The same is found in our Midland-specific data for 51 transactions for which we have acreage and dollar information. Approximately the same per acre dollar gains and losses are found in differently classified land.

However, the per-acre price of land sold did not always reflect the seller's actual returns from the sale. For example, Phineas Bailey's deed of October 1859 to Henry Patterson specified that the "parties of the first part reserving to themselves all pinetimber suitable for sawlogs or hewing timber now on said land and the right to enter upon such premise to remove the same." Similar provisions are found in deeds entered in 1861 and later. In one case, a time limit was added to the deed. For example, Alpheus Chapman held the right to certain specified acres he sold to Charles Wooden in 1863. There was a three-year time limit for exercising this right.

More information is needed in order to provide reasonably accurate estimates of rates of return on investments made in land. For example, information is needed on the cost of money, transaction costs, management fees, and taxes. Land prices were also distorted by tax sales. At least eleven residents acquired 19 or more deeds from tax auctions at low per-acre costs.[45] Sellers who only disposed of a portion of their earlier-acquired acres by patent or deed further complicated the analysis. Selling their less attractive acres at bargain prices could possibly enhance the value of the land the owners retained.[46]

Focusing on resident speculators masks the very large number of non-resident investors who suffered losses. As noted above, over one-fifth (26,506 acres) and probably more of all Midland lands patented through cash sales or military warrants (115,649 acres) were abandoned by their owners. We do not know the full universe of tax-forfeited land, as the deed books only record land that was sold at auction. Unsold land reverted to the state and taken off the county's tax rolls. This limits the generality of the following assessment.[47] Still, the imperfect market for land helps explain why so many investments were wasted rather than adding to the wealth of the nation by being invested elsewhere.

Forfeited patented lands were in sections with good as well as poor soils, and in sections with pine forests as well. Twenty percent of the auctioned parcels were in sections with good soils as the primary classification, and 27 percent were in sections with some pine.[48]

Non-residents were the primary buyers at Midland's tax auctions, and a relatively few buyers accounted for a major share of all properties acquired in this way. Three buyers acquired 58 percent of all the auctioned land.[49] Eight percent of Midland's 1860 residents who listed an occupation in the census of that year bought land at these tax auctions. Most (63 percent) of these resident buyers were farmers listed in the 1860 agricultural census. They presumably acquired useful information on which soils were worth an investment. But potential outside investors remained potential victims of an information-poor market.

Summary, Overview and Next Steps

10

Looking Back

We end this evidence-heavy market-oriented analysis of the closing of several American frontiers with two organizing themes taken from our introduction:

- There were diverse public and private owners and investors who intended to make wisely-informed choices in the lands they bought, sold, settled and farmed on the frontier.
- Investment and settlement decisions were made in information-poor markets that did not link the price of an acre of land to the potential of that land to be profitably cultivated.

Our chapters began with a top-down history of how the imperfect markets for land were legislatively created and then managed. Private contractors surveyed the land, laid out boundaries and made notes on the physical environment along section lines within individual counties. These imperfect and sometimes fallacious notes were the best information that potential investors and settlers had on where to close the American frontier.

After introducing and analyzing state and county-level soils, crop yields and population trends, we moved from a top-down to a more detailed bottom-up history of how one illustrative multi-soils county in Michigan was mapped, the surveyors' limited information and misinformation that was publicly available to potential investors in several different markets for land, and then the investment returns farmers realized from cultivating different quality soils. The bottom-up history and "findings" complement those discovered from a top-down analysis that was based on aggregated evidence subject to what statisticians label a possible ecological fallacy.

The bottom-up history covered how the land was surveyed, the limited and often fallacious information made available to potential investors, and the decisions individual farmers made within an information-poor market on what crops to cultivate on which soils. In the absence of a scientific understanding of soils together with other market imperfections, it is not surprising that farm frontiers were so wastefully closed. That may seem obvious, but the obvious still warrants documentation and explanation.

Antebellum markets for land on the expanding national frontiers and individual rational investors (decision-makers) were viewed from four perspectives:

- First, it was assumed that buyers and sellers of land strove to be rational decision-makers who acted to improve their own financial and family fortunes.[1]
- Second, the laws and institutions regulating and implementing the privatization of public lands affected the timing and locations of the choices of land that rational investors could make. Both national and local economies also affected these decisions.
- Third, the physical environment, the object of investment decisions, refers to soils, vegetation, climate, river systems, and, it should be re-emphasized, the location of earlier settlers.
- Fourth and finally, multiple forces influenced the *locational decisions* that actual settlers (not all investors) made. Some may have been more influenced by the decisions made by earlier settlers (a human rather than a soil gravity force) whereas others gave greater importance to the economic potential of the lands they acquired. Still other possible ways to understand how the frontier was closed are explored late in this chapter.

Perfect markets would assign different prices to lands that differed in their potential to repay what investors put into their land. But, as repeatedly emphasized throughout this study, despite the best intentions of legislators, the markets they created suffered imperfections that contributed to the wasted financial investments made during the closing of the frontier. Today we know much better how to structure honest, transparent and efficient markets. That suggests there would now be a closer overlap between two geographies, the physical one of soils and the human one of farmers.

Suggestions for Follow-on Research

We noted earlier that states and counties within them differ in their soil endowments as well as in their timing and pattern of settlement.

The present study provides guidelines on how to locate and analyze section-level numerical evidence that can be used in other place-specific bottom-up settlement histories.

These follow-on studies, it is hoped, will build on relatively recent trends in economics, geography and regional science.

Economists and others typically assume that investors in land were rational decision-makers who would in theory only invest in land that had a promise of yielding significant positive financial returns. This implies that the supply of the best soils and most marketable tree species would be procured before moving on to less-promising investments. Farmers would only cultivate the most productive soils. This, however, was not what often happened: physical and human geographies were not the same. Discrepancies between these two geographies are keys to documenting the wasteful way the American frontier was closed.

Were antebellum investors and settlers really irrational decision-makers and pre-modern capitalists? What were many settler-investors maximizing in addition to returns on capital? Possible alternative answers to these questions are introduced later in this concluding chapter.

This maximization question is relevant to how contemporary economists question the meaning of rational economic man, the investor-settler who Turner claimed closed the frontier. Nobel Award–winner Daniel Kahneman, for example, argued that investors base their decisions on what they might lose, not just on what they might gain.[2] And, as will be suggested later, financial returns were not the only criteria that settlers valued. But one feature that all settlers shared was the decision to move, not just to make a financial investment. There are reasons other than narrow returns on investments that might help us to better understand why and how America's antebellum frontiers were closed.

The present book has taken a fairly narrow focus on individual financial and human investments made in information-poor markets. Neither the public nor private markets for soils were able to provide reliable place-specific information on soils. The American frontier was closed before the advent of modern soil science made it possible to link soil-profiles to measurable crop harvests from different quality soils. The pre-science and sometimes invented field notes of the surveyors who mapped the external borders of sections, townships and counties were inadequate signals of the investment quality of different acres of soils whether marketed directly by the federal and state governments or by non-state owners of the land (speculators).

There is a large body of economic literature on perfect markets that are transparent and provide buyers with accurate information such as the potential productivity of different soils.[3] The market for land during the closing of the frontier was far from perfect, one of several reasons why so many farms were abandoned and others only provided bare subsistence for those who invested in farming.

Economics, markets and sustainable farming did not stop with the first plowing of land. We also need to link the spatial history of population movements with the decisions that cultivators made while farming their land. Rational decision-making did not end with the initial patent or deed to land. Earlier chapters placed farm-level decision-making in the context of what economists such as Lionel Robbins saw as a central theme in the science of economics: "rational behavior."

The American Economic Association defines the discipline as "the study of how people choose to use resources," while Noble Award-winning Paul Samuelson defined his discipline as the "study of how societies use scarce resources to produce valuable commodities and distribute them among different people." Adam Smith saw his field as "an enquiry into the nature and causes of the wealth of nations."[4]

Some critics will correctly argue that non-economists as well as non-historians also have much to contribute to our understanding of how different kinds of American frontiers were closed (prairie land, deserts, mountains). This is where we turn next.[5]

Thinking Outside the Economist's Model of Perfect Markets

Earlier chapters placed the economics of different markets for land in the context of two geographies, the physical geography of soils and the human geography of the farmers who cultivated the soils.[6]

Alan Baker's *Geography and History* covers different historical geographies or the geography of history. There are time geographies, geographies of temporality, historical biogeography, historical soil geography, hydrology, geomorphology, climatology, agriculture, urbanization, geosophy (perceptions of the natural environment) and more. The present study added another sub-specialty: the geography of information, a sub-discipline within regional science and regional economics concerned with how space, location, time and the physical environment relate to one another.[7]

Historical GIS and computer-based cartographical analyses (quantitative geography) provide investigators with new data-management and presentation tools useful in tracking the spatial diffusion of various items or traits (e.g., the adoption of new seeds) over time through different networks. Alex Pentland labeled this new craft *Social Physics*. Instead of the "old vocabulary of markets and class, capital and production," economists, according to Pentland, need to recognize that people and markets move more than goods and money: the flow of information and ideas is also important.[8]

Still other studies emphasize how "landscapes" change over time as well as the man-environment linkages that contributed to these changes.[9] With the ever-growing availability of mass data and methods to manipulate them, we can expect new man-environment analyses, including some that will no doubt qualify what is reported in the present study. That's progress.

Closing the American frontier is also a changing human geography of the original residents who were forced to relinquish their lands. Historical ethnography joins economics and geography in understanding the settlement history of Amerindian lands.

Jürgen Osterhammel reminds us that early settlers were colonizing other peoples' land and property.[10] Antebellum America was still in the early stages of becoming not just a nation but an empire as well. Whether they realized it or not, early settlers in Michigan and its neighboring states were inadvertent colonizers.

Osterhammel captured the difference between native and colonial understanding of the private land being closed on the frontier:

> The American Indians, like many other hunter-gatherers and farmers around the world, were perfectly familiar with private property, but for them it referred not to the land itself but to the things *on* the land. In principle, those who produced the crops also had them at their disposal. The idea of dividing up the land into fixed plots was as alien to the Indians as the idea that individual persons, households, or clans might take permanent possession of more land than they were able to cultivate.[11]

"Private" ownership is a socially-constructed concept that had different meanings at different times in different countries. The legal status of American lands and the markets for them evolved over time. Historians need to be aware of the ontology and epistemology of the language they use.

Amerindians trucked and traded what came from the land but not the land itself. Absent their written native languages, we lack the original occupants' understanding of and responses to their conquerors, just as we have few Michigan social histories authored by the earliest white settlers and travelers. (References, however, were made to the Saginaw experiences of Alexis de Tocqueville, Caroline Matilda Kirkland's memoir, and others.[12]) This chapter's final section will add other earlier-research studies that are relevant to the present one.

Additional Traditions of Historical Research

Narrative historians have their own story-telling practices and themes that include Turner's thesis on the closing of the American frontier including the boundaries of the five states carved of the Old Northwest Territory. Many of these historians correctly argued that settlers moved west for many reasons unrelated to the cost of land, the means to farm it, and the decisions that earlier arrivers had made.

One need not be limited to theories about irrational markets, rational investors and the wisdom of crowds to explain how the frontier was closed. Turner, however, gave the cheap price of land as the magnet that drew settlers to the American frontier. And as noted earlier, rather than the pull of cheap land, Stephen Thernstrom argued that migration was a safety value for the surplus labor force in Eastern urban centers. His "floating [labor force of] permanent transients," not stable settlers, seems to partially apply at least to Midland County.[13]

Institutional and legal scholars placed the marketing of land in what Gates labeled an "incongruous land system" and "the malfunctioning of an intended democratic system of land disposal." The system he explored included both laws and the ways they were administered.

Other comparative institutionalists such as the earlier-referenced John Weaver found that "components of the British and American property regimes were fraught with conflict, imprecision, impossible administrative burdens, economic risks, unfulfilled expectations, unintended consolidations, and corruption."[14] The Michigan privatization experience was not peculiar to the Old Northwest, the United States, or other former English colonies.

Gates, as with the present study, placed privatization and migration within a larger institutional and legal context—or what might be labeled institutional economics. That scholarly tradition evolved over time from the soft economics of John Commons and Thorstein Veblen to the methodological approach that Ronald Coase and others took on transaction costs and a property rights paradigm.[15] Douglass North and other institutional economists also published general economic histories relevant to the present study, one that consciously places the closing of the American frontier in the context of a mathematically less rigorous approach to institutional economics.[16]

Evidence on the "Social" in Social Histories

There are still other keys to understanding antebellum America's investment, marketing and settlement history. More biographical attention could be given to early market-makers, investors, settlers and farmers. Some families, for example, no doubt came to Midland with known neighbors and kinsmen. But a good majority was without the possible support that previously known neighbors might provide. At least at the beginning of their new lives in Midland there was little social support that might strengthen a commitment to stay in the county. On the other hand, some kinsmen (e.g., the DuPues from Upper Canada) paved the way for their immediate relatives to acquire land and begin farming. Another early arrival hosted his nephew who left New York for a new life in Midland.[17] These are examples of the complexity of different types of human and investor geographies.

Kinship, of course, was not the only force that gave a common culture if not the basis for seeking help from one's newly arrived fellow neighbors. Vedder and Gallaway's study of migration in the Old Northwest suggested that "migrants preferred to move, *ceteris paribus*, to areas with similar physical and cultural climates."[18] If this pattern applied to Midland, then it is reasonable to expect that the county's settlers would have come from the same general areas back East.

Eight of the ten Midland households in the 1850 census were born in New York, one in Vermont, and the other in Pennsylvania. New York was again the major supplier of immigrants statewide ten years later. Thirty-two percent of Michigan's entire population in 1860 was born in New York.[19] This is only slightly lower that the birth state of another sample of Michigan heads of household: 36 percent of them statewide were born in New York.[20]

Western New Yorkers were often seen as one-generation removed from New England,[21] so if the two sources (New York and New England) are considered as having a common culture, then 75 percent of Midland's native-born residents age 20 and older would have shared a common culture. To the degree that Ontario shared the same culture, then 70 percent of all (male and female) of the county's residents age 20 and older in 1860 came to Midland with a similar heritage that some labeled the "universal Yankee nation" or "Greater New England" and the "Yankee West."[22]

Lewis reported examples of groups of New Yorkers from the same county moving to a single Michigan county, and there are examples of particular counties drawing disproportionately large populations of Germans and Dutch.[23] Midland did not seem to follow the exact same gravity-model pattern. The 54 prominent ante-bellum citizens profiled in the county's previously referenced 1884 biographical and portrait album includes the names of three men from Penobscot, Maine and two each from three different counties in New York (Genesee, Monroe and Ontario). One New Yorker each came from 17 different counties. No single New York county was a significantly large source of Midland's immigrants.

Whatever the wisdom of the decisions made in moving to Midland, the county did not mark the end of the decision-making and investment process. Contrary to what some historians might have assumed, "mid-continent pioneering" was not necessarily "home seeking."[24] Nor does it seem reasonable to accept unverified ideological assertions that "on the whole, the family farm [in the 1850s] was largely independent of the ups and downs of the economic cycle.... Poverty existed, but it was usually due to physical or mental defects, misfortune, illness, or just plain laziness."[25] That is a questionable quantitative claim, one that is often found in even the best narrative histories. Readers need to be aware of a false sense of numerical precision.

Yes, investors made unwise decisions but they were not necessarily a decision-maker's ever-lasting fate. An investor could move on, just as many Midland residents in 1860 had moved one or more times before arriving in the county. Midland was a temporary home for a transient population on the move in search of wives, higher incomes, and better jobs and lives. The physical geography of the county was not an anchor holding farmers to the lands they were cultivating.

Again, neither Midland nor Michigan was unique, as Americans, according to some historians, were a "restless, migrating people."[26] And Americans (and immigrants) on the move did not just move once. Serial movement decisions were made. Based on the birthplaces of children enumerated in the1860 national census, Atack and Bateman reported that the "mean number of moves by migrants" in northern ante-bellum states was 1.27. In Michigan it was 1.34 moves.[27]

Perhaps because Midland was home to many young families, the county did not replicate the same multi-state pattern reported by Atack and Bateman. For the 135 families with children identified in the 1860 census, only one had children born in two states other than Michigan. Seventy-five families only had Michigan-born children.[28]

All these "findings" and the interpretations for them are based on imperfect and incomplete information on the exact locations of the most promising soils and vegetation. Yes, America's settlement history is also a history of politics, legislation and trends in the nation's economy. There are multiple histories and disciplines for writing them. We saw how the lottery for land was influenced by how the larger legal and institutional environments affected the timing, rate and spatial patterning of the privatization of land, settlement, farming and logging. These effects are seen in the increase in patent applications following passage of new federal land laws favorable to patentees. Trends in the national economy also had significant effects, especially following major financial panics, a constantly recurring crisis in American economic history. These panics exposed the adverse effects of a privatization system that enabled widespread speculation. At least one-fifth of all acres patented in Midland was auctioned for non-payment of property taxes prior to June 1, 1860. There was much wastage of financial and human resources.

If a major justification for a private sector capitalist economy is making the most efficient use of scarce resources, then America's settlement history is marred by widespread inefficiency and waste, a topic I explored in two of my recent publications.[29]

The State of Michigan and its private sector played mixed roles in the market for land and the encouragement of wise investments. After its early financial missteps, the state had only a minor role in providing infrastructure that would have facilitated settlement, and early poorly regulated reckless banking practices left small buyers without access to investment and working capital. At different times during its early statehood, Michigan suffered from inept leadership and widespread dishonesty on the part of prominent members of the private sector. Crony capitalism has a long destructive history in America.

While the institutional legal and economic environments had significant effects on the privatization process, it is again necessary to remember that individual investors, not the federal or state governments, decided which lands to buy. Those who made wise decisions benefited from them.

These are the "findings" from a study that placed individual decision-making within a larger physical and non-physical setting. The criteria or terms of reference used in this study narrowed the narrative. This is not a general history but it does contribute new information on antebellum America, the five states of the Old Northwest, the state of Michigan in particular, its Lower Peninsula counties, and one illustrative county. That is, this is a national, regional, state, sub-regional and local history.

Many rational investors learned that they had made unwise investments such as William Kelly, an 1853 settler in Midland. He reported that "The first settlers had little hopes that agriculture could be successfully prosecuted, and beyond raising of a limited quantity of potatoes and corn, farming was decidedly at a discount. The earliest attempts at growing grass and grain were practically failures."[30] Yet that is what Kelly and other investors did: they made unwise locational and investment decisions that might have been avoided if there had been an information-rich market for land.

Farmers continued to make unwise decisions. As already mentioned, Samuel Turner bought swampland from the state after 1865. "Much of the land in this vicinity [Jasper Township] is low and swampy, and Mr. T has had to encounter an unusual number of hardships as a pioneer. Sometimes the water covered the ground in places from one to two feet deep."[31] Since Turner lived in the county for several years before buying this swampland, there seems to be little excuse for such an unwise investment.

A good proportion of failed investors realized their errors and decided to move on. Margaret Walsh reported that "[a]nalyses of early decades of settlement in several parts of the Midwest point to a turnover of some 65 to 75 percent among farm operators.... The mobility of agricultural laborers was even higher."[32] These figures indicate that both the settlers and the economy more generally wasted limited financial and human investments, a loss we partially attribute to information-poor market for land. Still, the American frontier continued its wasteful closing, a history that goes well beyond Kuhn's two questions that opened the present study.

And the frontier of historical research on the closing American frontier is still open.

Chapter Notes

Preface

1. George Berkeley, *On the Prospect of Planting Arts and Learning in America* (1726).

2. In 1932, sixty percent of the leading history departments in the U.S. were teaching courses in frontier history along Turnerian lines. Allan G. Bogue, "Frederick Jackson Turner Reconsidered," *The History Teacher* 27:2 (1994): 195.

Introduction

1. George Iggers, *Historiography in the Twentieth Century* (Middletown, CT: Wesleyan University Press, 1997).

2. Richard Bushman's social and cultural (not economic nor market) history of American agriculture was limited primarily to the eighteenth-century eastern colonies whereas the present market-oriented study covers the third, fourth and parts of fifth decades of farming and settlement on the expanding western frontiers of the original five new states carved out of the Northwest Territory. See his *The American Farmer in the Eighteenth Century: A Social and Cultural History* (Yale, 2018). Minnesota was added later but is not included in the present analysis.

3. For other relatively recent histories of agriculture, see Giovanni Federico's *Feeding the World: An Economic History of Agriculture, 1800–2000* (Princeton, NJ: Princeton University Press, 2008), in which he synthesized two hundred years of agricultural development throughout the world in exploring the factors that affected agricultural performance: environment, accumulation of inputs, technical progress, institutional change, commercialization and agricultural policies. Christopher Isett and Stephen Miller's *The Social History of Agriculture: From the Origins to the Current Crisis* (Lanham, MD: Rowman & Littlefield, 2016) argued that people rather than markets were the primary agents of agricultural change. Wendell Berry argued that good farming is a cultural and spiritual discipline, not one limited to markets (*The Unsettling of America*, Counterpoint; reprint edition, 2015). These and other studies do not narrowly focus on how the markets for land influenced not just farming but settlement histories, a central concern of the present research.

4. Daniel Kahneman's "prospect theory" can be found in his *Thinking, Fast and Slow* (New York: Farrar, Straus & Giroux, 2011).

5. Gary Saul Morson and Morton Schapiro, Cents and Sensibility: What Economics Can Learn from the Humanities (Princeton NJ: Princeton University Press, 2017). According to Robert Skidelsky, "A dose of realism, or even a cursory knowledge of history, would have told these savants that markets do not work in this way." See his Money and Government: The Past and Future of Economics (Yale University Press, 2018).

6. For how mass humanities might fill some of the quantitative gaps in evidence, see Robert Mitchell's *Human Geographies Within the Pale of Settlement: Order and Disorder During the Eighteenth and Nineteenth Centuries* (New York: Macmillan-Palgrave, 2018, Chapter 9). And for the history of how the dictionary of economic terms influenced the questions and assumptions economists make, see Robert E. Mitchell *The Language of Economics: Socially Constructed Vocabulary and Assumptions* (New York: Macmillan-Palgrave, 2016) and *A Concise History of Economists' Assumptions about Markets: From Adam Smith to Joseph Schumpeter* (Santa Barbara, CA: Praeger, 2014).

7. Madison Kuhn, "Tiffin, Morse, and

the Reluctant Pioneer," *Michigan History*, L (1966), 111, 113. Kuhn does not attempt to answer his questions but instead covers the views and often questionable information that the public had about the Michigan Territory.

8. See *William Jarvis & the Merino Sheep Craze* on Vermont Historical Society's website at https://vermonthistory.org/educate/online-resources/an-era-of-great-change/work-changing-markets/william-jarvis-s-merino-sheep.

9. Donald Parkerson, *The Agricultural Transition in New York State: Markets and Migration in Mid-Nineteenth Century America* (Ames: Iowa State University Press, 1995).

10. Douglas Helms, "Soil and Southern History," *Agricultural History*, 74:4 (2000): 732–58.

11. David Hackett Fischer, *Albion's Seeds: Four British Folkways in America* (Oxford University Press, 1989).

12. Robert Darnton, *The Great Cat Massacre and Other Episodes in French Cultural History* (New York: Vintage Books, 1985).

13. See the concerns covered by the Agricultural History Society at http://www.aghistorysociety.org/. See Robert Sweirenga's "The New Rural History: Defining The Parameters," *Great Plains Quarterly* (Fall, 1981) available online at https://digitalcommons.unl.edu/cgi/viewcontent.cgi?article=2871&context=greatplainsquarterly. Most of the other schools of analysis have their own journals.

14. See Robert Fogel, "The New Economic History. Its Findings and Methods," *Economic History Review* (December, 1966). Also Claude Diebolt and Michael Haupert, "A Cliometric Counterfactual: What If There Had Been Neither Fogel nor North?" *Cliometrica* (September 2018, Vol. 12, Issue 3, 407–434.)

15. Frederick Jackson Turner, *The Frontier in American History* (New York: Henry Holt, 1920). Many historians savaged Turner's thesis. See William N. Parker, "From Northwest to Mid-West: Social Bases of a Regional History," in Klingaman and Vedder, *Essays in Nineteenth Century Economic History*, 3–34. Billington, among others, argued that many of Turner's assumptions could not be substantiated. Ray Allen Billington, "How the Frontier Shaped American Character," *American Heritage: The Magazine of History* (April, 1958). For other critics including Louis Hacker's attack on "Turner's Myopia" and "exceptionalism," see Richard Etulain, ed. *Does the Frontier Make America Exceptional?* (Boston, St. Martin's Press, 1999) at http://www.h-net.org/reviews/showrev.php?id=3689 Also see Ray Allen Billington and Martin Ridge, *Westward Expansion* (New York: Macmillan, 5th ed., 1982). For other works covering public-domain states, see Arlene Eakle and Johni Cerny, eds., *The Source: A Guidebook of American Genealogy* (Ancestry, 1984), 224 ff.

16. Stephen Thernstrom, *Poverty and Progress: Social Mobility in a Nineteenth Century City* (Cambridge, MA: Harvard University Press, 1964), 31.

17. I did not find any female-headed farmer-settler households in my research.

18. See Fred Block and Margaret Somers, The Power of Market Fundamentalism: Karl Polanyi's Critique (Harvard University Press, 2014). There is a vast literature on the different meanings of a "public good" such as something that is useful for the public generally, such as education and infrastructure, although these are not "public goods" in the economic sense. This is in contrast to a "common good," one that is non-excludable but is rivalrous to a certain degree. Polanyi and others argue that land was not humanly produced and thereby is something held in common by the general public. Nations differ in how they understand "land." Some countries only assign ownership to what is on top of the land, not the minerals, water and petroleum underneath it. In the United States, ownership covers both levels. Polanyi and others remind us in the United States that there are many ways to define markets, private vs. public property and how markets can be organized and managed. For an analysis of alternative ways to link political and market institutions supportive of economic development, see Yuen Yuen Ang, "Autocracy With Chinese Characteristics: Beijing's Behind-the-Scenes Reforms," Foreign Affairs (May/June, 2018).

19. Adam Smith saw wealth in the great variety of goods that people traded and consumed. He also argued that gold and silver (perhaps like land) did not have an absolute value. Instead there were commodities whose value rose and fell with supply and demand. Smith held that it is not the possession of gold and silver or other items of wealth that creates a nation's economic power; it is the production of what people want and can use.

20. Historians are aware of the multiple C's of historical thinking about change over time—causality, context, complexity, and contingency. See, for example, Sam Wineburg's *Historical Thinking and Other Unnatural Acts* (Philadelphia: Temple University Press, 2001) and George Iggers' critique of the Hegel school of history in his previously-referenced *Historiography in the*

Twentieth Century: From Scientific Objectivity to the Postmodern Challenge.

21. Paul W. Gates, *History of Public Land Law Development* (Superintendent of Documents, 1968); *The Jeffersonian Dream: Studies in the History of American Land Policy and Development* (University of New Mexico Press, 1996); "The Homestead Law in an Incongruous Land System," *American Historical Review* (XL, 1935–1936); *The Farmer's Age: Agriculture 1815–1860* (Armonk, NY: M.E. Sharpe, 1989).

22. In her *A History of the Modern Fact: Problems of Knowledge in the Sciences of Wealth and Society* and *Genres of the Credit Economy: Mediating Value in Eighteenth-and Nineteenth-Century Britain* Mary Poovey explored how key terms, metaphors, images, conjectures and mental models were "operationalized" as facts that could be counted (numbers became important) and combined with other numbered facts to create evidence-based hypotheses and models of markets and economies more generally. Facts, of course, do not add up to history, as Immanuel Wallerstein and others noted for decades. (Immanuel Wallerstein, *The Limits of Nineteenth-Century Paradigms: Unthinking Social Science*, Temple University Press, 2001, second edition.) Our knowledge and truths are "social creations" that we use to understand the world, including markets and economies. That is one of the reasons why it is helpful to understand the history of the different disciplines. See my *The Language of Economics: Socially Constructed Vocabularies and Assumptions* (Palgrave, 2016), as well as Paul Lazersfeld and Morris Rosenberg's classic *The Language of Social Research* (The Free Press, 1955).

23. For this and other fallacies, see David Hackett Fischer, *Historians' Fallacies: Toward a Logic of Historical Thought* (Harper Torchbooks, 1970).

Chapter 1

1. Edward G. Lengel, *First Entrepreneur: How George Washington Built His – and the Nation's – Prosperity.* (Boston: Da Capo Press, 2016).

2. Critics might correctly argue that these antebellum speculators were not bandits "taking" or stealing land, since the original inhabitants did not claim legal ownership of their collective property. Still, as some critics might claim, the new United States of America sold land that was forcefully expropriated first by England and then by force of arms transferred to the American enemy that defeated its colonial owners. National entities, England and the United States, had legal standing denied the original often roving inhabitants. That is, the closing of the American frontier was led by big government selling off other peoples' land to provide a significant source of public revenues. Mancur Olson's public choice theories on the stationary and roving bandits has yet to be recast for an understanding of America's own early history. See Mancur Olson, "Dictatorship, Democracy and Development," American Political Science Review (September, 1993) and, among his other public-choice writings, The Logic of Collective Action: Public Goods and the Theory of Groups (Harvard University Press, 1971). Olson was concerned with authoritarian heads of state, not settler-investors such as his father, a North Dakota wheat farmer, as well as my own maternal grandparents, Duncan and Maude Wayne, early non-pirate pioneer farmer-settlers in the middle of Michigan. An immigrant from Simcoe, Ontario, Duncan held the record for the longest elected official in Michigan. In addition to his services on the Midland Board of Supervisors, he was thrice elected to the Michigan House of Representatives.

3. The other additions were from two treaties with Spain in 1819 (72,003 square miles in primarily present-day Florida), the Texas accession in 1845 (390,143 square miles), border treaties with Great Britain that led to adding the Oregon Territory in 1846 (285,580 square miles), the Mexican Cession of 1848 (529,017 square miles) and the Gadsden Purchase of 1853 (29,640 square miles). Historical Statistics, Series J, 1–2. There are multiple settlement histories and disciplinary perspectives on them. For a recent narrative account of how prairie states' post-bellum lands were settled, see David Danbom, Sod Busting: How Families Made Farms on the Nineteenth-Century Plains (Johns Hopkins, 2014).

4. For expansion in Canada, see David Harvey, *Americans in Canada, Migration and Settlement Since 1840* (E. Mellen Press, 1991). John Ladell, *They Left Their Mark: Surveyors and Their Role in the Settlement of Ontario* (Dundurn Press, 1993). Gregory Rose, "The Origins of Canadian Settlers in Southern Michigan, 1820–1850," *Ontario History* 79:1 (1987): 31–52. For an example of Russia's expansion, see Fernand Braudel, *The Perspective of the World, Civilization & Capitalism 15th–18th Century* (New York: Harper & Row, 1984), 455–462. For a multi-country perspective, see John Weaver, *The Great Land Rush and the Makings of the Modern*

World, 1650–1900 (McGill-Queen's University Press, 2003). And for an eye-opening worldwide perspective, see Jürgen Osterhammel, *The Transformation of the World: A Global History of the Nineteenth Century* (Princeton University Press, 2014).

5. Paul W. Gates, *History of Public Land Law Development* (Superintendent of Documents, 1968), 285.

6. Gates, *History*, 72–73.

7. Thomas Cooley, *Michigan: A History of Governments* (New York: Houghton, Mifflin, 1906), 128–29. Also, among others, Andro Linklater, *Measuring America* (Walker, 2002), Chapter 6, including page 82.

8. Cooley, 128.

9. Linklater, *Measuring America*, 148–50; Gary Nash, *The Unknown American Revolution* (Viking, 2005), 171–2. In his letter of 1767 to his agent William Crawford, George Washington wrote "Any person ... who neglects the present opportunity of hunting out good lands, and in some measure making them for his own, in order to keep others from settling them, will never again regain them. From John C. Weaver, *The Great Land Rush and the Making of the Modern World, 1650–1900* (McGill-Queen's University Press, 2003), 88.

10. Gates, *History*, 124.

11. Gates, *History*, 91.

12. Gates, *History*, 91. Gates (p. 92) reported that Michigan had 280,769 acres of "confirmed private land claims" from pre-Revolutionary settlers.

13. Mancur Olson, *Dictatorship, Democracy, and Development* (American Political Science Review, Vol. 87, Issue 3, 1993).

14. Before 1796, at least in Ohio, a different numbering system was used during the first survey under the Land Ordnance of 1785. Surveyors' first partial section was set as number 1 in the lower right-hand corner.

15. Deed records indicate occasional deviations from this locational system.

16. Linklater, *Measuring America*; C. Albert White, *A History of the Rectangular Survey* (Superintendent of Documents, 1983); E. Wade Hone, *Land & Property Research in the United States* (Ancestry, 1997). This cadastral approach was different from the prose style metes and bounds procedures used in colonial America. Up to the time of the Revolutionary War, or until about the beginning of the nineteenth century, land, when parcelled out, and sold or granted, was described by "Metes and Bounds" and that system is still in existence in the following States, or in those portions of them which had been sold or granted when the present plan of surveys was adopted: New York, Pennsylvania, New Jersey, Delaware, Maryland, Virginia, North and South Carolina, Georgia, Tennessee, Kentucky, Texas and the six New England States. To describe land by "Metes and Bounds" is to have a known landmark for a place of beginning, and then follow a line according to the compass-needle (or magnetic bearing), or the course of a stream, or track of an ancient highway. This plan has resulted in endless confusion and litigation, as landmarks decay and change, and it is a well-known fact that the compass-needle varies and does not always point due North." See "Analysis of the System of United States Land Surveys" available online at http://www.surveyhistory.org/metes_&_bounds_vs__public_lands.htm Colorado and Hawaii use a lot and block designation system.

17. According to one source, a "hardwood stake was driven into the ground at each section corner, with about a foot length left showing above the ground." Willis Dunbar and George May, *Michigan: A History of the Wolverine State* (Eerdmans, 1995), 155. John Gordon wrote in the diary he kept during his 1836 visit to Michigan that "The 4 sides of sections are marked by blazed trees and the corners ... have 4 trees numbered ..." John M. Gordon, "A Speculator's Diary," Justin Kestenbaum, ed., *The Making of Michigan 1820–1860: A Pioneer Anthology* (Detroit: Wayne State University Press, 1990), 135.

18. Lowell O. Steward, *Public Land Surveys: History, Instructions, Methods* (Collegiate Press, 1935), 146. Also Hugh Prince, *Wetlands of the American Midwest: A Historical Geography of Changing Attitudes* (University of Chicago Geography Research Paper No. 241, 1997), 197.

19. Vernon Carstensen, "Introduction," in Vernon Carstensen, ed., *The Public Lands, Studies in the History of the Public Domain* (University of Wisconsin Press, 1968), xxii.

20. See Gates, *History*, 804–805 for the number of acres granted states for these different purposes. For other histories of laws governing the public domain, see Thomas Donaldson, *The Public Domain: Its History, with Statistics* (45th Cong., 3d sess., House. Ex. doc 47, pt. 4); Vernon Carstensen, *The Public Lands: Studies in the History of the Public Domain* (University of Wisconsin Press, 1968); Benjamin Hibbard, *A History of the Public Land Policies* (University of Wisconsin Press, 1965); Roy Robbins, *Our Landed Heritage: The Public Domain 1776–1936* (University of Nebraska Press, 1962); James W. Oberly, *Sixty Million Acres: American Veterans and the Public Lands before the Civil War* (Kent University Press, 1990). For

a list of annual reports of the Commissioner of General Land Office, see *CIS US Serial Set Index Part 1, American State Papers and the 15th–34th Congresses 1789–1857* and *Part II 35th–45th Congresses 1857–1879* Subject Indexes (Washington: Congressional Information Service, 2000).

21. For a history of GLO, see Milton Canover, *The General Land Office: Its History, Activities, Organization* (Johns Hopkins Press, 1923).

22. Patricia Kelly Hall and Steven Ruggles, "'Restless in the Midst of Their Prosperity': New Evidence on the Internal Migration of Americans, 1860–2000," *Journal of American History*, XCI (2004), 829–843.

23. *Ibid.*

24. Douglas Helms, "Soil and Southern History," *Agricultural History*, 74:4 (2000): 723–58.

25. Jeremy Atack and Fred Bateman, *To Their Own Soil: Agriculture in the Antebellum North* (Ames: Iowa State University Press, 1987). Their other research results will be referenced later.

26. The microfilms were kindly made available through a local open-access family history library supported by The Church of the Latter Day Saints (Mormons).

27. Including one or two prominent citizens who, according to other sources, were "half Indian."

28. For an overview of some of these analytical challenges, see Robert E Mitchell "Antebellum Farm-Settlement Patterns: A Three-Level Approach to Assessing the Effects of Soils," *Journal of Interdisciplinary History*, (Winter, 2011). This article did not place America's settlement history in the context covered in the present chapter.

29. Steven Stoll, *Larding the Lean Earth: Soil and Society in Nineteenth-Century America* (New York: Hill & Wang, 2002) 14.

30. As my 1950s graduate school neighbor and friend Robert Wiebe did in his The Search for Order, 1877–1920 (New York: Hill & Wang, 1966).

31. Miles Fairburn, *Social History: Problems, Strategies and Methods* (New York: St. Martin's 1999, 43. His reference is to T. Burnard, "Ethnicity in Colonial America Historiography: A New Organising Principle?" *Australasian Journal of American Studies*, Vol. 11 (July 1992), 4.

Chapter 2

1. Although there are many maps of the states carved out of the Northwest Territory, the federal, state and university archives as well as the online map sites the author contacted were unable to identify the original sources of these maps and if they are copyrighted. Among the many options I am unable to use can be found at http://www.ohiohistorycentral.org/w/Northwest_Territory; https://www.ultimateglobes.com/Northwest-Territory-1787-map-018-p/km-30053.htm and https://en.wikipedia.org/wiki/File:Northwest-territory-usa-1787.png#/media/File:Northwest-territory-usa-1787.png

2. Douglas Gordon and George May, eds., "Michigan Journal, 1836, John M. Gordon," *Michigan History* (43:3, September 1959): 258–59, 268–69.

3. Guy Smith and Andrew Aandahl, "Soil Classification and Surveys," in *Soil: The Yearbook of Agriculture 1957*, 396.

4. Hulbert, *Soil*, 70.

5. Gordon and May, "Michigan Journal," 270–71.

6. Kenneth Lewis, *West to Far Michigan: Settling the Lower Peninsula, 1815–1860* (Michigan State University Press), 35, 55.

7. Hulbert, *Soil*, 133.

8. Donald Parkerson, *The Agricultural Transition in New York State: Markets and Migration in Mid-Nineteenth Century America* (Ames: Iowa State University Press, 1995), 69.

9. Hulbert, *Soil* 63, 72.

10. The State Legislature meeting for the first time in 1837 established the State Geological Survey with Douglass Houghton holding the position of state geologist.

11. Gates, *The Farmer's Age Agriculture*, Chapters 15 and 16. Also see Atack, Bateman and Parker, "The Farm, the Farmer, and the Market," 270–74.

12. If Midland County, Michigan is any example, then the enumerators for the 1860 census also commented on the agricultural potential of areas in their census districts. There is no information on whether these observations were made public.

13. Prince, *Wetlands of the American Midwest*, 139.

14. Gates, *History of Public Land Law Development*, 263.

15. Prince, *Wetlands of the American Midwest*, 139.

16. Gates, *History of Public Land Law Development*, 325. Michigan and other states established their own land offices to administer the privatization of these and other lands granted to them. Gordon and May, "Michigan Journal," 281. The seasons during which surveys were made no doubt affected what the surveyors reported. Wintertime work

would miss frozen bogs and swamps. Gordon and May, "Michigan Journal," 281.

17. Mary Marjorie True Dooley, *The Andrews Bailiwick: A Geographic Study of Migration to the Settlement of Northern Macomb County, Michigan, 1810–1850, as Perceived by Selected Participants* (Ph.D. dissertation, Michigan State University, 1975), xviii.

18. Madison Kuhn, "Tiffin, Morse, and the Reluctant Pioneer," *Michigan History*, L (1966), 113. Surrounded by the large navigable Great Lakes, Michigan had a number of "port" cities. However, during the pre-1860s, these small ports served economically-weak hinterlands. The development of mining and lumbering industries certainly contributed to the sometimes temporary expansion of some ports. A history of Great Lakes port cities (american and Canadian) has yet to be written.

19. Lewis, *West to Far Michigan*, 25.

20. Prince, *Wetlands*, 119.

21. Prince, *Wetlands*, 27.

22. Gates, *History of Public Land Law Development*, 182. For swamps in Minnesota see Cheri Register, *The Big Marsh: The Story of a Lost Landscape* (St. Paul: Minnesota Historical Society, 2016).

23. Stoll, *Larding the Lean Earth*, 14.

24. Franklin Thomas, *The Environmental Basis of Society: A Study in the History of Sociological Theory* (Century, 1925), Chapter 6; Michael Conzen, "The Historical Impulse in Geographical Writing about the United States, 1850–1990," in Michael Conzen, Thomas Rumney and Graeme Wynn, eds., *A Scholar's Guide to Geographical Writing on the American and Canadian Past* (University of Chicago Press, 1993), 3–90; Douglas Helms, "Soil and Southern History," *Agricultural History*, 74:4 (2000); Walter Martin Kollmorgen, *The German-Swiss in Franklin County Tennessee: A Study of the Significance of Cultural Considerations in Farming Enterprises* (U.S. Department of Agriculture, Bureau of Economic Economics, 1940), 106–07; also references in Helms "Soil and Southern History", 756, and Stoll, *Larding the Lean Earth.*

25. *Soil: The Yearbook of Agriculture 1957* (Government Printing Office, 1957).

26. L.A. Dean, "Plant Nutrition and Soil Fertility," in *Soil: The Yearbook of Agriculture 1957*, 80.

27. Marlow Vesterby, Robbin Shoemaker, Ralph Heimlich and Margot Anderson, *1.3. Land and Soil Quality*, a United States Department of Agriculture online document at http://www.ers.usda.gov/publications/arei/ah712/AH71213a.PDF: 41.

28. Vesterby, *1.3. Land and Soil*, 47.

29. United States Department of Agriculture, National Resources Conservation Service, *State Soils*, an online publication at http://soils.usda.gov/gallery/state_soils/, 1.

30. *Average Crop, Pasture, and Forestry Productivity Ratings for Illinois Soils* (University of Illinois College of Agricultural, Consumer and Environmental Sciences, Bulletin 810, 2000):,4. Also see http://www.npwrc.usgs.gov/resource/1998/rlandscp/rlandscp.htm.

31. W.H. Allaway, "Cropping Systems and Soil," *Yearbook of Agriculture*, 387. These and other cropping evidence suggest, as did Arnaud Costinot and Dave Donaldson, that some areas (regions or soils, growing season and more) have a comparative advantage in some crops. See their "How Large Are the Gains from Economic Integration? Theory and Evidence from U.S Agriculture, 1880–1997," *Econometrica* (November 2016).

32. J. B. Fehrenbacher, et al, *Soils of Illinois* (University of Illinois Agricultural Experiment Station Bulletin 778, 1984), 69.

33. Susan E. Gray, *The Yankee West, Community Life on the Michigan Frontier* (Chapel Hill: University of North Carolina Press, 1996), 202.

34. Hulbert, *Soils*, 71–72; In addition to soil and vegetation classifications, there are environmental delineations, ecological regions, watersheds, and landscape ecosystems that combine biotic and abiotic dimensions. Dennis A. Albert, *Regional Landscape Ecosystems of Michigan, Minnesota, and Wisconsin: A Working Map and Classification* (U.S. Department of the Interior, U.S. Geological Survey, Northern Prairie Wildlife Research Center, 1994) available online at http://www.npwrc.usgs.gov/resource/1998/rlandscp/rlandscp.htm.

35. The 800 figure comes from *Average Crop, Pasture and Forestry Productivity Ratings for Illinois Soils*, 3. Associations appear to be similar to if not equivalent to "series." The 430 figure comes from Fehrenbacher, *Soils of Illinois*, 1.

36. *Introduction to the Soils of Wisconsin* (Wisconsin Geological and Natural History series, Education series No. 10, 1955), 8.

37. E. P. Whiteside, I.F. Schneider, and R. L. Cooke, *Soils of Michigan* (Soil Science Department, Agricultural Experiment Station, Michigan State University, 1956), 32.

38. See http://soils.usda.gov/survey/printed_surveys/ Some of the links cited in footnotes may have changed their address over time.

39. Douglas Helms, "The Development of the Land Capability Classification,"

in his *Readings in the History of the Soil Conservation Service* (Washington, D.C.: United States Department of Agriculture, Natural Resources Conservation Service, 1992), 1. Also available online at http://www.nrcs.usda.gov/about/history/articles/LandClassification.html.

40. Vesterby, *Land and Soil*, 42.

41. Gary Nash, *The Unknown American Revolution* (New York: Viking, 2005), 395.

42. Charles Freeman, *The Closing of the Western Mind: The Rise of Faith and the Fall of Reason* (New York: Alfred Knopf, 2003), 83.

43. Fernand Braudel, *The Wheels of Commerce* (New York: Harper & Row, 1982), 589. It appears that Braudel was referring to the Ming Dynasty (1368–1644).

44. Charles Ingrao, *The Habsburg Monarchy 1618–1815* (Cambridge, UK: Cambridge University Press, 2000), 171.

45. Helms, *The Development of Land Capability Classification*, 8.

46. "Productivity indices for crops provide a simple scale on which soils may be rated according to their suitability for several major crops under specified levels of management." *Average Crop, Pasture, and Forestry Productivity Ratings for Illinois Soils*, 61. As noted in the preface to the present book, all the sources cited in this and most other chapters were identified and recorded by the author before he moved from the Washington, DC area farther north.

47. Jeremy Atack and Fred Bateman, *To Their Own Soil, Agriculture in the Antebellum North*, 259–60, 175–179. This study is based on information taken from the individual agricultural and population schedules from a sample of townships enumerated in the 1860 census.

48. Richard A. Easterlin, "Farm Production and Income in Old and New Areas at Mid-Century," in David Klingaman and Richard Vedder, eds., *Essays in Nineteenth Century Economic History: The Old Northwest* (Ohio University Press, 1975), 81, 90–91. Later we will note questions raised about the published data Easterlin used. American yields per acre were low compared with those in Europe. Jeremy Atack, Fred Bateman, and William Parker, "The Farm, the Farmer, and the Market," in Stanley Engerman and Robert Gallman, eds., *The Cambridge Economic History of the United States* (Cambridge University Press, 1966), 260.

49. Atack and Bateman, *To Their Own Soil*, 164. 172–73.

50. P.W. Mausel, E.C.A. Runge, and S. G. Carmer, *Soil Productivity Indexes for Illinois Counties and Soil Associations* (University of Illinois, College of Agriculture, Agricultural Experiment Station Bulletin 752, 1975), 2.

51. *The 2000 Wisconsin Agricultural Statistics*, kindly provided the author by the Wisconsin Agricultural Statistics Service, 19–23.

52. Richard Easterlin, "Interregional Differences in Per Capita Income, Population, and Total Income, 1840–1950," in National Bureau of Economic Research, *Trends in the American Economy in the Nineteenth Century* (Princeton, NJ: Princeton University Press, 1960), 98.

53. Atack and Bateman, *To Their Own Soil*, 243.

54. Jeremy Atack and Fred Bateman, "Yeoman Farming: Antebellum America's Other 'Peculiar Institution,'" in Lou Ferleger, ed., *Agriculture and National Development: Views on the Nineteenth Century* (Iowa State University Press, 1990), 43.

55. Atack and Bateman, *To Their Own Soil*, 216

56. Atack and Bateman, *To Their Own Soil*, 256–57. It would have been helpful to have had more location-specific information on smaller and larger farms.

57. For other approaches, see Alan Bogue and Margaret Beattie Bogue, "Profits and the Frontier Land Speculator," *Journal of Economic History*, 17:1 9March 1957): 1–24. Robert Swierenga. "Quantitative Methods in Rural Landholding," *Journal of Interdisciplinary History*, 13:4 91983): 787–808.

58. J. O. Veatch, *Agricultural Land Classification and Land Types in Michigan* (Michigan State College Agricultural Experiment Station Special Bulletin 231, 1941), 65.

59. Thomas Pressly and William Scofield, *Farm Real Estate Values in the United States by Counties, 1850–1959* (University of Washington Press, 1965), 6.

60. Atack and Bateman, *To Their Own Soil*, 118.

61. Value refers to the value of money at each census date. Pressly and Scofield, *Farm Real Estate Values*, 11.

62. Atack and Bateman, *To Their Own Soil*, 32. Farm tenure information was not collected until the 1880 census.

63. Atack and Bateman, *To Their Own Soil*, 111. For another classification based on census and local land assessment records, see Gray, *The Yankee West*, 106.

64. Dong Hyu Yang, *Aspects of United States Agriculture Circa 1860* (Ph.D. Dissertation, Harvard University, 1985), 14.

65. Both Ohio and Indiana had a net outflow of the "native born." They were partially offset by a net immigration of foreign-born. Richard Vedder and Lowell Gallaway," Migra-

tion and the Old Northwest," in Klingaman and Vedder, *Essays in Nineteenth Century Economic History*, 162–65.

66. Population figures for the present discussion are taken from Vedder and Gallaway, "Migration and the Old Northwest." For rural population statistics, see *Historical Statistics of the United States*: Series A195–209.

67. From instructions given to the census enumerators. See Atack and Bateman, *To Their Own Soil*, 118. Also, *1860 Census Instructions to Marshals*, provided by IPUMS at http://www.ipums.umn.edu/usa/voliii/inst1860.html

68. Vedder and Gallaway, "Migration in the Old Northwest," 170, 173.

69. Many Canadians, as well as Michigan settlers, were enticed to the area by promoter speculators who painted a false picture of the land they owned. Rose Lockwood Moore, *Of Berry Pickers, Shanty Boys, and the Jack Pine Bird: Patterns of Settlement and Subsistence in Nineteenth Century Oscoda County (Michigan)* (Master's Thesis, Western Michigan University, 1990), 39, 78.

70. Helms provides examples in his "Soils and Southern History."

71. See Stoll's study for examples of both good and bad soil management, as well as the western-migration of farmers who abandoned the land their own practices depleted. *Larding the Earth.*

72. Lewis D. Stillwell, "Migration from Vermont, 1776–1860," *Proceedings of the Vermont Historical Society* V (1937): 232, quoted in Gates, *The Farmer's Age*, 401. For an early Michigan settler's description of his native Vermont's land that had only been farmed for about fifty years by the late 1830s, see Edward W. Barber, "A Zion in the Wilderness," in Kestenbaum, *The Making of Michigan*, 160.

73. But note the earlier mention of other influences such as the length of the growing season, drainage, and more.

74. Atack and Bateman, *To Their Own Soil*, 256–57.

75. Atack and Bateman, *To Their Own Soil*, 115. These cautions also apply to the Vedder and Gallaway's report that Michigan had the highest elasticity of migration with respect to per capita income, a finding that seems at odds with Michigan's low farm income and rates-of-return.

76. Robert E Mitchell, "Using Pre-Settlement Vegetation Maps to Understand the Early History of Michigan's Lumber Industry," *Michigan Historical Review*, 37:2 (Fall 2011), 1–28.

77. For statistics, listings and analyses of antebellum statutes on the public domain, see Donaldson, *The Public Domain;* Gates, *History of Public Land Law Development;* Carstensen, *The Public Lands;* Hibbard, *A History of the Public Land Policies;* Robbins, *Our Landed Heritage: The Public Domain;*. Oberly, *Sixty Million Acres*. For a list of annual reports of the Commissioner of General Land Office, see *CIS US Serial Set Index Part 1, American State Papers and the 15th–34th Congresses 1789–1857* and *Part II 35th–45th Congresses 1857–1879* Subject Indexes (Congressional Information Service, 2000).

78. Carstensen, *The Public Lands* 481.

79. Arthur H. Cole, "Cyclical and Sectional Variations in the Sale of Public Lands, 1816–1860," *Review of Economics and Statistics* (Vol. 9, 1927): 41–53. Also Oberly, *Sixty Million Acres.*

80. For the number of acres nationally in each of five classes whose prices declined from $1 per acre down to 12.5 cents per acre, see Gates, *History of Public Land Law Development*, 188.

81. Cole, "Cyclical and Sectional Variations in the Sale of Public Lands, 1816–1860," 45. Cole did not refer to cultural and information influences on land sales.

82. Paul W. Gates, *The Jeffersonian Dream, Studies in the History of American Land Policy and Development* (University of New Mexico Press, 1996) 12.

83. Gates, *The Farmer's Age*, 81. His *Large-Scale Farming in Illinois, 1850 to 1870* (A paper read on December 28, 1931, at the joint session of the Agricultural History Society with the American Historical Association in Minneapolis) is an interesting overview of larger farms in different Illinois counties. Gates general overview did not link settlement patterns to soil endowments and the role of market imperfections. This paper can be found at http://www.aghistorysociety.org/pdf/articles/ag000085.pdf.

84. Acres sold are found in the Annual Reports of the Commissioner of General Land Offices to the 32nd and 33rd Congresses, as referenced in the *CIS US Serial Set Index Part 1*, 998. Ohio's Western Reserve and private sales are not provided in these annual reports. The percentages reported here are approximations, for as noted earlier, farms that did not have produce of at least $100 were not included in the 1850 agricultural census. Also it does not seem that grants to states are included in the sales figures.

85. Kuhn, "Tiffin Morse," 112, 115, 117, 119, 121, 126, 130, 133, 136.

86. Later chapters will explore the contributions of different soils to productivity and land values.

Chapter 3

1. Paul W. Gates, "The Homestead Law in an Incongruous Land System," *American Historical Review* XL (1935–1936): 652–81. Also Reginold Horsman, "Changing Images of the Public Domain: Historians and the Shaping of the Midwest Frontiers," *This Land is Ours* (Indianapolis Indiana Historical Society, 1978), 61.

2. Dallas Lee Jones, *The Survey and Sale of the Public Land in Michigan, 1815–1862* (Master's Thesis, Cornell University, 1952).

3. Yes, in other states as well. See Paul W. Gates, *Farmer's Age Agriculture 1815–1860*, 432.

4. Lewis, *West to Far Michigan*, 1, 3.

5. Gray, *The Yankee West*, 1. Her Ph.D. dissertation on which the book is based is titled *Family, Land, and Credit: Yankee Communities on the Michigan Frontier, 1830–1860* (University of Chicago, 1985).

6. For the spread of rational choice theories and their limitations, see the author's two books on the intellectual history of economics.

7. Archer Butler Hulbert, *Soil, Its Influence on the History of the United States* (New York: Russell & Russell, 1930), 50.

8. Arthur Field, "Road Patterns of Michigan," *Papers of the Michigan Academy of Science, Arts and Letters*, Vol. 14 (1930), 312.

9. Benson, *Logs and Lumber*: 2. Lumberman David Ward recalled his travel by canoe in April, 1859 from St. Louis on the on Pine River to Midland on the Tittabawassee River and then to Saginaw. David Ward, *The Autobiography of David Ward* (New York: private printing, 1912), 106.

10. See Michael McDonnell, Masters of Empire: Great Lakes Indians and the Making of America, (New York: Hill & Wang, 2015).

11. The significance of this form of social organization can be seen by comparing the acephalous Balanta, Guinea-Bissau's largest ethnic group and the Muslim Fulas (Fulani) and Mandingas with their larger lineages. See Carey Lifton, *Social Soundness and WID Analysis for USAID Legal Reform Project Paper* (1991). Guinea-Bissau is an ex-Portuguese colony in West Africa. The present author, a development member of the United States Agency for International Development in this ex-Portuguese colony, designed, commissioned and oversaw Lifton's work.

12. Mary Margaret Montfort, *Ethnic and Tribal Identity Among the Saginaw Chippewa of Nineteenth Century Michigan* (Master's Thesis, Michigan State University, 1990).

13. Wilbur R. Jacobs, "The Indian and the Frontier in American History—A Need for Revision," in David Ward, ed., *Geographic Perspectives on America's Past* (Oxford University Press, 1979), 73. For an in-depth report on Michigan Amerindians, see Charles E. Cleland, *Rites of Conquest: The History and Cultures of Michigan's Native Americans* (University of Michigan Press, 1992). His maps following page 148 show only one "tribe" in the Lower Peninsula during 1600–1650, none in 1670, three in 1800 and 13 "bands" in the 1820 to 1840 period.

14. My maternal great grandmother's third of four husbands, James Whitman, a member of perhaps Midland's first white settler, reported on his "Indian" neighbors in "Has Lived in Midland County Longer Than Any Other Man," *The Midland Sun* (May 1, 1924).

15. Jacobs, "The Indian and the Frontier," 72.

16. Malcolm J. Rohrbough, *The Land Office Business, the Settlement and Administration of American Public Lands 1789–1837* (Wadsworth, 1990), 66.

17. Jones, *The Survey and Sale of the Public Land in Michigan, 1815–1862* (Cornell University Master of Arts Thesis, 1952): 4–6. For a history of treaties with Michigan Amerindians, see Helen Hornbeck Tanner, mapping the Grand Traverse Indian Country: The Contribution of Peter Dougherty," in *The Michigan Historical Review* (31:1, Spring 2005): 44–91. The Upper Peninsula was granted to Michigan in exchange for the Toledo area claimed by Ohio as part of the agreement that incorporated Michigan as the twenty-sixth state within the United States of America.

18. Cleland's Chapter 6 in his *Rites of Conquest* is titled "Not the Feelings of Their Hearts." Henry Schoolcraft was accused of trickery in his negotiations with the Saginaw Chippewa. Michael A. Leeson, *History of Saginaw County, Michigan* (Chapman, 1881), 157. For an international comparative history of land-taking among indigenous peoples, see John C. Weaver, *The Great Land Rush.*

19. Barbara E. Benson, *Logs and Lumber: The Development of Lumbering in Michigan's Lower Peninsula 1837–1870* (Clarke Historical Library, Central Michigan University, 1989), 27.

20. Harriette M. Dilla, *The Politics of Michigan 1865–1878* (AMS Press, 1970 reprint), 240; Jones, *The Survey and Sale*, 17.

21. Dunbar and May, *Michigan*, 93. Where possible, I will refer to sources specific to Michigan rather than to the excellent histories of American land disposal policies,

such as Gates' *History of Public Land Law Development.*

22. Robbins, *Our Landed Heritage*, 170. Greeley referred to the development of the Graduation Act.

23. Gates, *The Farmers Age*, 72.

24. Monica Prasad has written on the fallout of food gluts. See her *A Land of Too Much* (Harvard, 2012).

25. For a review of Canadian settlement policies in the 1840s, see John Laddell, *They Left Their Mark: Surveyors and Their Role in the Settlement of Ontario* (Dundurn, 1993), 133–35, 144. As noted earlier, American surveyors under contract to the General Land Office were required to assess the agricultural potential of the land they covered. These observations and the results of the surveyors' field notes were made readily available to the general public thus helping to reduce some information costs.

26. Jeremy Atack and Fred Bateman, "Yeoman Farming," 31–33.

27. The figures for 109 40-acre Michigan farms indicated that $754 for the (undefined term) farm, $47 for implements, and $171 for livestock. An 80-acre farm required $1,556 for these same expenses, while the 160-acre unit required $3,285. Atack and Bateman, "Yeoman Farming", 31–33.

28. Atack and Bateman, "Yeoman Farming," 33, 45.

29. For studies more generally on the private (not public) holders of debt, see Robert E. Wright, *One Nation Under Debt: Hamilton, Jefferson, and the History of What We Owe* (New York: McGraw-Hill, 2008), and *The Wealth of Nations Rediscovered* (Cambridge, 2002), as well as Robert E. Wright and Richard E. Sylla, *Genealogy of American Finance* (New York: Columbia University Press, 2015), and *U.S. Government Bond Trading Database, 1776–1835* at http://eh.net/database/u-s-government-bond-trading-database-1776-1835/.

30. James W. Oberly is a major source of information and analysis of the national acts. Oberly, *Sixty Million Acres*, Table 1 (p. 3) summarizes the different size warrants for the four national acts.

31. Benson, *Logs and Lumber*, 22.

32. Oberly, *Sixty Million Acres*, 162.

33. Oberly, *Sixty Million Acres*, 170.

34. Calculated from Oberly's Table 14, *Sixty Million Acres*, 86–87.

35. Benson, *Logs and Lumber*, 22–23.

36. Jones, *The Survey and Sale*, 26–27, as well as 17–20. For dates that sales began in different counties, see his page 40. For a history of surveys, see Linklater, *Measuring America.*

37. Prince, *Wetlands and the American Midwest*, 137. Canadian surveyors were also specifically instructed to look for good agricultural land. Laddell, *They Left Their Mark*, 135.

38. Thomas Vale, *Plants and People: Vegetation Change in North America* (Association of American Geographers, 1982), 57.

39. Jones, *The Survey and Sale*, 67.

40. From Vol. J1, page 52 in the surveyors' original notes available in the archives of the Bureau of Land Management.

41. Norman C. Caldwell, *Surveyors of the Public Lands in Michigan, 1808–2000* (N.C. Caldwell, 2001), 17.

42. The township names can be found in the non-indexed files RG 67–27 of the Michigan State Archives.

43. *Annual Report of the Commissioner of the State Land Office* (Joint Document No. 4 dated December 1, 1855, State of Michigan, Legislature, 1855), 11.

44. For the names and dates of these thirteen, see *Preliminary Inventory of Land-Entry Papers.* Congressional action was required to make additions and changes. See, for example, *Laws of the United States of a Local or Temporary Character and Exhibiting the Entire Legislation of Congress Upon Which the Public Land Titles in Each State and Territory Have Depended* (Government Printing Office, 1884), Vol. 1, 202, 213, 219.

45. For a brief summary of these operations, see *Preliminary Inventory of Land-Entry Papers*, 2–3.

46. Rohrbough, *The Land Office Business*: 197. Douglas H. Gordon and George S. May, eds., "Michigan Journal, 1836, John M. Gordon," *Michigan History* (43:3, September, 1959): 283.

47. Greffenius, *Development of Michigan Public Land Policy*, 240.

48. Harry N. Scheiber, "Land Reform, Speculation, and Governmental Failure: The Administration of Ohio's Canal Lands, 1836–60," *Prologue* (VII, 1975): 85.

49. Dorothy Langdon Yates, *Salt of the Earth: A History of Midland County Michigan* (The Midland County Historical Society, 1987), 27–28.

50. Benson, *Logs and Lumber*, 248.

51. Benson, *Logs and Lumber*, 18.

52. Lucile Kane, "Federal Protection of Public Timber in the Upper Great Lakes States," in Carstensn, *The Public Lands*, 441. For congressional opposition to federal enforcement efforts, see Gates, *History of Public Land Law Development*, 191.

53. Benson, *Logs and Lumber*, 20. For state efforts to avoid similar mischief in the purchase of primary school lands and the

credit provisions associated with these lands, see *Annual Report of the Commissioner of the State Land Office* (Joint Document No. 4 dated December 1, 1855, State of Michigan, Legislature 1855), 7.

54. Gates, *History of Public Land Law Development*, 536.

55. Benson, *Logs and Lumber*, 12.

56. Benson, *Logs and Lumber*, 235–37.

57. Farmers also sold timber from their clearing of land for cultivation.

58. Alan G. Bogue and Margaret Beattie Bogue, "'Profits' and the Frontier Land Speculator," in Carstenson, *The Public Lands*, 389.

59. John Clarke, *Land, Power, and Economics on the Frontier of Upper Canada* (McGill-Queen's University Press, 2001) from the online bibliographies of EH.NET reviewed by Douglas McCalla.

60. Gordon and May, "Michigan Journal," *Michigan History* (43:1, March, 1959): 10–14 and elsewhere in his journal published in three different issues of *Michigan History*.

61. Harold Reinholds, *The Free Banking Law: The Michigan Experience* (Ph.D. dissertation, Michigan State University, 1975), 91.

62. Gates. *The Farmer's Age*, 81.

63. Jones, *The Survey and Sale*, 134–35. Gates, *History of Public Land Law Development*, 168.The Carrolls were from a large slave-holding family in Maryland. See the various references to this family during the formative years of America in Nash, *The Unknown American Revolution*.

64. http://www.lib.cmich.edu/clarke/mpown.htm.

65. Moore, *Of Berry Pickers*, 88.

66. See for example, *Michigan Farmer* (1853): 7.

67. Benson, *Logs and Lumber*, 27. For the careful and systemic procedures one timber cruiser employer, see her description on page 27.

68. Jones, *The Survey and Sale*, 137.

69. "Higher" is in reference to the price proclaimed by law. This was a price-regulated market, and all land, regardless of soil quality or location, had the same fixed price. The Graduation Act introduced a sliding price scale.

70. Stephen Schoene, as reported in Oberly, *Sixty Million Acres*, 163–64.

71. Robert Fogel and Jack Rutner as referenced in Robert Swierenga, "Quantitative Methods in Rural Landholding," *Journal of Interdisciplinary History* (1983, 13:4): 802–03.

72. Lee Soltow, "The Growth of Wealth in Ohio, 1800–1969," in Klingaman and Vedder, *Essays in Nineteenth Century Economic History*, 191–207.

73. Andrew Cayton and Peter Onuf, *The Midwest and the Nation: Rethinking the History of an American Region* (Indiana University Press, 1990), 36.

74. Gates, *The Farmers Age*, 399. Atack, Bateman and Parker, "The Farm, the Farmer, and the Market", 278.

75. Ruben J. E. Greffenius, *Development of Michigan Public Land Policy* (University of Michigan Ph.D. dissertation, 1968) 149 (Table VI).

76. Gates, *History of Public Land Law Development*, 325, 384–85, 804–06.

77. Gates, *History of Public Land Law Development*, 296. This Act also provided 72 sections for what became the University of Michigan, 5 sections for public buildings, 46,080 acres of saline lands, and 5 percent "of the net proceeds from land sales for roads and canals."

78. Benson, *Logs and Lumber*, 29. University land was to be sold for $20 but lowered later to $12.

79. Benson, *Logs and Lumber*, 29.

80. A complete listing of these microfilm reports available at the Law Library of the Library of Congress appear in the *CIS US Serial Set Index, Part I: American State Papers and the 15th–34th Congresses 1789–1857, Subject Index, L–Z* and *Part II, 35th–45th Congresses 1857–1879, Subject Index, L–Z* (Congressional Information Service: n.d.). For Part I, see pages 998–1002, 1126–31. For Part II, see pages 630–31, 694–98. My subsequent references to the Commissioner's annual reports are specified in these two sets of indexes.

81. *Annual Report of the Commissioner of the State Land Office* (Joint Document No. 5 dated December 1, 1849, State of Michigan, Legislature, 1850), 6.

82. Only the surveyors' notes on township boundaries are in the archives of the Bureau of Land Management.

83. *Annual Report of the Commission of the State Land Office*, 10–11.

84. Gates, *History of Public Land Law Development*, 323.

85. Benson, *Logs and Lumber*, 29.

86. Jones, *The Survey and Sale*: 95. Benson, *Logs and Lumber*, 29.

87. For a brief description of each road, see Donaldson, *The Public Domain*, 798–800. Also see Graydon M. Meints, *Michigan Railroads & Railroad Companies* (Michigan State University Press, 1992). Gates lists 1,695,510 acres, but over time the total rose to 3,134,058. Gates, *History of Public Land Law Development*, 379, 384.

88. Karl Reynold Hosford, *Evolution of the Organizational Structuring and Land*

Resource Responsibilities of the Department of Natural Resources in Michigan, 1785–1978 (Ph.D. Dissertation, Michigan State University, 1979), 31. Greffenius, *Development of Michigan Public Land Policy*, 174.

89. Three other canal grants were approved in 1865 and 1866. Donaldson, *The Public Domain*, 258. This publication gives one of the earliest summaries of patent totals.

90. Greffenius, *Development of Michigan Public Land Policy*, 219.

91. See, for example, Greffenius, *Development of Michigan Public Land Policy*, 210. Speculators were said to have dominated Michigan's early legislatures. Robbins, *Our Landed Heritage*, 64.

92. Gates, *History of Public Land Law Development*, 336.

93. Jones, *The Survey and Sale*, 88, 203–04. No information is available on how much was actually in scrip form.

94. Saint Mary's Falls Ship Canal Company, *560,000 Acres Pine Lands in the State of Michigan* (Detroit: H. Barnes, 1857). Also, Ronald Maybee, *Michigan's White Pine Era, 1840–1900* (Michigan Historical Commission, 1960), 16. For mineral lands under the same grant, see Irene D. Neu, "The Mineral Lands of the St. Mary's Falls Ship Canal Company" in David Ellis, ed., *The Frontier in American Development* (Ithaca, NY: Cornell University Press, 1969), 162–191.

95. For a history of the debt and associated problems, see John D. Haeger, *The Investment Frontier: New York Businessmen and the Economic Development of the Old Northwest* (State University of New York, 1981), Chapter 11 "Eastern Capitalists and State Debts."

96. Among the several accounts of the causes and consequences of these events, see Ronald E. Seavoy, Borrowed Laws to Speed Development: Michigan 1835–1863," *Michigan History* (1975): 39–68.

97. 9. U.S. Statutes 519; 11. U.S. Statutes 251; 12. U.S. Statutes 3.

98. For Michigan's role in encouraging immigration, a pamphlet titled *The Emigrant's Guide to Michigan* in both German and English. See Dunbar and May, *Michigan*, 247.

99. Prince, *Wetlands*, 147.

100. LeRoy Barnett, "Roads, Railroads, Recreation: Swamplands and the Building of Michigan," *Michigan History* (72:4, 1988), 32.

101. For some of the illegal tricks banks employed, see Theodore H. Hinchman, *Banks and Banking in Michigan* (New York: Arno Press 1980 reprint of 1887 edition), 32–33; Gray, *Yankee West*, 45–46; and for general histories of banking in Michigan see Reinholds, *The Free Banking Law* and Carter Harry Golembe, *State Banks and the Economic Development of the West, 1830–44* (Ph.D. Dissertation, Columbia University, 1952). For a personal account of one Michigan county's bogus banking practices and the distress caused, especially among "the poorest classes of farmers," see Kirkland, *A New Home*, Chapters 31 and 32.

102. Seavoy, "Borrowed Laws", 45.

103. For examples, see Seavoy, "Borrowed Laws," 45.

104. Seavoy, "Borrowed Laws," 50.

105. For a list of banks, their location, capital and date they filed for organization with the Secretary of State, see Hinchman, *Banks and Banking*, 30–31, as well as 31–32 for private associations providing exchange and some banking functions.

106. Donald R. Adams, "The Role of Banks in the Economic Development of the Old North-West" in Klingaman and Vedder, *Essays in Nineteenth Century Economic History*, 223.

107. Hinchman, *Banks and Banking*, 56.

108. *Thompson's Bank Note and Commercial Reporter* (American Banker): August 21, 1854. This same source also listed retired banks, as well as three "private bankers" in its March 19, 1859 issue. For a recent history of Michigan banks, see Christopher Bailey, Tarique Hossain, Gary Pecquet, "Private banks in early Michigan, 1837–1884," *Cliometrica*, (January 2018, Vol. 12, Issue 1, pp 153–180).

109. William Parker, "The Finance of Capital Formation in Midwestern Development, 1800–1910," in Thomas Weiss and Donald Schaefer, eds., *American Economic Development in Historical Perspective* (Stanford University Press, 1994), 169.

110. Reinhold, "The Free Banking Law," 102–03.

111. John's relative James was my maternal great grandmother Elethier Whitman's third husband. She outlived all three as well as a fourth. See William A. and Laura McCreery, eds., *A Historical, Genealogical and Biographical Record of Some Members of the Alexander McCreery Clan of the United States and Canada* (privately published 1976.)

112. Prince, *Wetlands of the American West*, 162.

113. Weaver, *The Great Land Rush*, 249–50.

114. Atack, Bateman and Parker, "The Farm, the Farmer, and the Market," 274.

115. The title of his article in the *Review of Economic Statistics* (Harvard Univer-

sity Press, 1927): 41–53 and reprinted in Carstensen, *The Public Lands.*

116. For details, see Gates, *History of Public Land Law Development.* His chapter IX examines the effects of the Panic of 1837. Stanley Engerman and Robert Gallman, *The Cambridge Economic History of the United States* (New York: Cambridge University Press, 1996). Hugh Rockoff's contribution to this volume reports the stock of money fell 18.5 percent between 1856 and 1857. "Banking and Finance, 1789–1914": 667. Also see Oberly, "The Demand for Public Land, 1847–1860," Appendix D in his *Sixty Million Acres.* He argues that the Graduation Act was largely a southern phenomenon and therefore had little effect on the demand for land in the North—but that for "each rise of one cent in the wholesale price of wheat, nearly 79,000 additional acres of public lands were located by private individuals the next year..." (176). For the effects that crop failures in Europe had on the price of U.S. wheat and corn, see Robbins, *Our Landed Heritage,* 197. For a general economic history of pre-Civil War America, see Jeremy Atack and Peter Passell, *A New Economic View of American History* (Norton, 1994).

117. Greffenius suggests that Michigan's internal improvement lands listed as sold may have not been alienated—that is, sold to private owners. Instead, the state provided contractors with scrip for land in lieu of cash payments. I have not found information on how long it took for companies to sell the land to pay for their expenses. *Development of Michigan Public Land Policy,* 219.

Chapter 4

1. For the role that networks play in physical and human geographies, see the author's earlier-referenced *Human Geographies Within the Pale of Settlement: Order and Disorder During the Eighteenth and Nineteenth Centuries.*

2. The early parts of the present research overlaps with but is different from the innovative descriptive studies of Kenneth Lewis. He asked "What do we know about the course of agricultural colonization in antebellum Michigan and the variables that influenced this process?" Using maps, he tracked the population distribution using county population statistics, township formation dates, and post office establishment dates. Lewis, "Mapping Antebellum Euro-American Settlement Spread," *Michigan Historical* Review (Fall, 2004) 132.

3. This Lower Peninsula map is taken from Henry Francis Walling's *Atlas of the State of Michigan: Including Statistics and Descriptions of Its Topography, Hydrography, Climate, Natural and Civil History, Railways, Educational Institutions, Material Resources, etc.* courtesy of the Michigan County Histories and Atlases Digitization Project https://quod.lib.umich.edu/m/micounty/ Among the more recent Lower Peninsula maps are the readable http://diamant-ltd.com/michigan-county-map/mi-south-nice-michigan-county-map/

4. Arthur W. Bromage, "County Government in Michigan," *Papers of the Michigan Academy of Science, Arts and Literature* (Vol. 6, 1931), 440–41.

5. Cooley, *Michigan, A History of Governments,* Chapter 17 (818) Sec. 36.

6. For information on forfeited lands and tax sales, see the annual reports of both the Auditor General and the Commissioner of the State Land Office.

7. Formisano, *Birth of Mass Political Parties,* 60.

8. Gray, *The Yankee West,* 3–4, 151.

9. Sonya Salamon, *Prairie Patrimony, Family, Farming & Community in the Midwest* (Chapel Hill: University of North Carolina Press, 1992), 32.

10. Kirkland, Caroline Matilda, *A New Home or Life in the Clearing,* edited by John Nerber (New York: Putman's Sons, 1953).

11. For the quantitative evidence challenge, see Maris A. Vinovskis, *Toward a Social History of the American Civil War: Exploratory Essays* (New York: Cambridge University Press, 1990) as well as Tamara Hareven and Maris Vinovskis, *Family and Population in Nineteenth-Century America* (Princeton University Press: 1978). One can find occasional relevant local social case studies. See, for example, Walter Martin Kollmorgen, *The German-Swiss in Franklin County Tennessee: A Study of the Significance of Cultural Considerations in Farming Enterprises* (Washington, D.C.: U.S. Department of Agriculture, Bureau of Economic Economics, 1940). And I explore other options in my forthcoming tentatively titled *Order and Disorder in a Changing Pale of Settlement: Behavioral Science, Geographical and Economic Perspectives.*

12. Stall, *Larding the Lean Earth.*

13. Atack, Bateman and Parker, "The Farm, the Farmer, and the Market," 260.

14. For Ohio, see *Cultivator* (VI, 1849): 28. *Ohio Farmer* (VIII, 1859): 105. For Michigan, see *Cultivator* (V, 1848): 121. *Michigan Farmer* (8, July 1850): 195 and (Jan. 1851): 21. The annual reports of the Michigan Agricultural Society made similar references.

15. Veatch, *Agricultural Land Classification and Land Types in Michigan*, 57. Also see his *Soils and Land of Michigan* (Michigan State College Press, 1953).

16. Veatch, *Agricultural Land Classification and Land Types in Michigan*, 55.

17. Veatch, *Agricultural Land Classification and Land Types in Michigan* 54. Most soil surveys elsewhere in the U.S. since 1957 include "interpretations" of "[e]stimated yields of the common agricultural crops under defined levels of management." From an online report by the National Resources Conservation Services of the U.S. Department of Agriculture. See http://www.statlab.iastate.edu/soils/soildiv/sslists/sslisthome.html.

18. Veatch, *Agricultural Land Classification and Land Types in Michigan*, 57.

19. For Veatch's more detailed classifications of soils in the Lower Peninsula, see *Agricultural Land Classification and Land Types in Michigan*, 23–51. The description of the four-fold classification appears on pages 57–58.

20. Veatch, *Agricultural Land Classification and Land Types in Michigan*, 58. It is possible that the better class soils are increasingly overstated as we move from south to north in the state.

21. Paul Rood developed a "social productivity index" for his study of land use and fertility in 36 Lower Peninsula counties. See his *An Analysis of Land Use and Fertility in Michigan Counties* (Michigan State College, Soils Extension Service, 1943). Another report issued in 1956 includes a statewide map (with county boundaries) that is keyed to 26 land divisions and related "associations." E. P. Whiteside, I.F. Schneider and R. L. Cook, *Soils of Michigan* (Michigan State University, Agricultural Experiment Station, 1956). William Frederick of the National Resource Conservation Service kindly provided me with a detailed Midland County map using an eight-category land classification system. Private communication dated September 9, 2003.

22. Lewis describes each of these regions in his *West to Far Michigan*, 71–72. Other settlers used different criteria to identify six major soil types—four light-colored and two dark-colored.

23. Greffenius, *Development of Michigan Public Land Policy*, 9, 11. Michigan is the only state in the Old Northwest to adopt a non-agricultural soil (Kalkaska) as the state soil.

24. Benson, *Logs and Lumber*, 5–6 and footnote 11 on page 228.

25. Greffenius, *Development of Michigan Public Land Policy*, 12.

26. He also provides a 10-division phyteogeografic classification. Veatch, *Soils and Land of Michigan*, 9–10. Whiteside *et al* reported that the distribution of the state's native tree species was fairly closely related with soil types. The southern limit of White Pine was along the boundary between the Gray-Brown Podzolic and the Podzol regions. Whiteside, Schneider and, *Soils of Michigan*, 10.

27. Lumbermen gave the greatest attention to cork and pumpkin pine. This variety accounted for about 20 percent of Michigan's pine forests, and although "superior" pine stands were found throughout much of the Lower Peninsula, the state's "super pine belt" of the best trees were located in the center of the Peninsula. Maybee, *Michigan's White Pine Era*, 12–13; Benson, *Logs and Lumber*, 8.

28. Gray, *The Yankee West*, 202, *n*28.

29. Lewis, *West to Far Michigan*, 47. His chapter 3 is titled "The Environmental Context of Colonization."

30. For this map and other climagraphs, see http://www.geo.msu.edu/geo333/precip.html.

31. Lewis, *West to Far Michigan*, 41.

32. Prince, *Wetlands of the American Midwest*, 14.

33. A personal note: I contacted malaria while living and working as a Foreign Service Officer in Guinea-Bissau during the early 1990s. My daily anti-malaria prescriptions failed to protect me.

34. They do not attribute these differences to soil. Pressly and Scofield, *Farm Real Estate Values*, 9.

35. Since many farmers no doubt owned land not counted as farms in the census, the proportion of farmer-owned land was no doubt greater than "less than half."

36. Again, census numbers are approximations. For example, the state's 1864 census reported 11,096,472 taxable and non-taxable acres in the Lower Peninsula. This total was nearly four million fewer acres than were patented statewide by 1860 but at the same time more than four-million farm acres in the same year. The modest number of lands patented during the Civil War (perhaps around 700,000 acres from 1860 through 1864) might help explain these discrepancies. For further questions about census information, see the annex to this chapter. Also see Jones, *The Survey and Sale*, 19, 94. State land disbursements for these post-1860 years were not available to the author.

37. Lewis' Chapter 9 is titled "Population Expansion, Transportation, and Settlement Patterning on the Michigan Frontier, 1845–1860." Given the absence of reliable statistics

on many topics Lewis addresses, he occasionally uses such terms as "many" immigrants and "Most ... Michigan residents." Lewis, *West to Farm Michigan*, 121, 123.

38. Some new counties were attached to older ones, but if the 1860 population census for Midland is representative of other counties statewide, then the residents of unorganized and organized counties were listed separately from one another. It appears that there were no census reports submitted by some higher-tier counties. These counties are considered here to have been without residents and farms.

39. There were 35 counties but information is lacking on one, Huron.

40. If the incomplete published census figures are approximately correct, then Wayne and St. Clair counties had fewer farm acres in 1860 than in 1850.

41. Average Size Farm (total acres)

Tier	*1850*	*1860*
1	120.3	105.5
2	140.2	122.9
3	123.5	110.4
4	115.2	102.1
5	142.8	123.3
6	177.1	173.5
7–11	0	123.8

42. Gray, *The Yankee West*, 37.

43. Dooley, "The Andrews Bailiwick," xviii.

44. Moore, "Of Berry Pickers," 51.

45. Wayne and St. Clair counties added new farms during the decade, even though they had fewer acres in farms in 1860 than in 1850 Census errors could help explain some of these differences.

46. Charles M. Davis, "The Hydrographic Regions of Michigan, *Papers of the Michigan Academy of Sciences, Arts and Letters* (16: 1931): 211.

47. Benson, *Logs and Lumber*, 2. See her Map 1 on the Lower Peninsula's primary rivers and streams.

48. Prince, *Wetlands of the American Midwest*, 71.

49. "Michigan Journal, 1836, John M. Gordon," *Michigan History* (43:3, September, 1959): 257.

50. Anita Fisk, *The History of Saginaw County Medicine* (Pendell Print, 1986). 1–3. As Jeffrey Sachs noted, geography (as in the present case of swamps) does not equal determinism, as "... not all malarial regions [in Africa] are condemned to poverty. Rather, special investments are needed to fight poverty." Jeffrey Sachs, "Institutions Matter, But Not for Everything," *Finance and Development* (June, 2003): 40. In Michigan these investments were primarily private farmers draining their own land. As noted, the State dodged its drainage responsibilities called for under congressional acts granting Michigan its swamp lands.

51. Lewis, *West to Far Michigan*, 193–99 and his Chapter 13.

52. "Michigan Journal, 1836, John M. Gordon," *Michigan History* (43:3, September, 1959): 290.

53. Dooley, "The Andrews Bailiwick," 134.

54. Golembe, *State Banks*, 131.

55. Among the many references to the effects that improved transportation had on the farm sector, see Kuhn, "Tiffin, Morse, and the Reluctant Pioneer," 112, and Lewis, *West to Far Michigan*, 229.

Chapter 5

1. Emphasis added. Atack and Bateman, "Yeoman Farming," 26.

2. Atack and Bateman, *To Their Own Soil*.

3. Cited in Atack, Bateman and Parker, "The Farm, the Farmer and the Market," 276.

4. Atack, Bateman and Parker, "The Farm, the Farmer and the Market," 279.

5. Atack and Bateman, *To Their Own Soil*, 257.

6. Atack and Bateman, *To Their Own Soil*, 23–27.

7. Atack and Bateman, "Yeoman Farming," 43–47. In their *To Their Own Soil*, they reported a return of 11.5 percent rather than 12.5 percent on 160 acres. Page 257.

8. Atack and Bateman, *To Their Own Soil*, 252.

9. Atack and Bateman, "Yeoman Farming," 43.

10. Donald Parkerson, *The Agricultural Transition in New York State: Markets and Migration in Mid-Nineteenth Century America* (Iowa State University Press, 1995), 91.

11. Paul Wallace Gates, "The Role of the Land Speculator in Western Development," in Cartenson, *The Public Lands*, 371.

12. Allan G. Bogue and Margaret Beattie Bogue, "Profits and the Frontier Land Speculator," in Cartensen, *The Public Lands*, 374. Their research was limited to Grand Prairie, Illinois and eastern Nebraska.

13. Robert Swierenga, "Quantitative Methods in Rural Landholding," *Journal of Interdisciplinary History* (13:4, 1983): 802–03.

14. Atack and Bateman, "Yeoman Farmers," 32.

15. For two estimates of farm-making costs in Michigan, see Clarence H. Danhof, "Farm-Making Costs and the 'Safety Valve':

1859–1860," in Carstensen, *The Public Lands*, 258.

16. For some statewide estimates of "land clearing," see Martin Leonard Primack, *Farm Formed Capital in American Agriculture, 1850 to 1910* (New York: Arno Press, 1977 reprint).

17. Clarence H. Danhof, *Change in Agriculture; the Northern United States, 1820–1870* (Cambridge, MA: Harvard University Press, 1969), 120.

18. Michael Williams, *Americans and Their Forests: A Historical Geography* (Cambridge University Press, 1989), 115 and Table 5.1.

19. Parkerson, *The Agricultural Transition in New York State*, 70.

20. Edward H. Rastatter, "Nineteenth Century Public Land Policy: The Case for the Speculator," in Klingaman and Vedder, *Essays in Nineteenth Century Economic History*, 122; Dooley, "The Andrews Bailiwick," 64; Lewis, *West to Far Michigan*, 55, 106; Danhof, "Farm-Making Costs and the 'Safety Valve' 1859–1860," 286 (*n*286), 258; Danhof, *Change in Agriculture*, 117, 118 (*n*32); Gray, *The Yankee West*, 53.

21. As indicated, it appears that Atack and Bateman based their rates of return and related measures on total acres. Also as previously noted, they found that a "40-acre farm—the yeoman farm par excellence—was barely, if at all, profitable." A northeastern farmer "had to work about 60 acres, while a midwesterner should have had at least 80 acres." "Had" and "worked" are different concepts. See Atack and Bateman, "Yeoman Farming," 44–45.

22. Donald Winters, *Farmers Without Farms: Agricultural Tenancy in Nineteenth-Century Iowa* (Greenwood Press, 1978), 6–7.

23. Jeremy Atack, Fred Bateman, and William Parker, "Northern Agriculture and the Westward Movement," in Stanely L. Engerman and Robert E. Gallman, eds., *The Cambridge Economic History of the United States* (Cambridge University Press, 2000), 315.

24. Atack and Bateman, "Yeoman Farming," 315.

25. Atack and Bateman, *To Their Own Soil*, 243, Table 13.8. They refer to "Estimated per Capita Farm Income by State and Tenancy, 1859–60 ($)." Tenants, of course, did not realize any capital gains.

26. Oberly, *Sixty Million Acres*, 162. Atack and Bateman might not have imputed housing income and food grown on farmers' land in estimating farmer income.

27. References to such off-farm work appear in the pension files for Midland County's Union volunteers during the Civil War. These files were reviewed for the preparation of the author's "The Organizational Performances of Michigan's Adjutant General and the Federal Provost Marshal General in Recruiting Michigan's Boys in Blue."

28. Both the price of farm commodities and lumber varied over time with some years better or worse than others. The span of years selected for determining rates of return is affected by these variations. For example, American grain prices increased in 1855 when Russian supplies were cut off from European markets because of the Crimean War and by lowered French and British harvests at the same time. Lumber prices declined sharply after the Panic of 1857. Walter Smith and Arthur Cole, *Fluctuations in American Business, 1790–1860* (Russell & Russell, 1969), 99. Benson, *Logs and Lumber*, 154.

29. As noted earlier, cropping refers to "the kind and sequence of crops grown on a given area of soil over a period of time," while soil-management includes the cropping system plus other practices, such as the use of fertilizers and drainage. Allaway, "Cropping Systems and Soil," 387.

30. Danhof, *Change in Agriculture*, 262, 265.

31. Robert Russell, "Agricultural Notes in Ohio and Michigan," *Journal of Agriculture* (October, 1856): 8.

32. Quoted in Danhof, *Change in Agriculture*. See his chapter "Utilization of the Soil," *n*12.

33. *Effects of Soil Erosion on Soil Productivity and Soil Quality* (Soil Quality Institute, Technical Note No. 7, Soil Quality-Agronomy from the Soil Quality Institute, Natural Resources Conservation Service, United States Department of Agriculture, 1998), 2.

34. Danhof, *Change in Agriculture*. See his chapter "Utilization of the Soil," *n*11. Gates, *Farmer's Age Agriculture*, 168.

35. Atack, Bateman and Parker, "The Farm, the Farmer and the Market," 259. Erin Stewart Mauldin covers how the cultivation of cotton depleted southern soils. See his *Unredeemed Land: An Environmental History of Civil War and Emancipation in the Cotton South* (Oxford University Press, 2018).

36. Labor and total factor productivity (but not land productivity) increased in the latter half of the 19th Century, according to some researchers. See Atack, Bateman and Parker, "The Farm, the Farmer and the Market," 258–59. Richard A. Easterlin, "Farm Production and Income in Old and New Areas at Mid-Century" and Robert E. Gallman, "The Agricultural Sector and the Pace

of Economic Growth: U.S. Experience in the Nineteenth Century," both in Klingaman and Vedder, *Essays in Nineteenth Century Economic History*, 81, 105. Questions of labor productivity, new technologies, improved knowledge, and better management skills are beyond the scope of the present study. For relevant coverage of these topics, see Gates, *The Farmer's Age*, Chapter 16 as well as Chapter 13 for technologies in use before the Civil War. For example, Gates (p. 287) references Leo Rogin that "a man with a sickle could cut one half to three quarters of an acre of wheat in a day, with a cradle he could cut two to three acres per day. For the dates and names of farm journals specific to Michigan, as well as the organization of the State Agricultural Society in 1849 and the State Agricultural College, see Dunbar and May, *Michigan*, 279, 292.

37. Clayton and Onuf, *The Midwest and the Nation*, 39.

38. http://research.nres.uiuc.edu/soilproductivity, 4.

39. Kenneth C. Beeson, "Soil Management and Crop Quality," The United States Department of Agriculture, *Soil: The Yearbook of Agriculture 1957* (Government Printing Office, 1957), 258.

40. Lewis, *West to Far Michigan*, 235–46.

41. According to Atack and Bateman's sample, 93 percent of Michigan farmers grew corn, 66 percent grew wheat and 98 percent grew potatoes. These totals could be skewed by farmers practicing crop rotation and by the authors' sampling plan. *To Their Own Soil*, 171.

42. Atack and Bateman, *To Their Own Soil*, 164.

43. Stoll, *Larding the Lean Earth*, 63, 233 *n*84. American corn yields at mid-century were generally in the range of 25 to 60 bushels per acre and an average of around 30. Comparable corn yields for Europe are not available.

44. I did not explore the markets for these different crops.

45. *Third Annual Report of the Secretary of the State Board of Agriculture of the State of Michigan for the Year 1864* (Kerr, 1864).

46. Emphasis in the original. *Census and Statistics of the State of Michigan, 1864* (Kerr, 1865), iii–v. The state census of 1854 is equally if not more incomplete.

47. For the roles and performance of local and national officials during this time in Michigan, see the author's "The Organizational Performances of Michigan's Adjutant General and the Federal Provost Marshal General in Recruiting Michigan's Boys in Blue."

48. Michigan's own 1874 census summarizes information from the 1864 census but gives higher productivity yields for Berrien and Cass counties. *Census of the State of Michigan, 1874* (W.S. George, 1875).

49. Corn yields per acre were 6 bushels for Emmet and 36 for Oakland. Wheat yields were 4 for Mason and 17 for Berrien.

50. For the classic statement on potential ecological fallacies, see William S. Robinson, "Ecological Correlations and the Behavior of Individuals," *American Sociological Review* (1950, 15) 351–357.

51. Because lower tier counties had a longer history of farm settlement, one might expect that farms in these tiers would have more physical investments in them than found in higher tier farms. However, as we have seen earlier in this chapter, these older counties attracted the most new farms during the 1850s. Their sheer number would lower the average farm value and, hence, the per acre value.

52. The correlation between county population and corn yields per acre (both for 1863) is .39. Between population and wheat yields the correlation is .45.

53. These rates refer to a 10-year period without annual compounding. Of course, farmers were also earning (or losing) money from their farming activities. For the *Historic Consumer Price Index 1800–1998* from the University of Michigan's Documents Center online at http://www.lib.umich.edu/govdocs/historiccpi.html. Other indices can be found in John J. McCusker, *How Much is That in Real Money? A Historical Price Index for Use as a Deflator of Money Values in the Economy of the United States* (American Antiquarian Society, 1992), 328 where the Brady-David-Solar Index reports 94 in 1850 and100 in 1860; the Taylor-Hoover index for these years gives 90.6 in 1850 and 99.6 in 1860. A Composite Consumer Price Index reports 94 for 1850 and 100 for 1860.

54. As a child on my maternal ancestors' sizeable farm in Midland, I often wondered how my grandfather Duncan Wayne was able to clear the trees on the 50 acres in front of the farm house and another 50 acres behind the house as well as more contiguous acres at a later time. The house and its wraparound porch still stands (under new owners). Farmers always had challenging tasks waiting for them after their onerous work days. If Bette Davis was correct in saying old age is no place for sissies, then it is safe to say that farming is no place for lazies.

55. Fourteen units had a farmer, farm laborer, or day laborer listed both before and after the unoccupied units. Another two had

a farmer or farmer who was also a merchant either before or after the unit.

56. Daron Acemoglu, "Root Causes, A Historical Approach to Assessing the Role of Institutions in Economic Development," *Finance & Development* (January, 2003): 28.

57. David Ward, *Geographic Perspectives on America's Past*, 44.

58. However, see David Hackett Fischer's *Albion's Seed: Four British Folkways in America* (Oxford University Press, 1989).

59. The sample of counties used in Atack and Bateman's research did not permit them to analyze the effects of market size on the value of land.

60. Atack and Bateman, *To Their Own Soil*, 18, 21, 114.

61. Gates, *History of Public Land Law Development*, 431. Robbins, *Our Landed Heritage*, 291 *n*21.

62. See the author's "Survey Materials Collected in the Developing Countries: Sampling, Measurement, and Interviewing Obstacles to Intra- and Inter-National Comparisons," in *International Social Science Journal* (17:4, 1965): 665–685. Among other sources where this article has been reprinted, see Donald Warwick and Samuel Osherson, eds., *Comparative Research Methods* (Prentice-Hall, 1974).

63. For the instructions given to enumerators, see Atack and Bateman, *To Their Own Soil*, 118–120, and for the list of crops, see 108–09.

64. Pressly and Scofield, *Farm Real Estate Values*, 6, Table 1.

65. Stanley Engerman and Claudia Goldin, "Seasonality in Nineteen-Century Labor Markets," in Thomas Weiss and Donald Schaefer, eds., *American Economic Development in Historical Perspective* (Stanford University Press, 1994), 104.

66. Kenneth Winkle, *The Politics of Community: Migration and Politics in Antebellum Ohio* (Cambridge University Press, 1988), xi.

67. Atack and Bateman, *To Their Own Soil*, 119, 238. Pressly and Scofield, *Farm Real Estate Value*, 4.

68. Atack and Bateman, *To Their Own Soil*, 21.

69. Thomas M. Cooley, *Compiled Laws of the State of Michigan* (Hosman & Kerr, 1857), Chapter 17 (841) Sec. 59.

70. Atack and Bateman, *To Their Own Soil*, 118.

71. Gray noted that three of the ten Michigan counties in the Atack and Bateman analyses are north of the line that marks the limits of viable grained-based agriculture and, therefore, that the results of their research aggregated as the state level might underreport wheat yields for the state. Gray, *The Yankee West*, 202, *n*28. Atack and Bateman's sample included nine (not ten) counties. Atack and Bateman, *To Their Own Soil*, 25. The authors could have elaborated their description of their sampling design beyond stating that it was a "two-step, variable cluster sample from the manuscript censuses of agriculture and population." The county was the primary sampling unit; one non-urban township (the cluster) was selected. Although it appears that counties were not stratified by population size, it is likely that this was a partially self-weighting sample. Even if all the 233 farms in these three northern counties were taken (and this is not the case), they would only represent two percent of all the 11,136 farms the census reports for all the nine counties in this sample. The same three counties accounted for .04 percent of all farms in all counties in the 1860 census – although we recognize, as noted above, that the definition of a farm excluded farms from the census.

Chapter 6

1. George Fredrickson, "Nineteenth-Century American History" in Anthony Molho and Gordon S. Woods, eds., *Imagined Histories: American Historians Interpret the Past* (Princeton University Press, 1998), 165.

2. Although this refers to post-Civil War America, it can be applied to the entire century. Richard L. McCormick, "Public Life in Industrial America, 1877–1917," in Eric Foner, ed., *The New American History* (Temple University Press, 1990), 95.

3. This quote is from the editors' summary of Hull and Ruggles, "'Restless in the Midst of Their Prosperity': New Evidence on the Internal Migration of Americans 1850–2000," 827, 829–846.

4. Margaret Walsh refers to a constantly changing time-space matrix in the settlement of agricultural frontiers. See her *The American Frontier Revisited* (Humanities Press, 1981), 32.

5. That is, it is not possible in a statistical sense to hold the various components "constant" in order to assign the size of the contribution that one component makes to the others individually or to the matrix as a whole.

6. Robert H. Wiebe, *The Search for Order 1877–1920* (New York: Hill & Wang, 1967). Bob and his family were my wife's and my own friends when we were both Columbia University graduate school living on Morningside Drive.

7. Christopher Clark touches on some of these conflicting views in his *The Roots of Rural Capitalism: Western Massachusetts 1780–1860* (Cornell University Press, 1990), Chapter 1.

8. The Midland Genealogical Society's very useful "listing of all persons appearing on the official census rolls" misspells several names as well. See the Society's *Midland County, Michigan, Census Records 1850–1894* (Midland Genealogical Society, 1983).

9. Not all sections had 640 acres. Some had more, others had less. See Chapter 4.

10. The Bureau of Land Management's online patent-search service does not cover military warrants, swamp land grants to states, and state pass-through grants to canal and railroad companies. The Bureau's database is accessible at http://www.glorecords.blm.gov/. The same limitation applies to the Rootsweb listing of Midland patents at ftp://ftp.rootsweb.com/pub/usgenweb/mi/midland/multiple/deeds/midland.txt.

11. We will also see that some patents issued to railroads and possibly to the state under federal swampland acts overstated the number of acres covered by these patents.

12. Some historians no doubt believe that anecdotal information trumps the potentially "biased" and "incomplete" numerical evidence introduced in the following chapters. There are pluses and minuses in both soft and hard evidence. One review of competitive interpretations of soft data by ethnographers and historians suggests that apparently contrary views of truth can in fact be complimentary rather than diametrically opposed. To an unknown degree, the same might be said of studies based on hard versus soft "evidence." See Ron Robin's analysis of Derek Freeman's critique of Margaret Mead's *Coming of Age in Somoa* and other questions about "a single truth." Ron Robin, *Scandals & Scoundrels: Seven Cases that Shook the Academy* (University of California Press, 2004), Chapter 4. For a history of "facts" invented and honed by early economists, see Mary Poovey ibid. as well as two books by the present author: *A Concise History of Economists' Assumptions about Markets from Adam Smith to Joseph Schumpeter* and *The Language of Economics: Socially Constructed Vocabulary and Assumptions.*

Chapter 7

1. One author reported that Midland "embraced an area of some 538 square miles" when first laid out in 1831." Stan Berriman, *Upper Tittabawassee River Boom Towns* (Messersmith, 1979), 54. When organized as a county, Midland encompassed approximately 339,000 acres (530 square miles). *Midland City Directory* (Robinson Directories, 1992–93). Just as Midland was "attached" to another county prior to its formal organization, other unorganized counties were attached to Midland as well, a common theme in the history of local governments in America. As a result, the county's boundaries and size changed over time.

2. Each township would have 36 sections, each one square mile. A square mile has 640 acres. Townships farther north from the equator have shorter east-west lines. During my rechecking of sections with more acres patented than the model section of 640 acres, Walt Tennis, a surveyor at the Bureau of Land Management, gave me several reasons for these discrepancies. Where a surveyor began his work and the distance from the meridian were two reasons. The surveyor's map for T 13 N R 1E shows this township is not aligned perfectly with its adjacent western township. Discrepancies, according to Mr. Tennis, can be found in almost any section within a township. One result of this lack of perfect uniformity is that particular subsections will differ in their number of acres—for example, the SW ¼ of NW ¼ might have fewer or more than 40 acres.

3. Yates, *Salt of the Earth*, 53. A byproduct of this reduction was a lower information-collection and management task required for the present study.

4. John C. Hudson, "North American Origins of Middlewestern Frontier Populations," *Annals of the Association of American Geographers* (78: 1988): 406.

5. John C. Hudson, *Making the Corn Belt: A Geographic History of Middle-Western Agriculture*. The eastern boundary coordinate is –84.125 and its western coordinate is –84.625. (Indiana University Press, 1994).

6. *Soil Survey of Midland County, Michigan* (United States Department of Agriculture, Soil Conservation Service, 1979), 64–65.

7. http://www.geo.msu.edu/geo333/precip.html. For climographs, see http://www.geo.msu.edu/geo333/growseason&frost.html. Also see the precipitation and temperature graphs in M. Sommers, *Atlas of Michigan* (Michigan State University Press, 1977), 46–57 and Lewis, *West to Far Michigan*, 45–47.

8. Veatch, as noted in Chapter 3, did not use the same standard to classify soil percentages statewide. As a result, it is possible that less than 46 percent of Midland's soils were in the two best soil classes.

9. Bruce Catton, *Michigan: A History* (Norton, 1984), 137.

10. The Pine and Chippewa Rivers become a single channel before flowing into the Tittabawassee. The plats for T 14 N R 2E originally filed with the Office of the Surveyor General designated this channel as the Pine River, whereas it is currently designated to be the Chippewa.

11. Standard atlas of Midland County, Michigan: including a plat book of the villages, cities and townships of the county... patrons directory, reference business directory... / compiled and published by Geo. A. Ogle & Co.

12. *Soil Survey of Midland County.*

13. Charles M. Davis, "The Hydrographic Regions of Michigan," *Papers of the Michigan Academy of Science, Arts, and Letters* (16: 1931): 211.

14. Davis, "The Hydrographic Regions of Michigan," 215.

15. Davis, "The Hydrographic Regions of Michigan," 214.

16. Michigan Department of State, *Michigan and Its Resources* (Lansing: R. Smith, 1883), 260.

17. J. O. Veatch, *Soils and Land of Michigan* (Michigan College Press, 1953), Figure 13. For more recent water-related issues, see *The Final Impact Statement of Flood Control on the Tittabawassee River at Midland County* (Office of the Chief Engineer, Department of the Army, 1980).

18. State of Michigan Department of Environmental Quality, Office of the Great Lakes, *Historical Wetlands of the Saginaw Bay Watershed* (1993), 10. http://www.deq.state.mi.us/ogl/sagbay/histwet/htm.

19. For a series of articles on the mapping of Michigan, see the two special issues on "Mapping in Michigan and the Great Lakes" in *The Michigan Historical Review* (30:2, Fall 2004 and 31:1, Spring 2005). For the names of the federal surveyors and the instructions given them, see Caldwell, *Surveyors of the Public Lands in Michigan, 1808–2000.* Also Ralph Moore Berry, *Special instructions to Deputy Surveyors in Michigan, 1808–1854* (Michigan Museum of Surveying, 1990).

20. Andro Linklater, *Measuring America*, (Harper Collins: London (2002). Also see see Gary D. Libecap and Dean Lueck, *The Rectangular Survey Versus Metes and Bounds: Systematic and Unsystematic Land Demarcation* available online at https://law.yale.edu/system/files/documents/pdf/Intellectual_Life/Libecap_Lueck_LEO_Workshop_Nov_15_2007.pdf

21. Catton, *Michigan*, 70–71.As noted earlier, Ohio's numbering system evolved over time.

22. Gates, *History of Public Land Law Development*, 802. GLO, as noted earlier, was not always able to enforce the acreage caps set on patentees acquiring land under the Graduation Act.

23. Knox Jamison, "The Survey of the Public Lands in Michigan," *Michigan History* (42, 1958): 197–213.

24. Yates, *Salt of the Earth:* 13. Yates does not reference the source for this information.

25. All these quotations and the appropriate references to them are in Jones, *The Survey and Sale of the Public Land in Michigan*, 62–65.

26. Jamison, "Survey of the Public Lands," 202.

27. Richard Welch, *County Evolution in Michigan 1790–1897* (Michigan State Library Service, 1972), 11.

28. For the names and locations of these townships, see the unindexed materials in RG 67–27 of the Michigan State Archives.

29. Jamison, "Survey of the Public Lands," 206.

30. Punctuation and capitals as in the original, but emphasis added to "mostly." Taken from the field notes for Michigan, Vol. J1, pages 52–53 available at the Bureau of Land Management archives in Springfield, Virginia.

31. *Annual Report of the Commissioner of the State Land Office* (1855), 11.

32. These notes are found in the following Michigan volumes: 1J, 4J, 7C, 8C, 13D, 14D, 45J.

33. State of Michigan, Department of Environmental Quality, *Historical Wetlands*, 2–3.

34. Lowell O. Steward, *Public Land Surveys: History, Instructions, Methods* (Collegiate Press, 1935), 146.

35. Prince, *Wetlands of the American Midwest*, 12.

36. Saginaw's own elected government saw little potential in its neighbor Midland, an "Irreclaimable waste." Yates, *Salt of the Earth*, 19. One would think that early settlers were aware of this assessment and the basis on which it was made.

37. Fuller, *Economic and Social Beginnings*, 395.

38. Fisk, *The History of Saginaw County Medicine*, 3.

39. For a description of the evolving state road network, see Lewis, *West to Far Michigan*, 193–208. Also Charles Tuttle, *General History of the State of Michigan* (R.D.S. Tyler, 1873), 550–71.

40. Kirkland, *A NewHouse*, 59.

41. John M. Gordon, "A Speculator's Dairy" in Kestenbaum, *The Making of Michigan*, 120; also A. D .P. Van Buren, "Taking the Pledge," also in Kestenbaum, *The Making of Michigan*, 329.

42. NARA RG 110, File 5901 titled *Register of Letters Received by the Chief Mustering and Disbursing Officer 1863–65*, 305–06.

43. The exact reference is "to 40 or 50 miles above the mouth of the Pine River." John Blois, *Gazetteer of the State of Michigan* (S.L.Rood, 1839), 374. This was Edenville in T16 N R 1W.

44. Yates, *Salt of the Earth*, 152.

45. The steam engine boats were fired by wood that was bought from farmers who were clearing their land.

46. Atack and Batemen, *To Their Own Soil*, 229.

47. "In a large portion of New England, the roads are generally harder, better made, and less subject to deep mud than those of this State. Hence a horse of less weight would be required for the same purpose in the former section." *Third Annual Report of the Secretary of the State Board of Agriculture*, 82.

48. Atack and Bateman, "Yeoman Farming," 40.

49. River transport was an especially time and cost-efficient way to get logs from Midland to the major saw mills in Saginaw. (Midland only had two small mills in 1860.) Benson, *Logs and Lumber*, 150. River water levels also varied over the course of a year.

50. Further market boosts were given by other transportation developments—such as the Illinois and Michigan Canal that was completed in 1848.

51. Lewis, *West to Far Michigan*, 225.

Chapter 8

1. Taken from the Bureau of Land Management's web site at http://www.blm.gov. Some of the website addresses referenced in these footnotes may have changed since the author first recorded them in the late 1990s.

2. Thanks to Jennifer Spencer of this office for her kind assistance in helping me access these tract books and other materials. The major Michigan tract books are in NE vols. 3, 4, 13 and NW 16. Surveyors' field note are the Michigan volumes 1I, 4J, 7C, 8C, 13D, 14D, 45J and Res. 6000 ac. For a description of these sources, see Harry Yoshpe and Philip Brower, *Preliminary Inventory of the Land-entry Papers of the General Land Office* (National Archives, 1949). A second set of these tract books is housed in the State of Michigan's archives in Lansing, Michigan. My archives-based research was done over a number of months starting in the late 1990s.

3. The same limitation applies to Rootsweb, a genealogical service that provides access to patents with the names of Cash Act patentees. Rootsweb does not, however, provide dates or acres. See http://ftp.rootsweb.com/pub/usgenweb/mi/midland/multiple/deeds/midland.txt. Saginaw's deed books through 1857 include 144 land entries for Midland. The first five were entered in 1835 followed by 36 three years later in 1836. Seventeen of all the patentees listed in these tract books were enumerated in Midland's 1860 census.

4. Benson, *Logs and Lumber*, 23.

5. Also "deed" and "deed holder." A small number of patents were surrendered back to the General Land Office. These are excluded from the present analysis.

6. Walt Tennis, a surveyor at the BLM's patent archives in Springfield, Virginia commented to me that it is probably not possible to attain 100 percent accuracy using the available evidentiary sources.

7. Note the distinction between tract and deed books. The federal government was responsible for the former. Midland County was responsible for the latter. Indexes to Saginaw's early deed books do not distinguish between grantors and grantees. The author telephoned the register of deeds in three different counties. The Saginaw and Oakland offices claimed that no Midland deeds were in their books, while the Midland office claimed complete coverage. Saginaw's deed books for the 1835–1852 period list 23 patents for sections located in Midland County. There were also 42 tax sales, many of which lacked information on the dates of the auction sales. For the mechanics of auction sales, see later in this chapter. For an explanation of various types of deeds, see http://users.rcn.com/deeds/anatomy.htm, and the online lessons of the *International Internet Genealogical Society University* (among others) at http://users.arn.net/~billco/uslpr2.htm, http://users.arn.net/~billco/uslpr3.htm and http://users.arn.net/~billco/uslpr4.htm.

8. Because of "no information" and other similar considerations, there are several small discrepancies between tables in this chapter. The federal government stopped issuing railroad grants in 1871, and in 1872 "there was not a party platform which did not condemn the whole system and insist that the public domain be held for settlers." Quoted in Weaver, *The Great Land Rush*, 12. See the text above for reasons why the number of acres in some pass-through patents are overstated.

9. The primary concern in the present chapter and the only concern in Chapters 7 and 8 is with patents issued to individuals. Therefore, we do not use hypothetical percentages of adjust the number of acres covered by pass-through patents. Still, we note that 64 sections had 14.7 percent more acres than the possible maximum of 40,960 acres (64 × 640). If this percentage is applied to all patented acres under the railroad and swampland acts reported in Table 8.1, then all the pass-through patents would be reduced to 136,275 acres. These revised estimates can also be used to adjust the number of unpatented acres available at different times and the relative acres of individual and pass-through patents.

10. The first name listed varies for some of the partnerships. For example, Daniel Fitzhugh is listed before Edward Leroy in two of the patent decisions while Leroy is listed first in three others.

11. Six women are listed on patents. More appear on deeds (the after-patent land market). Michigan's Married Woman's Property Act of 1844 "gave married women the right to own property under some circumstances." It took time to remove coverture common at the time. See Marilyn Motz, *True Sisterhood: Michigan Women and Their Kin, 1820–1920* (State University of New York Press: 1983), 23.

12. Price-sensitivity is a line of analysis for economists, not the present author.

13. David Ward reported that Merrill cheated him on one of their land deals. Ward, ibid, 101–03.

14. Oberly, *Sixty Million Acres*, 138.

15. Benson, *Logs and Lumber*, 269.

16. Her totals are based on land records from 147 townships in 49 Lower Peninsula counties for the years 1818 to 1870. Benson, *Logs and Lumber*, 235.

17. Dunbar and Mays, *Michigan*, 178. Jones, *The Survey and Sale*, 84.

18. Jones, *The Survey and Sale*, 18. Also, see his map on page 40 delineating the counties opened at the same time as Midland for auction and private sale.

19. I designated patents as being under the Graduation Act if the patentee paid less than $1.25 per acre. The Graduation Act was not approved until August 1854, although Midland's first application under the Act was made in 1853. At the time, Michigan had 8,785,890 acres subject to these reduced per-acre prices. Despite the 320-acre cap on individual patentees, speculators (including some making applications to the Grand Rapids local GLO office) abused the law. Gates, *History of Public Land Law Development*, 187–90.

20. Cash sales were suspended for a number of townships while the railroad company made its selections. For the conditions under which grants were made to railroads, see Meints, *Michigan Railroads*: 7. Under conditions of the nearly forty-million acres granted to the state on June 3, 1856, "Washington set all the provisions that had to be met, and then gave the land to the state of Michigan to distribute. A railroad company had to build twenty miles of line to be eligible to receive any land. Then it would be awarded those odd-numbered sections of land lying within six miles on either side of the completed line that had not already been sold. If there was not sufficient land in the twelve-mile wide strip, the railroads could select farther away, but not more than fifteen miles from the rail line." Seventeen Midland patents issued to individuals were cancelled in favor of claims made by the railroad company. See the text above for questions about the accuracy of the number of acres patented to railroads.

21. Jones reported total acres patented. Oberle's acreage figures are based on a sample. Cole reported cash receipts that do not cover patents obtained through and military warrants (and, perhaps, the Graduation Act).

22. Jones, *The Survey and Sale*, 17–19, 94. Cole, "Cyclical and Sectional Variations in the Sale of Public Lands, 1816–1860," in Carstensen, *The Public Land*, 234–35. Oberle, *Sixty Million Acres*, 86–87.

23. Consumer price indices matched land sales after the Panic of 1837. For example, index numbers (using 1860 as the benchmark 100) dropped to below 100 during the 1840s land market doldrums. However, there is not a perfect match between land sales and indices of inflation and depression. Midland's fillip of sales in 1854 and 1855 matched a major increase in the consumer price index from 93 in 1853 to 101 the following year and 104 in 1855. John J. McCusker, *How Much Is That in Real Money? A Historical Price Index for Use as a Deflator of Money Values in the Economy of the United States* (American Antiquarian Society, 1992), 327–28. For the beginning and end years of selected periods of economic contraction from 1812 through 1931, see Ralph Andrews, ed., *New Views on American Economic Development* (Schenkman: 1965), 402, 424–25.

24. Gates, *Farmer's Age Agriculture, 1815–1860*, 410. Also see Chapter 2 in the present study.

25. Saginaw County's deed books record 42 tax sales in Midland for the period 1835–1852. A typical tax sale record read that the successful bidder (e.g., James Fraser on August 6, 1851) "became purchaser of

the rights of the State in and to the following land in the County of Saginaw [actually 298.24 acres in Midland's Edenville Township] which were bid off to the State for the taxes afixed (sic) thereon in the years 1845, 1846 and 1847."

26. Aside from bankruptcy, local courts handled other debts. Kirkland referred to "the satisfactory amount of business which is created by the collection of debts, a matter of 'glorious uncertainty' in Michigan. These suits are so frequent, that they pass as part and parcel of the regular course of things." Residents did not believe it "unfriendly in suing his next door neighbor for a debt of however a trifling amount." Kirkland, *A New Home*, 292. A Midland Sheriff's bankruptcy sale of February 6, 1858 reported that Charles Jacobs of Midland made a mortgage to John A. Whitman who in turn assigned it to James Fraser with a "power of sale" provision that became operative for reason of default.

27. The 10,240 acres in the 16 townships sections 16 are not included in the base for the percentages in this paragraph.

Chapter 9

1. A deed is a legal document recording the transfer of ownership from one party to another. Deed books record different types of transactions. The focus here is on the *deed of sale*, also known as an *indenture*. For a general overview of deeds, see Anatomy of a Deed at http://users.rcn.com/deeds/anatomy.htm. Also Park,"Perception of Land Quality," 11; The microfilms were obtained through the kind assistance of a local Family History Center (FHC). It appears that deeds for the same grantor and grantee are occasionally listed more than once. I suspect that I missed the deeds of some residents and may have double-counted others. The following Midland-specific FHC microfilm numbers in the U.S., Canada, and the Caribbean series were reviewed: 0946176 Deed Index A-C, 1855–77; 09466180 Deed Records A-B, 1855–60; 0946179 Deed Records V, 1856–59; 0946184 Deed Records V, G-H, 1858–98; 0946181 Deed Records V. C, 1860–64; 0946173 Mortgage Index A-C, 1856–1902; 0946186, Deed Records K-L, 1852–1935; 0945495 Index to Mortgages, Vol. 1–2, 1836–81; 0946471 Calendar 1850–1900 Probate File # 5, 1873. For the universe of Midland films available through the FHC, see http://www.familysearch.org/Eng/Library/fhlcatalog/supermainframeset.asp?display=titlefilmnotes&columns=*%2C180%2C0&titleno=245042&disp=Deed+records%2C+1855-1935%3B+index%2C+++. Also http://www.familysearch.org/Eng/Library/fhlcatalog/supermainframeset.asp?display=topicdetails&subject=379344&subject_disp=Michigan%2C+Midland+%2D+Land+and+property and http://www.familysearch.org/Eng/Library/fhlcatalog/supermainframeset.asp?display=localitydetails&subject=200075&subject_disp=Michigan%2C+Midland Not all these films had relevant information.

2. As noted earlier, these deed books only include a small proportion of all patents issued before 1855, the year Midland was organized and began to record deeds for the county. Some of these deeds are listed in Saginaw's early deed books, but that county's early index did not distinguish between grantor and grantee. Saginaw's deed records were viewed in Film 0966778, Deed Index V 1–4, 1824–67, Saginaw County. Not reported here is information taken from tax records that are archived by the Clarke Historical Library at Central Michigan University in Mt. Pleasant, Michigan. The tax files seem to provide names only for residents, although several non-residents are listed as well. (They might have left the county before the rolls were updated.) The much larger number of non-residents does not include names. Other records must have allowed the tax authorities to notify the appropriate owners of their tax obligations. These records do not record the name of the person or persons actually paying the tax. Moreover, as reported by Gray, some owners might have paid taxes on more acres than they actually owned. Gray, *The Yankee West*, 104. It is not clear whether the assessed values are adjusted for the exceptions applicable at the time according to Chapter XVII, Sect. 786 of the Michigan statutes. Bloise lists earlier exemptions that do not appear to have been carried forward after adoption of the 1850 constitution. See Bloise, *Gazetteer*, 69.

3. There were low or almost zero correlations among the measures of net acres, acres reported in the agricultural census, and taxable acres reported on the tax assessment rolls. And as noted earlier, the agricultural census has its own biases.

4. Forty-five percent of the 31 farms were still in the 1870 agricultural census; 46 percent of the other 41 were similarly persistent. These figures refer to farms still in the same farm family.

5. *Album of Midland County, Michigan* (Chicago: Chapman, 1884). A few of these 1884 men (no women had stand-alone biographical sketches) had moved in and out of the county. They were a mobile population. In 1860, most residents had newly arrived, and the housing vacancy rate of ten percent

suggests that many recent arrivals had already left the county. Gray also reported that many of Kalamazoo's early arrivals "bought land in several places and moved several times before settling permanently." This seems to generally describe the Midland experience as well. Gray, *The Yankee West*, 39 and 144.

6. Emphasis added. Quoted in *Third Annual Report of the Secretary of State Board of Agriculture*, 39.

7. Atack and Bateman, "Yeoman Farming," 256, 41–43. The authors also explain that "while these farms were earning less than the opportunity cost of the labor and capital they employed, it is unclear whether they incurred accounting losses as well," p. 251.

8. These comments appear at the bottom of Schedule 3 titled "Persons who Died during the Year ending 1st June, 1860." Midland and Jerome townships had multiple other townships attached to them. The county's single census enumerator crossed off his comments on Ingersoll township and added "The remarks in reference to the townships of Midland and Jerome will apply with equal propriety to this township," a difficult application given that only one township was seen to have clear farming potential.

9. *Michigan State Gazetteer and Business Directory for 1863/64* appears online in the Library of Congress's American Memory Series, "Pioneering the Upper Midwest: Books from Michigan, Minnesota, and Wisconsin, ca 1820–1910, 111.

10. Michigan Department of State, *Michigan and Its Resources* (R. Smith & Co.: 1893), 259–60.

11. For relevant guidance protocols and manuals, see the references in the USDA's *Soil Survey Geographic (SSURGO) Database for Midland County, Michigan*, 5 and 11, available at http://www.ftw.nrcs.usda.gov/ssurgo/metadata/mi111.html.

12. The soil survey team provides the number of acres for each of Midland's five capability classes. However, five soil types were not assigned capability classes. For this and perhaps other reasons, the acres reported in Table 6 of the report concerning capability classes are less than what the county had.

13. *Soil Survey of Midland*, 22. See Table 5 of this survey for the yields per soil name for seven different crops.

14. From personal information kindly provided me in April 2002 by William Frederick and Wilbur Sears of the Natural Resources Conservation Service regional office in Midland. This service also uses nine Soil Names for Midland's "Prime Farmland." All nine qualify as "Prime farmland if drained."

15. For the procedures used to develop these indices, see Sandra S. Batie, Mary A. Schulz, and David B. Schweikhardt, *A Continuation of Environmental Conservation Policy: The Conservation Reserve Program* (Department of Agricultural Economics, Michigan State University: March 1997): Staff Paper 97–16.

16. From a table titled *Soil/Payment Rate Table - For CRP Bid Caps, 2000 Approved Dryland Rates*, Document ID EPEB50-R001 dated September 22, 2000.

17. Only Lenawee ($83), Bay ($80), Saginaw ($80), Gratiot ($75) and Monroe ($75) had average rates higher than Midland's $70.

18. *Soil Survey Geographic (SSURGO) Database*, 8. For the great amount of digital data and information added to the initial 1979 survey, see 10–11.

19. See, for example, Atack and Bateman, *To Their Own Soil*: 116–117, 175–179, 259–60. Also Gray, *The Yankee West*, 179.

20. These 64,000 acres account for approximately 64 percent of the 99,840 "good" acres noted in Table 5.2.

21. Based on a tally of the information in the original census enumeration sheets.

22. Good and poor soils were not evenly distributed among the county's sixteen townships. Four townships were well endowed with over 60 percent of their sections having "primarily" good soils. In contrast, five other townships had fewer than ten percent of their sections similarly well endowed. There were three townships (T 14N R 1W 1, T 14N R 2W, and T 15N R 1W—Lee, Greendale and Jerome) without a single section with any good soil. (Today these townships do have farms.) Four townships offered the most promising soils: T 13N R 2E (Ingersoll), T 15N R 2E (Larkin) and T 13N R 1E (Mount Haley where much of my ancestors invested in land that they farmed). Settlers would have been advised (as some no doubt were) to avoid some townships and favor others.

23. These figures include the sixteen sections 16 (about 10,240 acres) not included in Table 6.4. Acreage in the county's croplands started a downward trend in the 1920s; 26,000 acres alone were withdrawn from farm use from 1949 to 1972. See *Soil Survey of Midland County*, 21.

24. Only three of Midland's current sixteen townships were recognized in the 1860 population census. The patent and deed records allow for locating 31 farms (other farms were not in these records so their exact locations and soils are not known and thereby excluded from this chapter's analysis. in all sixteen townships of which only half

were home to any of the 31 farms. These 31 included 13 (42 percent of the 31) in Ingersoll and seven in Midland. The other eleven farms were in Jasper (2), Homer (2), Lincoln (1), Jerome (2), Hope (1) and Edenville (1). One third of all 31 farms were in a section on the Tittabawassee River. Townships differed in their soil profiles and access to markets. All thirteen farms in Ingersoll Township were in sections with good soils (see the text for this classification), while only one of Midland Township's seven farms was similarly endowed. Townships also differed in their primary vegetation cover. All thirteen Ingersoll farms were in sections with maple trees. (Only three farms countywide had any pine trees.) Soils were not the only influences on the resources and advantages of farmers.

25. Gates, *Agriculture and the Civil War*, 223.

26. This arrangement was mentioned in the post-Civil War history of Herbert Fineout. He farmed 40 acres and lumbered for others, as reported in his pension file.

27. Wolves inhibited the expansion of animal husbandry. Ottawa County farmers were unable to keep sheep until "wolves and [wild] dogs" were controlled. *Third Annual Report*: 62. Minutes of the meetings of Midland's Board of Supervisors during the Civil War years report on bounties paid for wolf killings.

28. It is not possible to estimate per-acre yields because relevant acreage figures are not available.

29. Richard A. Easterlin, George Alter, and Gretchen A. Condran, "Farms and Farm Families in Old and New Areas: The Northern States in 1860," in Tamara Hareven and Maris Vinovskis, *Family and Population in Nineteenth-Century America*, 50.

30. $50 in 1860 is approximately equivalent to $1,385 in 2015.

31. Atack and Bateman, *To Their Own Soil*, 124.

32. Emphasis in the original. Kirkland is as close as we have to investigative journalism and popular ethnology on the Michigan frontier in the late 1830s and early 1840s. Kirkland, *A New Home*, 43. For a brief description of Nicolas Stoll's 1859 log cabin in southwest Michigan, see Annette Kolodny, *The Land Before Her: Fantasy and Experience of the American Frontiers, 1630–1860* (University of North Carolina Press, 1984), 229

33. Quoted by Gates in his "The Role of the Land Speculator in Western Development," in Carstenson, *The Public Lands*, 351.

34. Lesli Decker, "The Great Speculation: An Interpretation of Mid-Century Pioneering," in David Ellis, ed., *The Frontier in American Development* (Cornell University Press: 1968), 360.

35. Some state and county museums include early tools such as plows, harnesses, and cutting instruments available to farmers.

36. Forty-one percent of the farmers not enumerated in the agricultural census also moved.

37. Fifty-nine percent of the farmers included in the population census but not the agricultural one also persisted over the decade.

38. There were 185 farms in 1870, 31 of which were also in the agricultural census of 1860. *Statistics of the State of Michigan, 1870*, cxvii. Instead of the $100 threshold used for the 1860 agricultural census, a farm had to claim $500 in sold agricultural products to be included in the 1870 agricultural census. See Pressly and Scofield, *Farm Real Estate Values*, 6 (Table 1).

39. Local sheriffs were responsible for auctions resulting from bankruptcies involving mortgages and other debts to private parties (not non-payment of taxes to government). Article XVI of Michigan's 1850 constitution specified dollar and other exemptions from these auctions. Statutes provided further exemptions—for example, "spinning-wheels, weaving-looms ... stoves ... a seat, pew, or slip ... in any house or place of worship ... tools, implements ... team, vehicle, horse ... *The Business Man's Assistance and Legal Guide, Containing the Laws of Michigan, Indiana, Illinois, Iowa and Wisconsin* (Rufus Blanchard: 1856), 108–09. Parkerson found that "the probability of bankruptcy increased sharply among very recent arrivals to Lewis County" New York. Parkerson, *Agricultural Transition in New York State*, 109. Midland's deed books recorded fourteen bankruptcy cases prior to June 1, 1860. Three of twelve listed "defendants" (but none of the "complainants") were enumerated in the county's 1860 population census. Some of the other nine might have been former occupants of the uninhabited dwelling units recorded in this census. John Whitman was both a mortgagor and mortgagee. He and James Fraser were defendants in one bankruptcy case.

40. Deed holders had nearly twice the proportion of land purchases on the Tittabawassee River (34 percent for deeds vs. eighteen percent for patents).

41. For one review of early asset bubbles, see Peter Garber. 1990. "Famous First Bubbles." *Journal of Economic Perspectives*, (1990, 4(2): 35–54.

42. That Midland had more farmers than enumerated in the agricultural census is suggested by the 43 percent of the forty-two

other "farmers" (listed in the population census but not in the agricultural one) who at one time owned land. It is possible that some of these eighteen farmers were cultivators who did not meet the dollar criterion the census set for qualifying them for inclusion in the agricultural census. It is also possible that the census enumerator erred in not including them.

43. Insufficient information was available on three sellers. In addition, there were six patents issued by the State of Michigan.

44. As buyers and sellers of land, Midland residents were themselves promoting the county. John Larkin played a major role in this early development phase. He was an elected official, the local postmaster, hotel owner, part-owner of a river steamboat connecting Midland and Saginaw, part owner of a saw mill, and the primary force in developing and promoting the Village of Midland. Midland's deed books record nearly 120 land transactions by Larkin prior to June 1, 1860. These included several state patents (for Section 16 and swampland) that were acquired with favorable credit provisions. While he is most closely associated with the promotion of Midland Village, he also acquired land in Jasper and Mt. Haley Townships, along with acreage and lots in Midland Township. The bulk of his transactions were village lots he sold to residents and non-residents alike after the village's first plat was recorded in 1856. Larkin and other active resident land-market players warrant a separate analysis well beyond the present study's focus on the larger market for agricultural and pine acres. He specialized in village development and the sales of city lots (although he was also a farmer listed in the agricultural census).

45. The same auctioned land could be recorded two more times in the deed books. The eleven residents and their nineteen tax-auction acquisitions are minimum estimates. The point of presenting these numbers is to identify the obstacles to estimating rates of return.

46. Estimating rates of return requires information on the buyer's cost of borrowing (if mortgages were used), dollar investments in improving land, and the farmer's own sweat equity. This information is not available.

47. Tax sales (auctions) were important to state and local governments, for land taxes were the major source of government revenues. Swierenga reported that "In 1843, laws in nineteen out of twenty states in the Union provided for summary tax sales, and most of them made tax deeds prima facie evidence of title." Robert Swierenga, *Acres for Cents: Delinquent Tax Auctions in Frontier Iowa* (Greenwood Press, 1976), 10. Governments had an incentive to return their lands to the tax rolls as soon as possible. Under the state territorial laws, "Construction and maintenance of territorial roads were the responsibility of annually elected township highway commissioners, who organized corvees on which every able-bodied male over twenty-one had to serve or pay a fine." Gray, *The Yankee West*, 29. This was not an option for non-residents. Both residents and non-residents had to pay their taxes in specie. Michigan in general and Midland in particular lacked banks in which to deposit and then withdraw cash. Information from Civil War Veterans' pension files suggests that Midland residents operated in both a barter and cash economy. Since residents were not self-sufficient (producing all goods required for living and working), they needed the then-scarce specie for more than tax purposes. Little reliable evidence exists on how specie was acquired and more generally the survival strategies of farmers and others. The compiled laws of Michigan in effect in 1857 detail how "The Sale of Lands for Taxes, and the Conveyance and Redemption Thereof" are to be administered by the State's Auditor General. Cooley, *Compiled Laws of the State of Michigan*, 307 ff. Land with tax arrears was advertised in the county where the tracts or parcels were located. The lands were then auctioned on the first Monday of October by the county treasurer at a price "sufficient to pay the taxes, interest and charges thereon." The successful bidders were required to make payment "in specie, or its equivalent [!]" within twenty-four hours, a stipulation beneficial to buyers with access to financing.

48. The auctioned acres were in 23 percent of the county's 528 non-Section 16 sections. Seventy-one percent of Homer Township's 24 sections had tax-auctioned parcels. All three of the county's major rivers ran through this township (T 14N R 1E). Forty-four percent of the sections in the adjoining eastern township of Midland also had auction sales. Sections on all three major rivers were especially likely to have had auctioned parcels: 76 percent of the Tittabawassee's sections, 52 percent of Chippewa's, and 48 percent of the Pine's. In contrast, only 29 percent of the sections that were not on any river had tax-auctioned parcels.

49. James Jerome took 9,291 acres; Juan De Meir took 3,244 and James Fraser with his partners took 2,959. However, the overall figures must be considered approximations. Some tax parcels were listed as sold to the same buyer at two or more auctions. These

duplicates are not included in the above figures, an exclusion that most likely affected the total dollars paid. And, as noted earlier, lands not taken at auction reverted to the state. This means that tax-arrears land probably exceeded the 26,506 acres represented by these 240 auction transactions. It is possible (but not known) whether or not the non-auctioned parcels were in sections with the poorest soils and least pine forests.

Chapter 10

1. Behavioral economists and others have suggested that rational economic men may be an endangered species. See the author's *The Language of Economics: Socially Constructed Vocabularies and Assumptions*, a book that explores the socially-constructed meanings that economists have assigned to wealth and the distribution of wealth (inequality).

2. Daniel Kahneman's "prospect theory" can be found in his *Thinking, Fast and Slow* (New York: Farrar, Straus & Giroux, 2011).

3. I explore some of these themes in my *A Concise History of Economists' Assumptions About Markets* (Praeger, 2014) and in my *The Language of Economics: Socially Constructed Vocabularies and Assumptions* (Palgrave Macmillan, 2016).

4. Except for Robbins, "rationality" is not always central to an understanding of markets and economies. Many economists, however, still seem to agree with Robbins. Only Samuelson, however, specifically referenced "societies" rather than the unattached individual rational decision-maker.

5. Also see the earlier references to Morson and Schapiro in their *What Economics Can Learn from the Humanities: Cents and Sensibility*.

6. For a study that relates physical to human geographies, see Robert E Mitchell, Human Geographies Within the Pale of Settlement: Order and Disorder During the Eighteenth and Nineteenth Centuries (Palgrave Macmillan, 2019).

7. For some of the languages of the new regional sciences and regional systems theory, see Karl E. Ryavec and Mark Henderson, "Mapping Political Economies Over Time: Teaching Regional Systems Theory with G.W. Skinner's Historical GIS Datasets, " *Journal of World-Systems Research* (Vol. 24 Issue 2, 2018) -- for example: "Regional Systems Theory utilizes classic Land Use, Central Place, and Time Geography Theories to quantitatively map and measure how trade and marketing conditioned the human geography of traditional peasant societies, unlike the largely qualitative Marxist approach of Wallerstein's World-Systems Theory. Criticism of Skinner's Regional Systems approach largely stems from concern that as a spatial model it fetishizes the traditional marketing systems of peasant societies according to geometric zones of urban and rural land use, and that it is unable to take into account impacts from increasing modes of capitalist accumulation and global investment in the Modern Period."

8. Alex Pentland, Social Physics: How Social Networks Can Make Us Smarter (New York: Penguin Books, 2015).

9. Alan R. H. Baker, *Geography and History: Bridging the Divide* (Cambridge University Press, 2003), 56, 85 and 100, among his other references to different approaches to historical geography.

10. Jürgen Osterhammel, *The Transformation of the World: A Global History of the Nineteenth Century* (Princeton, 2014).

11. Osterhammel, 346. He references William Cronon's ethnohistory *Changes in the Land: Indians, Colonists and the Ecology of New England* (New York: Hill & Wang, 1983).

12. The Bentley Historical Library of the University of Michigan lists its Native American collections by location and tribe online at http://bentley.umich.edu/legacy-support/nativeamericans/nativeam_search.php?sort=collection.

13. We saw earlier that many if not most early settlers in that county bought their land from speculators rather than from the public agencies responsible for the privatizations of millions of newly acquired Amerindian land. The present study can be faulted for not having information on how railroad companies, the St. Mary's Canal Company and an array of different kinds of speculators priced and marketed their holdings. Did the after-market of private land-owners create a more knowledge-based pricing system for their holdings or did they generally follow the uniform pricing the practices specified in different legislative acts? That is a challenge for future researchers.

14. Weaver, *The Great Land Rush*, 43, 63–4.

15. For a bibliography and biographies of some of the major figures in the new institutional economics as well as the field of law and economics, see http://cepa.newschool.edu/het/schools/newinst.htm#newhist. Also http://www.isnie.org/readinglist.htm. For questions about the assumptions that economists make, see my two earlier-referenced books: *A Concise History* and The Language of Economics: Socially Constructed Vocabularies and Assumptions.

16. Douglass North, *Institutions, Institutional Change and Economic Performance* (Cambridge, UK: Cambridge University Press, 1990).

17. As happened with Herbert Fineout who stayed with his Uncle Harvey (perhaps really Jacob) Wiltsie, according to Fineout's pension file. Wiltsie was the holder of an 1856 land patent. Some Midland settlers (for example, the Whitman families) had relatives in the adjoining Tittabawassee Township within Saginaw County.

18. Richard L. Vedder and Lowell E. Galloway, "Migration and the Old Northwest," in Klingaman and Vedder, *Essays in Nineteenth Century Economic History,* 167. Note their use of non-quantified term "preferred."

19. New York contributed a larger absolute number of residents to Illinois, as 121,508 in that state came from New York. They accounted for eight percent of the state's population. Michigan had 191,128 from New York, and Wisconsin had 120,637, which was 24 percent of that state's 1860 population. Michigan lost some of its native-born to other states. For example 5,516 Michigan born people were included in the 1860 census for Illinois. *Statistics of the United States (including ...),* lxi-lxii.

20. Atack and Bateman, *To Their Own Soil,* 74. One-fifth of Midland's women and men age 20 or older in 1860 were foreign-born, with Canada providing 62 percent of these immigrants. (Upper Canada–which is Ontario–claimed one half of all of Midland's foreign-born residents.) Among the U.S.-born, 63 percent came from New York (which was one half of all native and foreign-born combined). That is four times as many residents as were born in Michigan itself. These were long-distance investors who presumably had less perfect market information.

21. Dunbar and May, *Michigan,* 91.

22. Gray, *The Yankee West,* Chapter 1.

23. Lewis, *West to Far Michigan,* 134–35.

24. For Leslie Decker's comments on this assumption, see his "The Great Speculation: An Interpretation of Mid-Continent Pioneering" in Ellis, ed., *The Frontier in American Development,* 360.

25. Dunbar and May, *Michigan,* 262.

26. Again, this quotation from Thermstrom is based on his studies of urban populations. See John C. Hudson, "Migration to an American Frontier," in Ward, *Geographic Perspectives on America's Past,* 95.

27. Atack and Bateman, *To Their Own Soil,* 83.

28. These are order-of-magnitude numbers based on assumptions about who was a child, a sibling or cousin.

29. *A Concise History of Economics from Adam Smith to Joseph Schumpeter* and *The Language of Economics: Socially Constructed Vocabulary and Assumptions.*

30. *Portrait and Biographical Album,* 338. Kelly's memory is not consistent with what farmers were actually cultivating and harvesting. See Chapter 7.

31. *Portrait and Biographical Album,* 353.

32. Margaret Walsh, *The American Frontier Revisited,* 65.

Works Cited

Acemoglu, Daron. "Root Causes: A Historical Approach to Assessing the Role of Institutions in Economic Development." *Finance & Development* (January 2003).

Adams, Donald R. "The Role of Banks in the Economic Development of the Old North-West." In *Essays in Nineteenth Century Economic Development*. Klingaman and Vedder. Athens: Ohio University Press, 1975.

Albert, Dennis A. *Regional Landscape Ecosystems of Michigan, Minnesota, and Wisconsin: A Working Map and Classification*. U.S. Department of the Interior, U.S. Geological Survey, Northern Prairie Wildlife Research Center, 1994). Available online at http://www.npwrc.usgs.gov/resource/1998/rlandscp/rlandscp.htm.

Allaway, W.H. "Cropping Systems and Soil." In *Soil: Yearbook of the Department of Agriculture*. Government Printing Office, 1957.

Andrews, Ralph, ed., *New Views on American Economic Development*. Cambridge, MA: Schenkman, 1965.

Ang, Yuen Yuen. "Autocracy with Chinese Characteristics: Beijing's Behind-the-Scenes Reforms." *Foreign Affairs* (May/June 2018).

Annual Report of the Commissioner of the State Land Office. Joint Document No. 5 dated December 1, 1849, State of Michigan, Legislature, 1850.

Annual Report of the Commissioner of the State Land Office. Joint Document No. 4 dated December 1, 1855, State of Michigan, Legislature, 1855.

Atack, Jeremy and Fred Bateman. *To Their Own Soil: Agriculture in the Antebellum North*. Ames: Iowa State University Press, 1987.

_____. "Yeoman Farming: Antebellum America's Other 'Peculiar Institution.'" In *Agriculture and National Development: Views on the Nineteenth Century*. Edited by Lou Ferleger. Ames: Iowa State University Press, 1990.

Atack, Jeremy, Fred Bateman and William N. Parker, "The Farm, the Farmer, and the Market." In *The Cambridge Economic History of the United States*. Edited by Stanley L. Engerman and Robert E. Gallman, Chapter 6. Cambridge: Cambridge University Press, 2008.

_____. "Northern Agriculture and the Westward Movement." In *The Cambridge Economic History of the United States*. Edited by Stanley L. Engerman and Robert E. Gallman. Cambridge: Cambridge University Press, 2008.

Atack, Jeremy and Peter Passell. *A New Economic View of American History*. New York: Norton, 1994.

Average Crop, Pasture, and Forestry Productivity Ratings for Illinois Soils. Urbana-Champaign, University of Illinois College of Agricultural, Consumer and Environmental Sciences, Bulletin 810, 2000. Also see http://www.npwrc.usgs.gov/resource/1998/rlandscp/rlandscp.htm.

Baily, Christopher, and Tarique Hossain and Gary Pecquet. "Private Banks in Early Michigan, 1837–1884." *Cliometrica* 12, issue 1 (January 2018): 153–180.

Baker, Alan R. H. *Geography and History: Bridging the Divide*. Cambridge, UK: Cambridge University Press, 2003.

Barber, Edward W. "A Zion in the Wilderness." In *The Making of Michigan, 1820–1860: A Pioneer Anthology*. Edited by Justin L. Kestenbaum. Detroit: Wayne State University Press, 1990.

Barnett, LeRoy. "Roads, Railroads, Recreation: Swamplands and the Building of Michigan." *Michigan History* 72, no. 4 (1988).

Batie, Sandra S, and Mary A. Schulz, and David B. Schweikhardt. *A Continuation of Environ-*

mental Conservation Policy: The Conservation Reserve Program. East Lansing: Michigan State University Department of Agricultural Economics, 1997: Staff Paper 97–16.
Beeson, Kenneth C. "Soil Management and Crop Quality." In *Soil: Yearbook of the Department of Agriculture.* Government Printing Office, 1957.
Benson, Barbara E. *Logs and Lumber: The Development of Lumbering in Michigan's Lower Peninsula 1837–1870.* Mount Pleasant: Clarke Historical Library, Central Michigan University, 1989.
Berkeley, George. "On the Prospect of Planting Arts and Learning in America. (1726)" In *Poems of Places: An Anthology in 31 Volumes.* Edited by Henry Wadsworth Longfellow. Boston: Osgood, 1876–1879.
Berriman, Stan. *Upper Tittabawassee River Boom Towns.* Midland, MI: Messersmith, 1979.
Berry, Ralph Moore. *Special instructions to Deputy Surveyors in Michigan, 1808–1854.* Lansing, MI: Michigan Museum of Surveying, 1990.
Berry, Wendell. *The Unsettling of America.* Berkeley: Counterpoint, 2015.
Billington, Ray Allen. "How the Frontier Shaped American Character." *American Heritage: The Magazine of History,* April 1958.
Billington, Ray Allen and Martin Ridge. *Westward Expansion, 5th ed.* New York: Macmillan, 1982.
Block, Fred, and Margaret R. Somers. *The Power of Market Fundamentalism: Karl Polanyi's Critique.* Cambridge, MA: Harvard University Press, 2014.
Blois, John. *Gazetteer of the State of Michigan.* Detroit: S.L. Rood, 1838.
Bogue, Alan, and Margaret Beattie Bogue. "Profits and the Frontier Land Speculator." *Journal of Economic History,* 17, no. 1 (1957). Also in Carstensen, Vernon. *The Public Lands: Studies in the History of the Public Domain.* Madison: University of Wisconsin Pres, 1963.
Bogue, Allan G. "Frederick Jackson Turner Reconsidered." *The History Teacher* 27, no. 2 (February 1994).
Braudel, Fernand. *The Perspective of the World, Civilization and Capitalism 15th–18th Century.* New York: Harper & Row, 1984.
_____. *The Wheels of Commerce.* New York: Harper and Row, 1982.
Bromage, Arthur W. "County Government in Michigan" *Papers of the Michigan Academy of Science, Arts and Literature* 6 (1931).
Buck, John Lossing. *Chinese Farm Economy.* University of Chicago, 1930.
_____. *Land Utilization in China.* University of Chicago, 1937.
Buck, Pearl. *The Good Earth.* New York: John Day, 1941.
Burnard, T. "Ethnicity in Colonial America Historiography: A New Organizing Principle?" *Australasian Journal of American Studies* 11 (July 1992).
Burnham, W. Dean. *Presidential Ballots 1836–1892.* Baltimore: John Hopkins Press, 1955.
Burns, Sarah. *Pastoral Inventions: Rural Life in Nineteenth-Century American Art and Culture.* Philadelphia: Temple University Press, 1989.
Bushman, Richard. *The American Farmer in the Eighteenth Century: A Social and Cultural History.* New Haven, CT: Yale University Press, 2018.
The Business Man's Assistance and Legal Guide, Containing the Laws of Michigan, Indiana, Illinois, Iowa and Wisconsin Chicago: Rufus Blanchard: 1856.
Caldwell, Norman C. *Surveyors of the Public Lands in Michigan, 1808–2000.* Owosso, MI: N.C. Caldwell, 2001.
Canover, Milton. *The General Land Office: Its History, Activities, Organization.* Baltimore: Johns Hopkins Press, 1923.
Carstensen, Vernon, ed. "Introduction." In *The Public Lands: Studies in the History of the Public Domain.* Edited by Vernon Carstensen. Madison: University of Wisconsin Press, 1968.
_____. *The Public Lands: Studies in the History of the Public Domain.* Madison: University of Wisconsin Press, 1968.
Catton, Bruce. *Michigan: A History.* New York: Norton, 1984.
Cayton, Andrew, and Peter Onuf. *The Midwest and the Nation, Rethinking the History of an American Region.* Bloomington: Indiana University Press, 1990.
Census and Statistics of the State of Michigan, May 1854. Lansing, MI: Geo. W. Peck, 1854.
Census and Statistics of the State of Michigan, 1864. Lansing, MI: Kerr, 1865.
Census of the State of Michigan, 1874. Lansing, MI: W.S. George, 1875.
CIS US Serial Set Index Part 1, American State Papers and the 15th–34th Congresses 1789–1857 and *Part II 35th–45th Congresses 1857–1879* Subject Indexes. Washington, D.C.: Congressional Information Service, 2000.

Clark, Christopher. *The Roots of Rural Capitalism: Western Massachusetts 1780–1860*. Ithaca, NY: Cornell University Press, 1990.
Clarke, John. *Land, Power, and Economics on the Frontier of Upper Canada*. Montreal: McGill-Queen's University Press, 2001.
Cleland, Charles E. *Rites of Conquest: The History and Cultures of Michigan's Native Americans*. Ann Arbor: University of Michigan Press, 1992.
Cole, Arthur H. "Cyclical and Sectional Variations in the Sale of Public Lands, 1816–1860" *Review of Economics and Statistics* 9 (1927). Also in Carstensen, *The Public Land*.
Comer, Patrick J. *Michigan Natural Features Inventory (MNFI)*, Report 1995–006, December 1995. Also see http://biology.usgs.gov/luhna/refer.html. and http://www.gap.uidaho.edu/Meetings/1998/abstracts.htm.
Conover, Milton. *The General Land Office: Its History, Activities and Organization*. Baltimore: Johns Hopkins University Press, 1923.
Conzen, Michael. "The Historical Impulse in Geographical Writing About the United States, 1850–1990." In *A Scholar's Guide to Geographical Writing on the American and Canadian Past*. Edited by Michael Conzen, Thomas Rumney and Graeme Wynn. Chicago: University of Chicago Press, 1993.
Conzen, Michael, and Thomas Rumney, and Graeme Wynn, eds. *A Scholar's Guide to Geographical Writing on the American and Canadian Past*. University of Chicago Press, 1993.
Cooley, Thomas M. *Compiled Laws of the State of Michigan*. Lansing, MI: Hosman & Kerr, 1857.
_____. *Michigan: A History of Governments*. Boston: Houghton, Mifflin, 1906.
Costinot, Arnaud, and Dave Donaldson. "How Large Are the Gains from Economic Integration? Theory and Evidence from U.S." *Econometrica*, November 2016.
The Counties and Townships of Michigan, Past and Present. A Michigan Heritage Publication, 1972.
Cronon, William. *Changes in the Land: Indians, Colonists, and the Ecology of New England*. New York: Hill & Wang, 1983.
Cultivator (V, 1848 and VI, 1849).
Danbom, David. *Sod Busting: How Families Made Farms on the Nineteenth-Century Plains*. Baltimore: Johns Hopkins, 2014.
Danhof, Clarence H. *Change in Agriculture: The Northern United States, 1820–1870*. Cambridge, MA: Harvard University Press, 1969.
_____. "Farm-Making Costs and the 'Safety Valve': 1859–1860." In *The Public Lands: Studies in the History of the Public Domain*. Edited by Vernon Carstensen. Madison: University of Wisconsin Press, 1968.
Darnton, Robert. *The Great Cat Massacre and Other Episodes in French Cultural History*. New York: Vintage Books, 1985.
Davis, Charles M. "The Hydrographic Regions of Michigan." *Papers of the Michigan Academy of Sciences, Arts and Letters* 16 (1931).
Dean, L.A. "Plant Nutrition and Soil Fertility." In *Soil: Yearbook of the Department of Agriculture*. Government Printing Office, 1957.
Deciker, Leslie. "The Great Speculation: An Interpretation of Mid-Continent Pioneering." In *The Frontier in American Development*. Edited by David Ellis. Ithaca, NY: Cornell University Press, 1969.
Department of Commerce, Bureau of the Census. *Historical Statistics of the United States, Colonial Times to 1970*. House document - 93d Congress, 1st session; no. 93–78. (Series) Bicentennial ed., Series A-8, J 1–2.
Dicks, W. Bruce. "A Study of Settlement and Land Use in Livingston County Michigan." *Papers of the Michigan Academy of Sciences, Arts and Letters* 26 (1940).
Dilla, Harriette M. *The Politics of Michigan 1865–1878*. New York: AMS Press, 1970.
Donaldson, Thomas. *The Public Domain: Its History, with Statistics*. 45th Congress, 3d session. House. Ex.doc 47, pt. 4.
Dooley, Marjorie True. "The Andrews Bailiwick: A Geographic Study of Migration to the Settlement of Northern Macomb County, Michigan, 1810–1850, as Perceived by Selected Participants." Ph.D. diss., Michigan State University, 1975.
Dunbar, Willis, and George May. *Michigan: A History of the Wolverine State*. Grand Rapids, MI: Eerdmans, 1995.
Eakle, Arlene, and Johni Cerny, eds. *The Source: A Guidebook of American Genealogy*. Salt Lake City: Ancestry, 1984.
Easterlin, Richard A. "Farm Production and Income in Old and New Areas at Mid-Century."

In *Essays in Nineteenth Century Economic History: The Old Northwest.* Edited by David Klingaman and Richard Vedder. Athens, OH: Ohio University Press, 1975.
_____. "Interregional Differences in Per Capita Income, Population, and Total Income, 1840–1950." in National Bureau of Economic Research, *Trends in the American Economy in the Nineteenth Century.* Princeton, NJ: Princeton University Press, 1960.
Easterlin, Richard A., George Alter and Gretchen A. Condran. "Farms and Farm Families in Old and New Areas: The Northern States in 1860." In *Family and Population in Nineteenth-Century America.* Edited by Tamara K. Hareven and Maris A. Vinovskis. Princeton: Princeton University Press, 1978.
Effects of Soil Erosion on Soil Productivity and Soil Quality. Soil Quality Institute, Technical Note No. 7, Soil Quality-Agronomy from the Soil Quality Institute, Natural Resources Conservation Service, United States Department of Agriculture, 1998.
1860 Census Instructions to Marshals at http://www.ipums.umn.edu/usa/voliii/inst1860.html.
Ellis, David, ed. *The Frontier in American Development.* Ithaca, NY: Cornell University Press, 1969.
Engerman, Stanley, and Claudia Goldin, "Seasonality in Nineteen-Century Labor Markets." In *American Economic Development in Historical Perspective.* Edited by Thomas Weiss and Donald Schaefer. Stanford, CA: Stanford University Press, 1994.
Engerman, Stanley, and Robert Gallman, eds. *The Cambridge Economic History of the United States.* New York: Cambridge University Press, 1966.
Etulain, Richard. Does the Frontier Make America Exceptional? Boston: St. Martin's Press, 1999.
Fairburn, Miles. *Social History: Problems, Strategies and Methods.* Boston: St. Martin's 1999.
Federico, Giovanni. *Feeding the World: An Economic History of Agriculture, 1800–2000.* Princeton, NJ: Princeton University Press, 2008.
Fehrenbacher, J. B., et al. *Soils of Illinois.* Urbana-Champaign: University of Illinois Agricultural Experiment Station Bulletin 778, 1984.
Ferleger, Lou, ed. *Agriculture and National Development: Views on the Nineteenth Century.* Ames: Iowa State University Press, 1990.
Field, Arthur. "Road Patterns of Michigan." *Papers of the Michigan Academy of Science, Arts and Letters* 14 (1930).
Final Environmental Impact Statement Flood Control on the Tittabawassee River at Midland, Michigan. Washington, D.C.: Office of the Chief of Engineers, Department of the Army, 1980.
The Final Impact Statement of Flood Control on the Tittabawassee River at Midland County. Washington, D.C.: Office of the Chief Engineer, Department of the Army, 1980.
Fischer, David Hackett. *Albion's Seeds: Four British Folkways in America.* Oxford University Press, 1989.
Fisk, Anita. *The History of Saginaw County Medicine.* Midland, MI: Pendell Print, 1986.
Fogel, Robert, and Jack Rutner as referenced in Robert Swierenga. "Quantitative Methods in Rural Landholding." *Journal of Interdisciplinary History* 13, no. 4 (1983).
Foner, Eric, ed. *The New American History.* Philadelphia: Temple University Press, 1990.
Formisano, Ronald. *Birth of Mass Political Parties, Michigan, 1827–1861.* Princeton, NJ: Princeton University Press, 1971.
Fredrickson, George. "Nineteenth-Century American History." In *Imagined Histories: American Historians Interpret the Past.* Edited by Anthony Molho and Gordan S. Woods. Princeton, NJ: Princeton University Press, 1998.
Freeman, Charles. *The Closing of the Western Mind: The Rise of Faith and the Fall of Reason.* New York: Alfred Knopf, 2003.
Frurip, David J., ed. *The Cater Site: The Archaeology, History, Artifacts and Activities at This Early 19th Century Midland County Site.* Midland, MI: Chippewa Nature Center, 2001.
Gallman, Robert E. "The Agricultural Sector and the Pace of Economic Growth: U.S. Experience in the Nineteenth Century." In *Essays in Nineteenth Century Economic History: The Old Northwest.* Edited by David Klingaman and Richard Vedder. Athens: Ohio University Press, 1975.
Garber, Peter. "Famous First Bubbles." *Journal of Economic Perspectives* (1990).
Gates, Paul W. *Farmer's Age Agriculture 1815–1860.* Armonk, NY: M. E. Sharpe, 1989.
_____. *History of Public Land Law Development.* Washington, D.C.: Superintendent of Documents, 1968.
_____. "The Homestead Law in an Incongruous Land System." *American Historical Review* XL (1935–1936).

_____. *The Jeffersonian Dream: Studies in the History of American Land Policy and Development.* Albuquerque: University of New Mexico Press, 1996.
_____. *Large-Scale Farming in Illinois, 1850 to 1870.* A paper read on December 28, 1931, at the joint session of the Agricultural History Society with the American Historical Association in Minneapolis. http://www.aghistorysociety.org/pdf/articles/ag000085.pdf.
_____. "The Role of the Land Speculator in Western Development." In *The Public Lands: Studies in the History of the Public Domain.* Edited by Vernon Carstensen. Madison: University of Wisconsin Press, 1968.
Golembe, Carter Harry. "State Banks and the Economic Development of the West, 1830–44." Ph.D. Diss., Columbia University, 1952.
Gordon, Douglas, and George May, eds. "Michigan Journal, 1836, John M. Gordon." *Michigan History* 43, no. 3 (September 1959).
Gordon, John M. "A Speculator's Diary." In *The Making of Michigan, 1820–1860: A Pioneer Anthology.* Edited by Justin L. Kestenbaum. Detroit: Wayne State University Press, 1990.
Gray, Susan E. "Family, Land, and Credit: Yankee Communities on the Michigan Frontier, 1830–1860." Ph.D. diss., University of Chicago, 1985.
_____. *The Yankee West: Community Life on the Michigan Frontier.* Chapel Hill: University of North Carolina Press, 1996.
Greffenius, Ruben J. E. "Development of Michigan Public Land Policy." Ph.D. diss., University of Michigan, 1968.
Grossberg, Michael. *Governing the Hearth: Law and the Family in Nineteenth-Century America.* Chapel Hill: University of North Carolina Press, 1985.
Hacker, Louis. "Sections or Classes." *Nation,* July 26, 1933.
Haeger, John D. *The Investment Frontier: New York Businessmen and the Economic Development of the Old Northwest.* Albany: State University of New York, 1981.
Hall, Patricia Kelly, and Steven Ruggles. "'Restless in the Midst of Their Prosperity': New Evidence on the Internal Migration of Americans, 1850–2000." *Journal of American History* 91, no. 3 (December 2004).
Hareven, Tamara K., and Maris A. Vinovskis, eds. *Family and Population in Nineteenth-Century America.* Princeton, NJ: Princeton University Press, 1978.
Harvey, David. *Americans in Canada, Migration and Settlement Since 1840.* Lewiston, NY: E. Mellen Press, 1991.
Helms, Douglas. "The Development of the Land Capability Classification." In *Readings in the History of the Soil Conservation Service.* Edited by Douglas Helms. Washington, D.C.: United States Department of Agriculture, Natural Resources Conservation Service, 1992.
_____. *Readings in the History of the Soil Conservation Service.* Washington, D.C.: United States Department of Agriculture, Natural Resources Conservation Service, 1992. Also available online at http://www.nrcs.usda.gov/about/history/articles/LandClassification.html.
_____. "Soil and Southern History." *Agricultural History* 74, no. 4 (2000): 723–58.
Hibbard, Benjamin, *A History of the Public Land Policies* Madison: University of Wisconsin Press, 1965.
Hinchman, Theodore H. *Banks and Banking in Michigan.* New York: Arno Press, 1980 (reprint of 1887 edition).
Historic Consumer Price Index 1800–1998. The University of Michigan's Documents Center online at http://www.lib.umich.edu/govdocs/historiccpi.html.
Historical Statistics of the United States: Colonial Times to 1870.
Historical Statistics of the United States: Series A195–209.
Hone, E. Wade. *Land & Property Research in the United States.* Salt Lake City: Ancestry, 1997.
Horsman, Reginold. "Changing Images of the Public Domain: Historians and the Shaping of the Midwest Frontiers." In *This Land is Ours.* Indianapolis: Indiana Historical Society, 1978.
Hosford, Karl Reynold. "Evolution of the Organizational Structuring and Land Resource Responsibilities of the Department of Natural Resources in Michigan, 1785–1978." Ph.D. diss., Michigan State University, 1979.
Hudson, John C. *Making the Corn Belt: A Geographic History of Middle-Western Agriculture.* Bloomington: Indiana University Press, 1994.
_____. "Migration to an American Frontier." In *Geographic Perspectives on America's Past.* Edited by David Ward and Thomas S. Flory. Oxford: Oxford University Press, 1979.
_____. "North American Origins of Middlewestern Frontier Populations." *Annals of the Association of American Geographers* 78 (1988).
Hulbert, Archer Butler. *Soil: Its Influence on the History of the United States.* New York: Russell & Russell, 1930.

Hull, Patricia Kelly, and Steven Ruggles. "'Restless in the Midst of Their Prosperity': New Evidence on the Internal Migration of Americans 1850–2000." *The Journal of American History* 91, no. 3 (December 2004).
Iggers, Georg. *Historiography in the Twentieth Century: From Scientific Objectivity to the Postmodern Challenge.* Middletown, CT: Wesleyan University Press, 1997.
Ingrao, Charles. *The Habsburg Monarchy 1618–1815.* New York: Cambridge University Press, 2000.
Introduction to the Soils of Wisconsin. Madison: Wisconsin Geological and Natural History series, Education series No. 10, 1955.
Isett, Christopher and Stephen Miller. *The Social History of Agriculture.* Lanham, MD: Rowman & Littlefield, 2017.
Jacobs, Wilbur R. "The Indian and the Frontier in American History—A Need for Revision." In *Geographic Perspectives on America's Past.* Edited by David Ward and Thomas S. Flory. Oxford: Oxford University Press, 1979.
Jamison, Knox. "The Survey of the Public Lands in Michigan." *Michigan History* 42 (1958).
Jones, Dallas Lee. "The Survey and Sale of the Public Land in Michigan, 1815–1862." Master's thesis, Cornell University, 1952.
Joy, Mark S. *American Expansionism 1783–1860.* London: Routledge, 2014.
Kahneman, Daniel. *Thinking, Fast and Slow.* New York: Farrar, Straus & Giroux, 2011.
Kane, Lucile. "Federal Protection of Public Timber in the Upper Great Lakes States." In *The Public Lands: Studies in the History of the Public Domain.* Edited by Vernon Carstensen. Madison: University of Wisconsin Press, 1968.
Kennedy, Joseph C.G. *Agriculture of The United States in 1860; Compiled from the Original Returns of The Eighth Census.* Washington, D.C.: Government Printing Office, 1864.
_____. *Preliminary Report on the Eighth Census. 1860.* Washington, D.C.: Government Printing Office, 1862.
Kestenbaum, John, ed. *The Making of Michigan 1820–1860: A Pioneer Anthology.* Detroit: Wayne State University Press, 1990.
Kirkland, Caroline Matilda. *A New Home, or Life in the Clearings.* Edited by John Nerber. New York: Putnam's Sons, 1953.
Kleppner, Paul. *The Cross of Culture: A Social Analysis of Midwestern Politics, 1850–1900.* New York: Free Press, 1970.
Klingaman, David, and Richard Vedder, eds. *Essays in Nineteenth Century Economic History: The Old Northwest.* Athens: Ohio University Press, 1975.
Kollmorgen, Walter Martin. *The German-Swiss in Franklin County Tennessee: A Study of the Significance of Cultural Considerations in Farming Enterprises.* Washington, D.C.: U.S. Department of Agriculture, Bureau of Economics, 1940.
Kolodny, Annette. *The Land Before Her: Fantasy and Experience of the American Frontiers, 1630–1860.* Chapel Hill: University of North Carolina Press, 1984.
Kuhn, Madison. "Tiffin Morse, and the Reluctant Pioneer." *Michigan History* 5, no. 2 (1966).
Ladell, John. *They Left Their Mark: Surveyors and Their Role in the Settlement of Ontario.* Toronto: Dundurn Press, 1993.
Lamoreaux, Naomi. "Rethinking the Transition to Capitalism in the Early American Northeast." *The Journal of American History* 90, no. 2 (2003).
Laws of the United States of a Local or Temporary Character and Exhibiting the Entire Legislation of Congress Upon Which the Public Land Titles in Each State and Territory Have Depended. Washington, D.C.: Government Printing Office, 1884.
Lazersfeld, Paul, and Morris Rosenberg. *The Language of Social Research.* New York: Free Press, 1955.
Leeson, Michael A. *History of Saginaw County, Michigan.* Chicago: Chapman, 1881.
Lengel, Edward G. *First Entrepreneur: How George Washington Built His—and the Nation's—Prosperity.* Boston: Da Capo Press, 2016.
Lewis, Kenneth E. "Mapping Antebellum Euro-American Settlement Spread in Southern Lower Michigan." *Michigan Historical Review* 30, no. 2 (Fall 2004).
_____. *West to Far Michigan: Settling the Lower Peninsula, 1815–1860.* East Lansing: Michigan State University Press, 2002.
Libecap, Gary D and Dean Lueck. *The Rectangular Survey Versus Metes and Bounds: Systematic and Unsystematic Land Demarcation.* https://law.yale.edu/system/files/documents/pdf/Intellectual_Life/Libecap_Lueck_LEO_Workshop_Nov_15_2007.pdf.
Lifton, Carey. *Social Soundness and WID Analysis for USAID Legal Reform Project Paper.* (1991).

Linklater, Andro. *Measuring America*. New York: Walker, 2002.
"Mapping in Michigan and the Great Lakes." *The Michigan Historical Review* 30, no. 2 (Fall 2004).
"Mapping in Michigan and the Great Lakes." *The Michigan Historical Review* 31, no. 1 (Spring 2005).
Mauldin, Erin Stewart. *Unredeemed Land: An Environmental History of Civil War and Emancipation in the Cotton South*. Oxford: Oxford University Press, 2018.
Mausel, P.W., E.C.A. Runge, and S.G. Carmer. *Soil Productivity Indexes for Illinois Counties and Soil Associations*. Champaign: University of Illinois, College of Agriculture, Agricultural Experiment Station Bulletin 752, 1975.
Maybee, Ronald. *Michigan's White Pine Era, 1840–1900*. Lansing, MI: Michigan Historical Commission, 1960.
McCalla, Douglas. "Review of *Land, Power and Economics of the Frontier of Upper Canada*." Economic History Association, April 2002. http://eh.net/book_reviews/land-power-and-economics-on-the-frontier-of-upper-canada/.
McCormick, Richard L. "Public Life in Industrial America, 1877–1917." In *The New American History*. Edited by Eric Foner. Philadelphia: Temple University Press, 1990.
McCreery, William A., and Laura McCreery, eds. *A Historical, Genealogical and Biographical Record of Some Members of the Alexander McCreery Clan of the United States and Canada*. Privately published, 1976.
McCusker, John J. *How Much Is That in Real Money? A Historical Price Index for Use as a Deflator of Money Values in the Economy of the United States*. Worcester: American Antiquarian Society, 1992.
McDonnell, Michael. *Masters of Empire: Great Lakes Indians and the Making of America*. New York: Hill & Wang, 2015.
Meints, Graydon M. *Michigan Railroads and Railroad Companies*. East Lansing: Michigan State University Press, 1992.
Michigan Department of State. *Michigan and Its Resources* Lansing. MI: R. Smith, 1883.
Michigan Farmer (magazine).
"Michigan Journal, 1836, John M. Gordon." *Michigan History* 43, no. 3 (September, 1959).
Michigan State Gazetteer and Business Directory for 1863/64. Reproduced in the Library of Congress's online *American Memory* service under "Pioneering the Upper Midwest: Books from Michigan, Minnesota, and Wisconsin, ca. 1820–1910."
Midland City Directory. Hillsdale, MI: Robinson Directories, 1992–93.
Midland County, Michigan Census Records 1850–1894. Midland, MI: Midland Genealogical Society, 1983.
Midland County, Michigan Miscellaneous Record Book, Marriages 1855–1871. Saginaw, MI: Saginaw Genealogical Society, 1976.
Mitchell, Robert E. "Antebellum Farm-Settlement Patterns: A Three-Level Approach to Assessing the Effects of Soils." *Journal of Interdisciplinary History* xli, no. 3 (Winter 2011): 393–420.
_____. "Antebellum Michigan Farmers and Their Soils: Choices Had Consequences." *Michigan Academician* XL (2010): 1–21.
_____. "Civil War Recruiting and Recruits from Ever-Changing Labor Pools: Midland County Michigan as a Case Study." *Michigan Historical Review* 35 (Spring 2009): 29–60.
_____. *A Concise History of Economists' Assumptions about Markets from Adam Smith to Joseph Schumpeter*. West Port, CT: Praeger, 2014.
_____. *Human Geographies Within the Pale of Settlement: Order and Disorder During the Eighteenth and Nineteenth Centuries*. London: Palgrave Macmillan, 2019.
_____. *The Language of Economics: Socially Constructed Vocabularies and Assumptions*. London: Palgrave Macmillan, 2016.
_____. "The Organizational Performance of Michigan's Adjutant General and the Federal Provost Marshal General in Recruiting Michigan's Boys in Blue." *Michigan Historical Review* 28, no. 2 (Fall 2002).
_____. "Survey Materials Collected in the Developing Countries: Sampling, Measurement, and Interviewing Obstacles to Intra- and Inter-National Comparisons." *International Social Science Journal* 17, no. 4 (1965): 665–685. Also in Donald Warwick and Samuel Osherson, eds. *Comparative Research Methods*. Upper Saddle River, NJ: Prentice-Hall, 1974.
_____. "Towards a History of Privatizing Public Lands in Michigan, 1785–1860." *Michigan Academician* 38, no. 3 (2008): 121–148.
_____. "Using Pre-Settlement Vegetation Maps to Understand the Early History of Michigan's Lumber Industry." *Michigan Historical Review* 37, no. 2 (Fall 2011): 1–28.

Molho, Anthony, and Gordon S. Woods, eds. *Imagined Histories: American Historians Interpret the Past.* Princeton, NJ: Princeton University Press, 1998.
Montfort, Mary Margaret. *Ethnic and Tribal Identity Among the Saginaw Chippewa of Nineteenth Century Michigan.* Master's thesis, Michigan State University, 1990.
Moore, Rose Lockwood. "Of Berry Pickers, Shanty Boys, and the Jack Pine Bird: Patterns of Settlement and Subsistence in Nineteenth Century Oscoda County (Michigan)." Master's thesis, Western Michigan University, 1990.
Morson, Gary Saul, and Morton Schapiro. *Cents and Sensibility: What Economics Can Learn from the Humanities* Princeton, 2017.
Motz, Marilyn. *True Sisterhood: Michigan Women and Their Kin, 1820–1920.* Albany: State University of New York Press, 1983.
Nash, Gary. *The Unknown American Revolution.* New York: Viking, 2005.
National Bureau of Economic Research. *Trends in the American Economy in the Nineteenth Century.* Princeton, NJ: Princeton University Press, 1960.
Neu, Irene D. "The Mineral Lands of the St. Mary's Falls Ship Canal Company" In *The Frontier in American Development.* Edited by David Ellis. Ithaca, NY: Cornell University Press, 1969.
North, Douglass C. *Institutions, Institutional Change and Economic Performance* Cambridge: Cambridge University Press, 1990.
Oberly, James W. *Sixty Million Acres: American Veterans and the Public Lands before the Civil War* Kent, Ohio: Kent University Press, 1990.
Ohio Farmer (VIII, 1859).
Olson, Mancur. "Dictatorship, Democracy and Development." American Political Science Review (September 1993).
_____. The Logic of Collective Action: Public Goods and the Theory of Groups. Cambridge, MA: Harvard University Press, 1971.
Osterhammel, Jürgen. The Transformation of the World: A Global History of the Nineteenth Century. Princeton, NJ: Princeton University Press, 2014.
Park, Siyoung. "Perception of Land Quality and the Settlement of Northern Pike County, 1821–1836." Western Illinois Regional Studies (Spring 1980).
Parker, William. "The Finance of Capital Formation in Midwestern Development, 1800–1910." In American Economic Development in Historical Perspective. Edited by Thomas Weiss and Donald Schaefer. Stanford, CA: Stanford University Press, 1994.
Parker, William N. "From Northwest to Mid-West: Social Bases of a Regional History." In *Essays in Nineteenth Century Economic History, The Old Northwest.* Edited by David Klingaman and Richard Vedder. Athens: Ohio University Press, 1975.
Parkerson, Donald H. *The Agricultural Transition in New York State: Markets and Migration in Mid-Nineteenth-Century America.* Ames: Iowa State University Press, 1995.
Pentland, Alex. *Social Physics: How Social Networks Can Make Us Smarter.* London: Penguin Books, 2015.
Portrait and Biographical Album of Midland County, Michigan. Chicago: Chapman Brothers, 1884.
Prasad, Monica. *A Land of Too Much.* Cambridge, MA: Harvard University Press, 2012.
Preliminary Inventory of Land-Entry Papers of the General Land Office, Preliminary Inventory No. 22. Washington, D.C.: The National Archives, 1949.
Pressly, Thomas, and William Scofield. *Farm Real Estate Values in the United States by Counties, 1850–1959.* Seattle: University of Washington Press, 1965.
Primack, Martin Leonard. *Farm Formed Capital in American Agriculture, 1850 to 1910.* New York: Arno Press, 1977.
Prince, Hugh. *Wetlands of the American Midwest: A Historical Geography of Changing Attitudes.* Chicago: University of Chicago Geography Research Paper No. 241, 1997.
Rastatter, Edward H. "Nineteenth Century Public Land Policy: The Case for the Speculator." In *Essays in Nineteenth Century Economic History: The Old Northwest.* Edited by David Klingaman and Richard Vedder. Athens: Ohio University Press, 1975.
Register of Letters Received by the Chief Mustering and Disbursing Officer 1863–65. Register NARA RG 110, File 5901.
Reinholds, Harold. "The Free Banking Law: The Michigan Experience." Ph.D. diss., Michigan State University, 1975.
Revel, Jacques, and Lynn Hunt. *Histories, French Constructions of the Past, Postwar French Thought, Volume I.* New York: New Press, 1955.
Robbins, Roy. *Our Landed Heritage: The Public Domain 1776–1936.* Lincoln: University of Nebraska Press, 1962.

Robin, Ron. *Scandals & Scoundrels, Seven Cases that Shook the Academy*. Berkeley: University of California Press, 2004.
Robinson, William, S. "Ecological Correlations and the Behavior of Individuals." American Sociological Review (1950).
Rockoff, Hugh. "Banking and Finance, 1789–1914." In *The Cambridge Economic History of the United States*. Edited by Stanley Engerman and Robert Gallman. New York: Cambridge University Press, 1996.
Rohrbough, Malcolm. *The Land Office Business: The Settlement and Administration of American Public Lands 1789–1837*. Belmont, CA: Wadsworth, 1990.
Rood, Paul. *An Analysis of Land Use and Fertility in Michigan Counties*. East Lansing: Michigan State College, Soils Extension Service, 1943.
Rose, Gregory. "The Origins of Canadian Settlers in Southern Michigan, 1820–1850." *Ontario History* 79, no. 1 (1987).
Russell, Robert. "Agricultural Notes in Ohio and Michigan." *Journal of Agriculture* (October 1856).
Ryavec, Karl E., and Mark Henderson. "Mapping Political Economies Over Time: Teaching Regional Systems Theory with G.W. Skinner's Historical GIS Datasets." *Journal of World-Systems Research* 24, issue 2 (2018).
Sachs, Jeffrey. "Institutions Matter, but Not for Everything." *Finance and Development* (June 2003).
Saint Mary's Falls Ship Canal Company. *560,000 Acres Pine Lands in the State of Michigan.* Detroit: H. Barnes, 1857.
Salamon, Sonya. *Prairie Patrimony: Family, Farming and Community in the Midwest*. Chapel Hill: University of North Carolina Press, 1992.
Scheiber, Harry N. "Land Reform, Speculation, and Governmental Failure: The Administration of Ohio's Canal Lands, 1836–60." *Prologue* (VII, 1975).
Seavoy, Ronald E. "Borrowed Laws to Speed Development: Michigan 1835–1863." *Michigan History* (1975).
Skidelsky, Robert. *Money and Government: The Past and Future of Economics Yale University Press, 2018.*
Skocpol, Theda. *Protecting Soldiers and Mothers: The Political Origin of Social Policy in the United States* Cambridge: The Belknap Press, 1992.
Smith, Guy and Andrew Aandahl. "Soil Classification and Surveys." In *The Yearbook of Agriculture 1957.*
Smith, Walter and Arthur Cole. *Fluctuations in American Business, 1790–1860*. New York: Russell & Russell, 1969.
Soil Survey Geographic (SSURGO) database.
Soil Survey of Midland County, Michigan. United States Department of Agriculture, Soil Conservation Service, 1979, 64–65.
Soil Taxonomy: A Basic System of Soil Classification for Making and Interpreting Soil Surveys. 2nd edition. Natural Resources Conservation Service. U.S. Department of Agriculture Handbook
Soltow, Lee. "The Growth of Wealth in Ohio, 1800–1969." In Klingaman and Vedder, *Essays in Nineteenth Century Economic History.*
Sommers, Lawrence M. *Atlas of Michigan* Michigan State University Press, 1977.
State of Michigan Department of Environmental Quality, Office of the Great Lakes, *Historical Wetlands of the Saginaw Bay Watershed* (1993) at http://www.deq.state.mi.us/ogl/sagbay/histwet/htm.
"Statistics of the State of Michigan in 1854." In *Census and Statistics of the State of Michigan, 1864.*
Steward, Lowell O. *Public Land Surveys: History, Instructions, Methods*. Ames, Iowa: Collegiate Press, 1935.
Stillwell, Lewis D. "Migration from Vermont, 1776–1860." *Proceedings of the Vermont Historical Society* V (1937).
Stoll, Steven. *Larding the Lean Earth: Soil and Society in Nineteenth-Century America*. New York: Hill and Wang, 2002.
Sutherland, Daniel. *The Expansion of Everyday Life, 1860–1876*. New York: Harper & Row, 1989.
Swierenga, Robert. *Acres for Cents: Delinquent Tax Auctions in Frontier Iowa*. Westport, CT: Greenwood Press, 1976.
_____. "The New Rural History: Defining The Parameters." *Great Plains Quarterly* (Fall, 1981

_____. "Quantitative Methods in Rural Landholding." *Journal of Interdisciplinary History,* 13:4 1983).
Tanner, Helen Hornbeck. "Mapping the Grand Traverse Indian Country: The Contribution of Peter Dougherty." In *The Michigan Historical Review* (31:1, Spring 2005).
The 2000 Wisconsin Agricultural Statistics. Wisconsin Agricultural Statistics Service.
Thernstrom, Stephen. *Poverty and Progress: Social Mobility in a Nineteenth Century City.* Cambridge, MA: Harvard University Press, 1964.
Third Annual Report of the Secretary of the State Board of Agriculture of the State of Michigan for the Year 1864. Lansing: John A. Kerr, 1864.
Thomas, Franklin. *The Environmental Basis of Society.* New York: Century, 1925.
Thompson's Bank Note and Commercial Reporter. New York: American Banker: August 21, 1854.
Tocqueville, Alexis de. "A Fortnight in the Wilderness." In Kestenbaum, *The Making of Michigan.*
Turner, Frederick Jackson. *The Frontier in American History.* New York: Henry Holt, 1920.
Tuttle, Charles. *General History of the State of Michigan.* Detroit: R.D.S. Tyler, 1873.
United States Department of Agriculture, *Soil: The Yearbook of Agriculture.* Washington: Government Printing Office, 1957.
United States Department of Agriculture, National Resources Conservation Service, *State Soils,* an online publication at http://soils.usda.gov/gallery/state_soils/
United States Department of Commerce, Bureau of the Census, *Historical Statistics of the United States, Colonial Times to 1970.* House document - 93d Congress, 1st session, no. 93–78. (Series) Bicentennial ed., Series A-8, J 1–2.
United States Geological Survey "The Land Use History of North America." Available online at http://biology.usgs.gov/luhna/refer.html
Vale, Thomas. *Plants and People: Vegetation Change in North America.* Washington, D.C.: Association of American Geographers, 1982.
Van Buren, A. D .P. "Taking the Pledge." In Kestenbaum, *The Making of Michigan.*
Veatch, J.O. *Agricultural Land Classification and Land Types in Michigan* East Lansing: Michigan State College, Agricultural Experiment Station Special Bulletin 231, 1941.
_____. *Soils and Land of Michigan.* East Lansing: Michigan State College Press, 1953.
Vedder, Richard and Lowell Gallaway." Migration and the Old Northwest." In Klingaman and Vedder, *Essays in Nineteenth Century Economic History.*
Vesterby, Marlow, and Robbin Shoemaker, and Ralph Heimlich, and Margot Anderson. *1.3. Land and Soil Quality.* A United States Department of Agriculture online document at http://www.ers.usda.gov/publications/arei/ah712/AH71213a.PDF
Vilar, Pierre. "History After Marx." In Revel and Hunt, *Histories: French Constructions of the Past, Postwar French Thought,* Vol. I. New York: New Press, 1955.
Vinovskis, Maris A. *Toward a Social History of the American Civil War: Exploratory Essays.* New York: Cambridge University Press, 1990.
Walsh, Margaret Walsh. *The American Frontier Revisited.* Atlantic Highlands, NJ: Humanities Press, 1981.
Ward, David. *The Autobiography of David Ward.* New York: Private printing, 1912.
Ward, David, ed. *Geographic Perspectives on America's Past.* New York: Oxford University Press, 1979.
Warwick, Donald and Samuel Osherson, eds. *Comparative Research Methods.* Englewood Cliffs, N.J.: Prentice-Hall, 1974.
Weaver, John C. *The Great Land Rush and the Making of the Modern World, 1650–1900.* Montreal: McGill-Queen's University Press, 2003.
Weiss, Thomas and Donald Schaefer, eds. *American Economic Development in Historical Perspective.* Stanford, CA: Stanford University Press, 1994.
Welch, Richard. *County Evolution in Michigan 1790–1897.* Lansing: Michigan State Library Service, 1972.
_____. *County Evolution in Michigan; Evolution of Michigan Townships.* Lansing: The Mid-Michigan Genealogical Society, Occasional Paper No. 4, 1972.
Wiebe, Robert H. *The Search for Order 1877–1920.* New York: Hill & Wang, 1967.
Wineburg, Sam. *Historical Thinking and Other Unnatural Acts. Philadelphia:* Temple University Press, 2001.
Winkle, Kenneth. *The Politics of Community: Migration and Politics in Antebellum Ohio.* New York: Cambridge University Press, 1988.
White, C. Albert. *A History of the Rectangular Survey.* Washington: Superintendent of Documents, 1983.

Whiteside, E. P., and I.F. Schneider, and R. L. Cooke. *Soils of Michigan*. East Lansing: Soil Science Department, Agricultural Experiment Station, Michigan State University, 1956.
Williams, Michael. *Americans and Their Forests: A Historical Geography* New York: Cambridge University Press, 1989.
Winters, Donald. *Farmers Without Farms: Agricultural Tenancy in Nineteenth-Century Iowa*. Westport, CT: Greenwood Press, 1978.
Wright, Robert. *One Nation Under Debt: Hamilton, Jefferson, and the History of What We Owe* McGraw-Hill, 2008.
_____. *The Wealth of Nations Rediscovered*. Cambridge, 2002.
Wright, Robert E., and Richard E. Sylla, Richard E. *Genealogy of American Finance*. New York: Columbia University Press, 2015.
Yang, Dong Hyu. *Aspects of United States Agriculture Circa 1860*. Ph.D. Dissertation, Harvard University, 1985.
Yates, Dorothy Langdon. *Salt of the Earth: A History of Midland County Michigan*. Midland, MI: The Midland County Historical Society, 1987.
Yoshpe, Harry, and Philip Brower. *Preliminary Inventory of the Land-entry Papers of the General Land Office*. Washington: National Archives, 1949.

Index

www.ingramcontent.com/pod-product-compliance
Ingram Content Group UK Ltd.
Pitfield, Milton Keynes, MK11 3LW, UK
UKHW041835100926
8556IPUK00018B/976

9 781476 680675